CW00738426

ROGUES, REBELS AND MAVERICKS OF THE MIDDLE AGES

Psalter depicting an early Wheel of Fortune by William de Brailes, *c.* 1240. The original is held by the Fitzwilliam Museum. A youth ascends on the left; at the top is a seated king – 'I exalt on high.' On the right is a falling figure and at the bottom a dying man: 'Lowest, I am ground by the wheel.'

ROGUES, REBELS AND MAVERICKS OF THE MIDDLE AGES

John Brunton

AMBERLEY

First published 2022

Amberley Publishing
The Hill, Stroud
Gloucestershire, GL5 4EP

www.amberley-books.com

British Library Cataloguing in Publication Data.
A catalogue record for this book is available from the British Library.

ISBN 978 1 3981 0440 2 (hardback)
ISBN 978 1 3981 0441 9 (ebook)

1 2 3 4 5 6 7 8 9 10

Typesetting by SJmagic DESIGN SERVICES, India.
Printed in the UK.

Contents

Introduction

Storytelling has always been present in the study of history. Everyone who has lived has a story, and many such stories in the context of the society and events of their time are of interest to whoever wishes to understand history. In the period from the eleventh century to the early sixteenth that we know of as the High to Later Middle Ages, many such stories beg to be told.

Medieval society was rigid in its control over people, and everyone had their lives circumscribed, their financial means, their standing in society, even their beliefs and opinions, and any deviations were severely dealt with. From the peasant who was practically owned by the lord of the manor to the noble and even the king there were serious restrictions, obligations and little scope for respite and improvement. Women of all social classes found their lives limited, from those who laboured to aristocratic ladies who were married by arrangement for reasons of inheritance and political alliance, and afterwards expected to produce a quota of children for similar purposes. There was little opportunity for improvement of whatever situation they were placed in.

This book looks at some of those who did not fit so easily into the model their society dictated. Some were rebels, some eccentrics, some downright villains and manipulators. Each is shown in the context of their own medieval world, and their deviation is often the exception that proves the rule. Some of them are not sympathetic characters and most died by violent means, some on the executioner's block. Some stories might appeal to a black sense of humour. Others show the tragedies of living in those times. The tale of a dedicated hermit browbeaten into becoming pope contrasts with a monk who took to outlawry and piracy, and many were marauders who despoiled or harmed as they went, often according to whoever licensed them to do so. The intelligent young widow forced to support her family as a professional writer, when most women – and in fact most men too – were denied even a basic education is a gentler tale. The last story shows the dangers of being in the service of a princess fallen into disfavour to one already under suspicion as the last of the Plantagenets, regardless of her own real opinions.

While choosing the people concerned, I have limited selection to those not as well known to history. Joan of Arc would have been a likely candidate, but there is already much written of her. The subjects do not often appear in many history books, or at best as fleeting references. It has intrigued me at times to read of the blind king who charged into the fight and to his inevitable death at the Battle of Crécy and the intriguing townsman who sought to use the dynastic dispute for the crown of France to his town's advantage. There has been coverage of some of these people since I started this project, although I might question the treatment of some, There are certainly many such stories, some of which cannot be told for lack of documentation, but there is enough material to fill several books, hence this strict selection.

1

Earl Waltheof

Rebel and Collaborator

Of all dates in British history, the best known has always been 1066. It was the year that opened with the death of Edward the Confessor, last of the Wessex kings of England and the succession controversy which gained Edward's brother-in-law Harold Godwinson the crown of England. It was the same year that the Norman army landed in England and under the leadership of their Duke William defeated the Saxon army at Hastings where King Harold fell, and before 1066 ended William was king in his place. One could wonder, however, how long it really took before William really was king of England, and what was in fact involved to transform the country to suit the new regime. One could also wonder what the English people did when the Normans conquered, and how they addressed the changes. Thus was the experience of Earl Waltheof.

For many centuries the title of earl has been a grade of higher nobility. One is an earl of a place, either of a county or a city. It is the oldest English title, but in the eleventh century it was in fact an office, a form of governorship and not strictly by nature hereditary.

When King Edward the Elder, son of Alfred of Wessex, waged his war of conquest of central England which was then held by the Danes in the early tenth century he created administrative units of the territories he gained, thus marking out the shires as we know them. To each he appointed an official then called an *ealdorman* who had wide military and administrative powers and who acted as king's representative in that region. This practice continued when Edward's son Athelstan succeeded in 924 and created a united England as we now know it. At times an ealdorman governed a much larger area, such as all East Anglia or Mercia; more often the practice in the next century. It resembled the continental title of count, which had itself become hereditary, as the ruling house of Wessex had established itself as a line of kings of all the English from the tenth century, although not as securely as they believed. In the period from 1016 to 1042 when the Danish king Cnut and then two of his sons in turn ruled England, the office continued, but known as that of earl from the time, a corruption of the Danish title of *jarl*, or lord.

Waltheof was born about 1050, possibly as early as 1045, the second son of Earl Siward of Northumbria. His father was a Danish earl who had served Cnut from 1016, but had since pledged loyalty to Edward the Confessor when he regained the English throne for the House of Wessex in 1042 on the death of the third Danish king. Waltheof's mother was Alflaed, daughter and granddaughter of previous English earls. Siward gained lordship over Northumberland and possibly also Cumbria, a region then disputed by Celtic and Danish rulers. As he grew up, it first seemed that Waltheof would be destined for the Church, as many a younger son would be pointed that way in those days.

The events of 1054 to 1055 changed such plans. King Edward, who had been sheltering Malcolm Canmore, pretender to the Scottish throne, now ordered Siward to invade Scotland and aid Malcolm against the usurper Macbeth. The sequence in the Shakespeare play is hardly a reliable account, in the final act showing the tyrant himself killing Siward's son in combat. It is not known how Osbearn the eldest son of Siward really died, but this made Waltheof, though still a child, heir to his father's wealth and political aspirations.

Earldoms were subject to royal appointment, although it was often politic to keep the office within the same powerful family. In this case the king had to look elsewhere when Siward himself died in 1055, as Waltheof could hardly as a minor perform the necessary duties in such a sensitive region. Edward was close to the family of the Norman Earl Godwin, having married his daughter and gave this northern earldom to Tostig, one of Godwin's sons. Another son Harold, later the last Saxon king, was already Earl of East Anglia.

Tostig was a disastrous appointment, for within ten years he had alienated many important elements and in 1065 the aging king had a revolt on his hands. Edward then replaced Tostig with Morcar, brother of Earl Edwin of Mercia. At the same time he appointed Waltheof Earl of Huntingdon, as an astute move to placate his dispossessed family.

In his teens Waltheof was still too young and inexperienced for such an appointment as Northumbria and this earldom of Huntingdon, which comprised western Mercia and was sometimes known as the earldom of Northampton, was a reasonable opening. It was comparatively quiet and less volatile than the north, ideal for a first appointment.

Edward the Confessor died without issue the following year. Much has already been written of the succession controversy then waiting to happen. Essentially Edward's nearest relatives on his mother's side were of the ducal house of Normandy, and his nephew Duke William claimed to have had his promise of succession to the English throne. The Saxon lords predictably opposed this idea and favoured Harold Godwinson, the old king's brother-in-law. They claimed that King Edward had named Harold his successor on his deathbed in January 1066, which carried the force of law in English custom. William of course rejected this, and maintained that not only had his uncle promised him the throne, but that Harold himself had once sworn over the relics of saints to aid the duke in his claim as king of England. It was a messy controversy which involved different interpretations of separate legal customs and could only be resolved by force of arms.

There is some debate over where Waltheof was involved in resisting the two invasions of 1066. In the summer of that year King Harald Hardrada of Norway landed in Yorkshire intent on adding England to his domains, with Tostig and his supporters rallying to his banner. Harold Godwinson, the new King of England was obliged to lead his army north in a successful defence and his victories at Fulford and Stamford Bridge ended the Norwegian threat.

But William of Normandy invaded so soon afterwards that Harold was placed at a disadvantage. Forced to speed south again he left most of his army behind, whose progress to rejoin him was far too slow. This was perhaps only one factor that saw Harold defeated and killed at Senlac Hill near Hastings on 19 October 1066 when he met the Normans with a shortage of seasoned troops.

Some Icelandic sources, themselves not considered too reliable, place Waltheof at the battles of Fulford, Stamford Bridge and Hastings. It is almost certain that as an earl he would be expected to lead the men of West Anglia to war, but some believe that he did not reach Hastings, as William later ordered that everyone who fought against him there would be put to death and the ultimate sanction was not applied to Waltheof. It is reasonable to conclude that he followed Harold to the north and it is likely that he fought the Norwegians, but was not among the small number that Harold rode to Sussex with; he was probably still bringing his own following south when the fateful battle took place.

What exactly changed when the Normans conquered England? One change was to reverse the trend that was bringing England into the Scandinavian world and link it instead with continental Europe. From the ninth century onwards the Danes (and some Norwegians also) had settled in England rather than just raid it and there had been a large Danish population in the centre of the island and in Yorkshire. Waltheof himself was of a Danish family in the service of the last Saxon kings. Cnut and his sons ruled England in personal union with Denmark and Norway, and the Norwegian Harald Hardrada claimed the English crown, having conquered the rest of Cnut's empire. This would have linked England culturally with Scandinavia, but from 1066 its orientation was fixed towards France, both in culture and in enmity.

The Normans, though descended from Danes who settled at the mouth of the Seine about 900, were French in language and culture by the mid-eleventh century. Norman adventurers Robert and Roger Guiscard captured both Sicily and southern Italy in this time, independently of William.

It is not as widely known how much of this Norman culture preceded the Conquest into England once Edward the Confessor gained the throne in 1042. Edward had spent his exile between 1016 and 1042 in Normandy, and had returned not only steeped in Norman ways but with a following from the duchy. Many Normans had become well placed in the reign: the Archbishop of Canterbury, William of Champart was a Norman. There had been unease among the Saxon notables during the reign and a revolt headed by Earl Godwin in 1052 had attacked the Normans, driving away the Archbishop. Perhaps Norman French was spoken at Edward's court more often than Anglo-Saxon. The latter language, then sounding more like German and incomprehensible to the modern English, was clearly different from that of the incomers.

Many volumes have been written on English feudal society after the Conquest. School history textbooks always emphasise a strong social divide of French-speaking knights and nobles holding and exacting revenues on manors where the Saxon peasants laboured to survive under this harsh regime. While it is true that the Normans introduced a continental manorial system, the real process was much longer and more haphazard, and the changes imposed were not as radical in places as believed. According to Domesday Book, in 1086 about five per cent of land was still held by Anglo-Saxon landowners, the rest having Norman lords. The timetable of such a handover is unclear.

A misconception appeared in the Victorian era of a free, almost egalitarian and even democratic Anglo-Saxon England, which has coloured our perception ever since. Just as elsewhere in western Europe, Saxon England had a warrior class supported by peasant labour and society was still divided. This elite had an economic basis to its membership: to qualify one needed the means to equip oneself for battle. One who owned at least five *hides* or units of land could notionally be counted a *thegn*, as such a holding was deemed to ensure he could afford the military commitment and he was liable to military service when his locality was under attack. Alternatively, the separate owners of every five hides were expected to provide a single equipped warrior between them when the *fyrd*, or militia, was called out. Whoever held the office of earl would need to own, or be granted, much larger resources.

The English thegn was therefore not too different from the continental knight, while the restriction of the military class to those born into it had not yet been fully imposed. Before 1066, although there was slavery in certain circumstances, a Saxon peasant might consider himself free, but economic dependence on his lord, on whose land he worked, restricted his options. As in later centuries a peasant would perform labour services or pay rents. There was nothing to prevent him leaving his lord's estate, but his need for a livelihood was the obstacle that kept him there. In fact, to live as a wanderer without a lord was truly a sorry state for a Saxon to have come to; there is even a surviving poem that laments such a plight. The Normans did impose a strict burden of control over the peasants of each manor, reducing them to virtual slavery with dues and labour services, although conditions varied immensely between regions and individual manors.

The Normans in October 1066 could be cautious over too many changes. At Hastings they had killed the principal Saxon claimant to the throne and destroyed his army, but there was still potential for resistance and William could not consider himself secure on the throne for some time to come. Part of his policy to bring the country under his control involved gaining recognition of his kingship from the Saxon earls and thegns. This is not as difficult as it appears; the Saxons had served under Danish kings within living memory and King Edward had been very Norman in his ways. The stigma we now associate with collaborators did not exist at the time, and many English were pragmatic enough to accept the new status quo. Waltheof had himself offered allegiance to William by the end of the year and was confirmed in his earldom.

Waltheof was one of those William took as hostage with him to Normandy later in 1066, as were Morcar, Edwin and Archbishop Stigand among others. Apart from a measure of surety this was a way to bond with such men, as they were useful to have on his side. They lived well at his court as his guests while he sought to convince them what a good idea it would be to serve him. William had tried a similar approach to Harold Godwinson when a storm washed him up in Normandy in 1064, but this was not so successful when Harold should have supported William's bid to gain the crown. It did seem that when Waltheof and the others returned to England the following year that they were William's men.

But England was far from subdued so soon after Hastings. William had problems when the city of Exeter refused to recognise him as king, even though most of the thegns of Devon had submitted. He besieged the city and it surrendered when he agreed to their previous privileges. He also placated Gloucester and Bristol. Thus most of the country acquiesced to the new king, mostly from a sense of realism.

Others of the Saxon nobility showed their opposition: Hereward the Wake waged a guerrilla war from what was then the Isle of Ely and Edric the Wild would rise in Shropshire. Even Count Eustace of Boulogne, who had fought on the Norman side at Hastings, rose in revolt. There was also Edgar Atheling, of the Saxon royal house but too young to succeed in 1066, who had taken refuge in Scotland and was growing up quickly.

William was building castles, previously almost unknown in England. As a beginning the motte-and-bailey form appeared, a construction of a wooden tower on a mound of earth with an enclosure at its foot, all as a preliminary to building a stone castle. The Normans had brought the Forest Laws to England. These had less to do with trees than with a status *outside* the common law (from the Latin *foris*) where terrible penalties could be exacted against those who hunted or gathered without licence.

Earl Waltheof seems to have embraced the new regime with little dissent. For two years he conducted his duties without incident, for at this time it made little difference which king he served while he still held his wealth and power. But like many English he might have considered his options and loyalties as events unfolded.

The north of England was still a problem for William; too many dissenting elements made the region difficult to keep at peace. A follower of Tostig named Copsi had deputised for Morcar while the latter was in Normandy. William replaced him with one Gospatric, a descendant of the Northumbrian kings, who bought the earldom and who turned out to be untrustworthy. There were many factions, and a general lack of enthusiasm for this new Norman monarchy. The north could detach itself from the rest of England easily, and it had done so before.

Swein Estrithson, King of Denmark, sought to invade. In 1067 there had been an appeal from English elements that he claim the crown, and he was determined to avenge the fall of his kinsman Harald Hardrada in 1066. It was only in 1069 that he ordered his force to sail, and then he sent his brother Asbjorn to lead the invasion where a personal appearance might have served his cause much better.

At least a quarter of those living in England were Danish in language, culture and ancestry, the result of previous waves of colonisation. There was a large Danish population in Yorkshire and an independent kingdom had briefly risen there in the 950s. For more than a century the Wessex kings ruled over these Danes, but it appears they could be rebellious at times.

After an attempted revolt in 1068 Gospatric fled to Scotland. The following year there took place a more serious rebellion. William had given up on native earls and had appointed Robert of Commines to take Gospatric's place, but the northerners were even more unwilling to accept a Norman to rule over them than the rest of the country. Early in 1069 rebels attacked Robert in Durham market and burned him to death in his home. They also killed many of the Normans he had brought, and legend has only one escaping to tell the tale.

This sparked revolt all over the north, and the people of York rose to kill the Norman commander but could not take the newly built castles there. By Easter, all the region had rebelled under one faction or another, and William was riding north with his army.

It was then that Waltheof rebelled. In September he met with the Danes at the Humber, and with Edgar Atheling and Gospatric. It can only be speculated as to why Waltheof turned against the Norman monarchy at this time. Perhaps he was moved by the treatment of the people of Yorkshire, where he still had strong family connections.

He might easily have seen Sweyn as a viable alternative king; Waltheof was part-Danish himself. He could have had designs on the earldom of Northumbria, remembering his father, but at any rate he had little reason to stay loyal to William,

The Norman garrisons of York had turned on the citizens and the city was burning down. They left their castles to face the invading forces and 3,000 of them were massacred according to some accounts. Waltheof was said to have personally beheaded many with his long axe and his exploits on this campaign were told in sagas. He was known for his strength.

But there was no one leader that all the north recognised, and the lack of concerted action failed to stop William's army when he ravaged the entire north of England. Large regions were laid waste and the north did not recover for generations. William paid the Danes to leave, a common remedy in times gone by, and pursued a remarkably harsh policy that involved burning down buildings, slaughtering animals and killing thousands of people.

Waltheof was left holding out with a small following at Coatham on the north Yorkshire coast and eventually surrendered. By late 1070 all the leading rebels were either killed or had fled, and the worst challenge to the Norman monarchy over. But Waltheof was pardoned.

It may seem remarkable that William spared Waltheof after he had done so much damage, and even to make him the new Earl of Northumberland two years later when Gospatric was finally expelled. It was part of the *Realpolitik* associated with rebellions. The north was always a problem for the Normans, too far away to police with their army and steeped in regional loyalties. Laying the north waste was illustrative of their recognition that it could not really be integrated into this Norman kingdom. But it was a sensitive area, where invasion from Scotland or Norway and further conspiracies were likely. Where the best policy was maintaining a complaisant earl, and where the northerners showed their dislike of southerners and Norman impositions on them, Waltheof was an astute appointment given his connections with York.

William appears to have been remarkably generous towards the repentant rebel. He was allowed to keep the lands he held in his capacity as Earl of Huntingdon-Northampton. It seems he may have been allowed to retain that earldom too. Before 1070 was over the king gave his niece Judith in marriage to Waltheof. Judith was daughter of Lambert, Count of Lens and William's sister Adelaide, and Waltheof made over his Huntingdon estates to her according to the Saxon custom, which gave her means of her own. They had three children.

As the new earl of his home area Waltheof took advantage of his powers by settling an old feud, and sent his housecarls to kill the Carlson brothers and their household in 1074. Their family and his had been enemies for generations, since the Carlsons killed Waltheof's ancestors Uhtred and Ealdred in 1016. The housecarls ambushed them, killing two of the four brothers. They had fought on the same side during the revolt.

But it was not the north of England Waltheof had known when William's reprisals had left a near-wilderness north of the Humber. It could only be speculated what Waltheof could have done to restore normal life in the region, if anything. He appears to have based himself at Hallam, south of what is now Sheffield, York having burnt down. Domesday Book, the survey of lands in England William would commission in 1086, talks of the hall he had there, then held by Roger de Busli from Judith.

Waltheof was credited with the promotion of religious houses. He financed the refounding of the monastery at Jarrow where Aldwin Prior of Winchcombe set up a small community. Waltheof granted them lands at Tynemouth that had belonged to the Church and also entrusted his nephew Morcar to them for his education. There were other awards, including the founding of a nunnery at Elstow near Bedford, but his greatest endowment was to the Abbey at Crowland, not far from Hallam.

He was remembered for such acts of piety. This was not much different from similar grants of land and other material endowments most men of wealth and power made to the Church, for many had individual monasteries as their favourite charity. Harold had made Waltham Abbey his own concern. They believed that it scored points for them in heaven, and that they would benefit when the monks remembered them in their prayers. From a practical standpoint Waltheof probably understood the importance of the monasteries and churches as a stabilizing influence. But much damage had been done, and the north of England remained underpopulated and economically backward for generations.

Waltheof was nevertheless probably the best earl that Northumbria could have in the circumstances, even if there was little he could do. In 1075, either by duplicity or his misfortune, Waltheof fell in a spectacular manner. Whether he did plot with other earls that year is not certain, but he was believed guilty of doing so. William had remained in Normandy since 1073, and there was tension among certain earls over the king's refusal to sanction a marriage of one's daughter. Earl Ralf of East Anglia married the sister of Earl Roger de Breteuil of Herefordshire, and when Waltheof attended the wedding feast these two sought to recruit him into a new rebellion. They valued his participation, partially as his Midland estates linked the other two earldoms.

The sources are divided as to whether Waltheof agreed to join the revolt. The chroniclers Orderic Vitalis and William of Malmesbury believe that he refused, but that he had previously sworn an oath not to betray what was said at the meeting. Whether this is so, or whether Waltheof decided that the revolt was a mistake, he quickly decided to dissociate himself. There is also a legend that he learned that Judith was in the process of betraying him to her uncle, and he acted to pre-empt royal anger. He rushed to London the next day, sought out Archbishop Lanfranc and confessed all to him. He acted in a contrite manner, professing a desire to become a monk. Lanfranc advised him to throw himself on William's mercy, which he did, travelling to Normandy with expensive gifts for the king.

The Revolt of the Earls as it was called was the last serious resistance to the Norman monarchy. Even though William benefited from knowing about it by Waltheof's confession, it was serious. Lanfranc excommunicated everyone involved. Bishop Wulfstan raised the Worcestershire *fyrd* and held Roger at the Severn. The Norman bishops Odo of Bayeux and Geoffrey de Mowbray met Ralf at Cambridge and put him to flight. Ralf then went to Denmark, leaving his wife in charge in Norwich castle. He soon returned with 200 Danish ships, but these warriors accomplished little. Ralf and Roger lost their lands and offices, and Roger was sentenced to perpetual imprisonment. He was released on William's death.

Waltheof's fate was sealed. He remained under close arrest and was brought twice before the Council, where, although he maintained his innocence throughout, he was declared guilty and sentenced to death. Many of the court, both English and Norman, felt this unjust; Lanfranc protested to his dying day that Waltheof was innocent. At Giles Hill near Winchester on 31 May 1076 Waltheof was brought out in his earl's robes for execution. Up to the last, many believed the sentence would not be carried out. Ironically for Waltheof, he received the penalty for rebellion specified in English law, which was death, while Roger as a Norman was only imprisoned under Norman law.

And here began a curious legend. After Waltheof had given his clothes to the poor, he bent to say his final prayer. The executioner was impatient, and probably nervous over possible crowd reaction, and when the earl seemed to take too long on his recitation of the Lord's Prayer, he struck off Waltheof's head just as he said 'Lead us not into temptation.' Witnesses testified to the severed head falling on the ground and still speaking the words 'but deliver us from evil. Amen' after it landed.

But even this did not quite mean the end for Waltheof. His body lay for two weeks in unconsecrated ground, but Abbot Ulfketel of Crowland petitioned successfully to take it to the Abbey for reburial, where the medieval cult of saints and miracles now found in him a new protagonist. In 1092 there was a fire in the chapter house at Crowland, and the abbot of the time had Waltheof's remains moved to a place in the abbey church. This entailed opening the coffin. The monks remarked that the body was now intact, the severed head rejoined fully to the trunk.

This was a miracle, they decided; it might have been someone else's body, but this was apparently not considered. Like many another religious houses they took advantage and publicised the marvel and soon there was a modest procession of pilgrims to the tomb. A few years later there were reports of miracles of healing among them, mostly those of restored sight. There was some attempt to have Waltheof canonised, but Rome paid little attention to it. His patronage for the abbey and other religious houses was remembered, and he acquired the reputation of a religious man. But Waltheof never became a fully fledged saint; he was not ideal material for such a role. Perhaps he was more a focus for the suffering of Saxons under the Norman yoke.

Judith was still alive at the end of William's reign. At one point William tried to make her marry his knight Simon of Senlis, which she refused 'because he was lame of leg'. Waltheof and Judith's eldest daughter Maud eventually married first that same Simon, who became Earl of Huntingdon, and then King David I of Scotland. Another daughter Adelise married the Norman baron Raoul of Tosny. His son Uhtred of Tynedale married a daughter of King Donald III of Scotland. One of Waltheof's grandsons and a namesake was Abbot of Melrose and was himself canonised.

William the Conqueror lived on until 1087. He had no serious revolts that threatened his regime after 1075, but from 1066 there was scarcely a year when he did not have some unrest or other to deal with. Two of his sons succeeded him in turn and the succession of his granddaughter Matilda was disputed by her cousin Stephen, bringing a long civil war. In 1154 the Angevin or Plantagenet dynasty gained England through marriage to Matilda, and Norman rule in England, Sicily and Normandy itself had all disappeared by 1204.

Waltheof was no saint, it is certain. He was a typical Saxon lord forced to make whatever way he could in the circumstances. Perhaps he had ambitions for the earldom his father held in the region of his upbringing, and perhaps he also understood how the rulership of England was hardly settled – William after all did not exactly have a divine right to be king. Waltheof might have been drawn to a Danish option under Sweyn; England was still at the crossroads, looking either to the Scandinavian world or to Normandy and France.

It is almost certain that his submission to William in 1070 entailed an oath not to rebel again. We do not know if he really did, for many believed his association with Roger and Ralf was not by his choice: he did repudiate it almost immediately. Perhaps William over-reacted, remembering the previous betrayal.

Waltheof was the last Saxon earl after the Norman Conquest, and his story marks one failure of William the Conqueror to reconcile the Saxon nobility to his rule. In the earlier years it served to his advantage that he was a Saxon noble willing to cooperate. But in later years as the only Saxon earl remaining it made him a focus for English discontent, and with one revolt to his discredit it was cause to make William wary. Waltheof was one more man of his time forced to live in a world that had changed from one he knew, and where simply to survive could be a challenge.

2

Reynald of Châtillon

Firebrand of the Crusader States

On 27 November 1095 the world changed. On that day Pope Urban II, then officiating at the Council of Clermont in France, made a dramatic address exhorting the faithful to go forth and liberate the Holy Land from the Saracens by force of arms. In this speech he created an institution that radically altered the lives of millions in Europe and the Near East for centuries. He had produced an acceptable hybrid of Christian zeal and feudal militarism.

Four years later, the First Crusade as inspired by this address finally charged through the gates of Jerusalem itself. It had been a long and bloody journey where an army of European knights and soldiers fought their way through Asia Minor and Syria and celebrated their victory by indiscriminately slaughtering everyone they found within the walls of the Holy City. For two centuries after this event, European Christians ruled in the Levantine region, their territory ever growing and contracting. The institution of crusading would last for centuries in one form or another, even to the present day.

The Franks, as the Moslems called the European Christians, created four separate states stretching along the Mediterranean seaboard of the region. The Kingdom of Jerusalem was the largest and most prestigious, and included many places mentioned in the Bible. There were also the Principality of Antioch and the counties of Tripoli and Edessa. Attitudes towards the Moslems varied throughout this period: from attempted total genocide in 1099 through their subsequent employment of Moslems as feudal tenants, to strong friendships and cultural contacts. The shortage of labour in the region alone persuaded the Franks that exterminating the native population was not the best policy. Frankish Syria, or Outremer, lived under continual threat of destruction by its Moslem neighbours, and its need to survive called for a range of measures, from conciliation to warfare.

Where Reynald of Châtillon fits into this picture depends on such varying realities. He is known to posterity as instinctively aggressive, cruel to Moslem and Christian enemies alike, a truce-breaker and warlike firebrand. He is credited with single-handedly bringing the wrath of Saladin on the Franks, which almost destroyed the Kingdom of Jerusalem in 1187. Yet this image is simplistic, based on the words of hostile chroniclers; perhaps he was simply blamed for what would have happened anyway.

Antioch was the first acquisition of the First Crusade. In October 1097 the army of knights and nobles set about an eight-month siege about the city's walls until its petty Turkish despot was forced to capitulate. A city with a long Roman and Biblical heritage, Antioch with its region was created a principality under the crusader Bohemund of Taranto and his family. This first Bohemund died in 1103, and the second succeeded as a minor. It was a precarious state, often under threat from attack. In 1130 Bohemund II in turn met his death fighting, leaving his daughter Constance as heiress.

In the struggle for this important lordship that ensued, Alice, Bohemund's widow, was thwarted in an attempt to assume the regency by King Fulk of Jerusalem, who had plans of his own for the principality. The Patriarch of Antioch, possibly at Fulk's urging, was said to have led Alice to believe that Roger, a son of the Count of Poitiers, was coming to marry her, but on arrival he married Constance. Roger was himself killed in battle in 1149, and Baldwin III, the reigning King of Jerusalem, again sought to impose a regency.

This political vacuum created an opening for a new, flamboyant figure, Reynald of Châtillon. Constance, widowed with four young children, was under pressure to take a new husband. She shocked everyone by marrying this landless newcomer from France. A handsome young man, he apparently charmed Constance into choosing him.

Reynald of Châtillon-sur-Loing was a son of the Lord of Gien, in the Orleans region of France, and was probably attracted to the east for the opportunities to be had. He certainly gained one of the best lordships there. With Constance's eldest son Bohemund then a minor, Reynald assumed the title of Prince of Antioch.

The year of Reynald's birth is unknown. If as believed he came to Outremer with the Second Crusade from 1146 he would have been born in the mid-1120s or earlier. While he was documented as a young man in 1153, he could then have been in his twenties or early thirties. His youth was then thought the cause for his turbulent and aggressive manner, although he was still as aggressive and unruly over thirty years later.

Reynald had much of his bad press from the chronicler William Archbishop of Tyre, writing late in Reynald's career. He described Reynald as a petty French aristocrat, but this was not the case; his family, lords of Donzy, Puisany and Berry, descended from Merovingian nobility. It was said that he could have married the Duke of Burgundy's daughter but went east instead to seek his fortune. Reynald was a younger son, which traditionally limited his possibilities. When the eldest son of an aristocratic family inherited his father's estates and titles, the other sons could not hope for any of it. This is why it was common practice for at least one younger son to pursue a career in the Church, but this of course was not ideal for all of them. Apart from seeking an heiress or a dowager, many a younger son could only gain advancement as a knight in the service of a greater lord or a king. Once the Levant was colonized by the Franks there were plenty of new opportunities, even after the territories had reached their fullest expansion. As a vassal of Louis VII of France, he could easily have followed him on the Second Crusade and decided to stay on in Outremer and try his luck. On the other hand, he could have journeyed east on his own some time before 1153; Frankish Syria was then a land of opportunity for many Europeans.

In the previous decades the Turkish Amir of Mosul, Imad-ad-Din Zangi, had taken an aggressive stance towards the Franks and raided periodically from the east. The easternmost possession of the Franks, the County of Edessa, was regained for Islam in 1146, and the Second Crusade, which was raised in response, accomplished little. Zangi died soon after his conquest and his son Nur-ad-Din Mahmud led the ongoing confrontation with the westerners. To the south, the Fatimid Caliphate, a Shi'ite dynasty, had long ruled over Egypt, the regime now sunk into a state of terminal decay. Until 1153 the Fatimids still held the fortified town of Ascalon on the Palestinian coast.

There was considerable opposition to Reynald's marrying Constance. Her sons being small boys, it would entail him effectively taking over the estate of prince. The Patriarch Aimery of Limoge was the most vociferous objector. Reynald had him arrested and imprisoned. This act hints that he had some support among the powerful elements of the principality, for he could not attack an established figure without a following. Perhaps many saw him as a leader they could rally around against the Zangid threat.

For all this wooing, and that of Reynald's rivals, the King of Jerusalem had to give his consent before the princess could marry anyone. Reynald then rode south and sought out the king. At the time Baldwin was besieging Ascalon, and when Reynald joined him there he appeared to have made enough of an impression on Baldwin to gain his assent; the king seems to have considered Reynald a safe pair of hands for the principality. He must have given a totally different impression to Baldwin than he had to Antioch. Or perhaps the king decided that Antioch being continually at war with the Moslems was to the advantage of the Kingdom. Reynald could keep Nur-ad-Din occupied for a time, at the very least.

Having assumed the title of prince, Reynald did address the problems of the principality. He spent much time and diplomacy attempting to marry his stepchildren to important allies. Otherwise his boundless energies were occupied in campaigns against the Nurids, attacking Aleppo in 1155 and in 1158 while Baldwin and the host of Jerusalem besieged Banyas. So far it could be said that Reynald was performing as needed by repeatedly attacking the enemy, not that it could have had any decisive effect given the strength of the Moslem rulers.

Technically, as Prince of Antioch Reynald's overlord was the Byzantine emperor; Antioch had once been a province of his empire. As Prince Reynald was expected to act on Constantinople's behalf, and in 1156 he conducted a punitive attack on Cilicia, an Armenian kingdom of Anatolia, which was also a Byzantine vassal state. But when he was not paid the amount he expected, he and King Thoros of Cilicia set about a joint naval attack on Byzantine Cyprus. The result brought no lasting result, but inevitably made Reynald the subject of the emperor's wrath.

Again, there was opposition in the principality to this expedition, in particular from the Patriarch. Reynald had Aimery seized, coated in honey and chained on the citadel roof at the mercy of the heat and the flies. Aimery eventually left for Jerusalem, preferring to live far away from Reynald for many years.

Three years later, when Manuel led an army eastwards on campaign against the Nurids, Reynald was taught a lesson in the practicalities of ruling in the Near East. He could not afford to have both Nur-ad-Din and Manuel as enemies, so performed an act of contrition and affirmed his homage. Reynald came to the emperor's camp at Mamistra dressed in rags, barefooted and with a rope around his neck. It was the *Realpolitik* of feudal monarchy: Manuel could not easily dislodge Reynald and had to content himself with bringing him to heel. Reynald had learned something of what he could not afford to do.

In 1157, Reynald and another newcomer, Thierry of Flanders, led an expedition to the Orontes valley. They besieged Sheizar, but their cooperation did not last. Baldwin gave Thierry the lordship they were creating, and Reynald, himself claiming suzerainty over the region, objected. The siege was eventually lifted after the two commanders fell to squabbling and ceased to provide leadership.

Reynald's time as usurper Prince of Antioch ended abruptly in 1160. While leading a skirmish against the Nurids (some say while attacking Armenian peasants) he was captured in the Marash region. He was certainly held to be ransomed, but in the event remained imprisoned by Nur-ad-Din for fifteen years. One could wonder why he stayed there so long without ransom; perhaps few were prepared to pay for his return. He spent his time in prison learning Arabic and Turkish, but this long imprisonment must have been frustrating for such a man of action.

In 1175 Reynald was finally released as a gesture by Nur-ad-Din's son, but he found that much had changed in those wasted years. He was no longer prince of Antioch. Constance had died and the nobles of the principality had sworn fealty to his stepson as Bohemund III. This was to be expected for the designated heir, but it shows how little personal credibility Reynald now had. He was considered little use to Antioch spending year after year in his Aleppine prison, and many in the principality must have felt relieved at his absence.

But for all Reynald's unruly behaviour, it cannot be denied that he could bounce back quickly. Soon he found another heiress and became Lord of Oultrejordain. His marriage to Stephanie, heiress of the lordship and widow of Humphrey of Toron, now made Reynald an important noble of the Kingdom of Jerusalem. His domain included the castles of Krak des Moabites and Shawbak, which aided the defence of the kingdom in the south-east. No longer a prince, he was now a serious player and politician of the Kingdom. For Jerusalem itself, this would later prove disastrous.

The time Reynald had spent in captivity had seen such changes in the political landscape that he surely found it difficult to recognise the world as it now was. Nur-ad-Din had been replaced by an equally able but just as aggressive leader. In 1168 an attempted Frankish invasion of Egypt had enabled Nur-ad-Din to send in his general Shirkuh as Sunni protector of the Shi'ite Caliphate, forcing the Franks to withdraw. The following year, Shirkuh returned to make the protectorate permanent but died soon after. His nephew and lieutenant, Salah-ad-Din Yusuf, or Saladin as the west knew him, now came into his own.

Having succeeded his uncle as virtual governor of Egypt, Saladin soon ended the Fatimid Caliphate, restoring Sunni Islam to the land, and when Nur-ad-Din died in 1174 began the conquest of the Moslem Levant. He gained Damascus fairly early but the regions of Aleppo and Mosul in Iraq, where others governed in the names of Nur-ad-Din's two underaged sons, took far longer to subdue. Committed as he was to the eventual driving of the Franks into the sea, he knew that this would need to wait. He needed the resources of Syria to accomplish this, given the demands of raising and supplying the forces needed. Considering his Moslem enemies he also needed to guard his own rear. At times, Saladin was amenable to making truces with the Christians, but such actions were pragmatic in their intent and only postponed his long-term objective.

Having received the endorsement of the Sunni Caliph in Baghdad, Saladin was now *sultan,* or 'executive power' over all Islam, which brought the responsibility of leading the jihad, or war of conquest on behalf of Islam. The threat to Outremer was now serious, and the newly released Reynald was in his element. But this was not a situation that either Reynald or his kind could resolve by simply fighting any Moslems they encountered.

Baldwin III had died during Reynald's time in prison, as had his successor Amalric I, who had pursued an aggressive policy towards his Moslem neighbours. Amalric on his death in 1174 had left the makings of a political disaster, for his successor the fourteen-year-old Baldwin IV was a leper.

An illness then widespread both in Europe and the East, leprosy involved rotting flesh, noisome odours and disfigurement. It had negative Biblical connotations: Pope Alexander III equated Baldwin's leprosy with his sins. But once he came to the throne Baldwin put all his efforts into maintaining his kingdom against the new threat. He even led armies to victory while he could, but at times his illness prevented him from governing, and regents would be appointed. Once, in 1178, the regency fell to Reynald for two years. By 1183 the disease had so ravaged the young king that he had lost the use of his hands and feet and was blind. Such constraints on the leadership were hardly what the Franks needed in such times.

The politics of the kingdom from 1174 to 1187 are often thought to have taken the form of factions divided over aggressive action towards the Moslems and those of conciliation. In reality, both sides alternated between the two stances. In retrospect, the wisdom of attacking the Moslem lands is questionable now that Saladin was in the process of uniting the former Nurid and Fatimid empires against the Christians, and Frankish depredations aided his cause.

On the other hand, Saladin was committed in the long term to the destruction of Frankish Syria, and his offers of conciliation were simply gaining him time to deal with his Moslem enemies and postponing the inevitable. Perhaps only a major war of conquest against Saladin's empire could have halted this threat, and this was hardly practicable without a mass of volunteers from Europe.

Nevertheless, there was a belligerent tendency among those who associated with Agnes, the young king's mother. Many were comparative newcomers from Europe, in particular the Poitevin adventurer Guy of Lusignan, who married Baldwin's sister Sibylla. The Master of the Templars, Gerard de Ridefort was also known for his impulsive behaviour and associated with this clique, in which Reynald himself figured prominently. Their leading opponent was Count Raymond III of Tripoli, the king's cousin on his father's side, who had also been a prisoner of the Moslems for several years but showed himself a far more cautious figure than Reynald. King Baldwin did not trust him but made him regent in 1183 when he himself knew that he was soon to die. Raymond had the support of many of the established barons of the kingdom.

The reign of Baldwin IV had proceeded under continual threat of invasion. The kingdom's military resources were poor while its well-built castles and fortified towns had a shortage of warriors to garrison them. The Templars and Hospitallers, together with the smaller military orders, provided reliable armies to aid the defence, but these together with the nobles and knights of the kingdom were not numerous enough to appear reassuring. Losses in territory impaired military strength further, for feudal resources were lost with them. Nor did crusading fervour in Europe turn into very much action, and relations with Constantinople, which had never been at all amicable, had turned particularly sour.

It was a very serious state of affairs for a realm weakened by such a king. Guy and Sybilla's faction, to which Reynald belonged, had few options. In 1181 and 1184 they sent missions to Europe hoping for a new crusade. At best they gained promises from some kings and nobles, but very few knights arrived to aid the kingdom in the ensuing years. There were fights with Moslem invaders. In July 1182, carried in a litter, Baldwin headed an army that thwarted one such attack at Le Forbelet in Galilee. After this, blind and immobile, he was incapable of any further activity.

The following year, Guy as regent rode out with the muster of the kingdom to meet a new invasion, and succeeded in standing firm until Saladin, his army low on supplies, withdrew without fighting. Guy had avoided engagement and had accomplished what was needed for that time, but this strategy was seen as so dishonourable that he was soon after deprived of the regency. Raymond of Tripoli then took over, but he had no new ideas. He succeeded in making yet another truce with Saladin but knew it would not last.

Reynald during these years was in his element, fighting Saracens. As his lordship of Oultrejordan bordered on a junction of Moslem Syria, the Hijaz and the Kingdom, he saw plenty of action as Saladin's armies often invaded through this region. His attack on a large caravan at Taima in 1181 violated an existing truce. In 1182 Reynald was trapped in the castle at Kerak while Saladin's armies laid siege. For a time, it was a match even for Reynald, as the Moslem siege engines were damaging the walls. Fortunately, Raymond of Tripoli arrived with a relieving force just in time

Late in 1182 he embarked on the most spectacular of campaigns. He had five ships brought overland to the Gulf of Aqaba and sailed them in the Red Sea. Frankish vessels had never been seen there before and they had the advantage of surprise. Throughout the winter Reynald and his men harried merchant ships, and – much worse – those laden with Moslem pilgrims bound for the Holy Places. Once they even menaced Medina itself with Bedouin allies. Eventually, Saladin launched a counterattack with Egyptian ships and drove the Frankish raiders ashore where some were captured, although Reynald himself was absent. They were all put to death, two in Mecca itself in a horrific public execution. Moslem hatred for the Franks was far from surprising. Saladin's personal animosity for Reynald himself was a driving issue in later events.

Perhaps the traditional view of Reynald as a firebrand who exhibited indiscriminate aggression against Moslems is simplistic. He is often contrasted with Raymond's cautious approach. In reality, the situation was becoming increasingly dire and the best action for the time was probably to harm the enemy as much as possible and impair his strength, but even this was futile in the long term. The very continued existence of Frankish Syria was remarkable; involving as it did a long sea voyage from Europe, being surrounded by enemies and with meagre military resources. Such a perspective makes the end of the Crusader states seem inevitable; that is if varying political conditions in the Moslem lands are not taken into account. Perhaps only ongoing crusading from Europe would have saved Outremer, but as this did not happen it is remarkable that the territories survived so long.

To make peace with Saladin was not viable in the long term, committed as he was as sultan to conduct the *jihad*. Whatever truces he made were designed to neutralise the Franks while he turned his attention on subduing Nurid resistance in the east. Between 1174 and 1183 Saladin reunited the Islamic lordships of the region and such conciliatory actions towards the Franks only aided this ultimate aim. As appeasement in the 1930s is seen with hindsight, this policy could only be disastrous in the endgame. Conciliation did buy time for the Franks, but they could do little to take advantage of it. They had tried to enlist aid from the West, and this policy failed as the Europeans were either too nearsighted or unwilling to crusade.

The institution of crusading was impromptu in its nature, and only an ongoing commitment on the part of the European states to supply armies could have maintained Outremer. Similar to military activities in Vietnam and Afghanistan in modern times, only a standing army and serious expenditure could have maintained their defence and none of the feudal monarchies of Europe in the twelfth and thirteenth centuries could ever sustain this. While the military orders recruited knights throughout the West for this purpose there was never more than a few hundred of each in Syria at any one time. In 1177 the Franks made an alliance with Aleppo against Saladin, but this accomplished little, and any attempt to rally the Kurdish interloper's enemies against him came to nothing. Still no crusade came. At times the truces were broken, often by Reynald himself when he ambushed trade caravans.

Reynald and those of similar mind were acting in the only way they thought could produce results. Of course, they knew they could do little without a much larger army, but perhaps they could frustrate Saladin's attempts to unite Egypt, Syria and the Hijaz and even this was not easy. It is possible that Reynald wanted to damage Saladin's prestige by striking at his role as protector of the Holy Cities. He could also hope to harm the Egyptian economy, reliant as it was on trade from the East. We do not know how knowledgeable he was about Islamic affairs, but this would explain his ostensibly wild acts of piracy. If Saladin had not put a stop to it at an early stage Reynald would have seriously undermined his position. There was some justification for his continual depredations, if only in the context of slowly wearing the Moslems down, but like conciliation, this policy only postponed the coming war of conquest. From 1183, once Saladin had seized Aleppo, the last remaining Nurid principality, he had attained a much stronger position.

There was an element of a personal duel between Reynald and Saladin in these later years. Saladin saw Reynald as representing everything about the Franks that he despised. Reynald's naval expedition had hit hard, not only at Saladin's role as protector of Moslems but at his sense of what was good behaviour. He might have resolved at this stage on revenge, should Reynald ever fall under his power.

In 1183 Saladin again attacked Reynald in Krak. The Franks were then celebrating the marriage of Reynald's stepson Humphrey of Toron, but as all assembled were in the mood for revelry, the party carried on as the Moslem artillery bombarded the castle. Lady Stephanie even sent food from the banquet out to Saladin's tent, as the unexpected guest at the wedding. The amir graciously enquired where the bridal pair was lodging and ordered that the bombarding be diverted from that part of the castle.

In 1185 Baldwin IV died, and his nine-year-old successor Baldwin V followed him within the year. Sibylla was now the heiress and Raymond's faction, which included many of the noble families of the kingdom, objected to her husband's succeeding, but Reynald, together with Gerard, Patriarch Heraclius and others, insisted on Guy. They had their way through a ruse but the result was divisive. Raymond even made an alliance with Saladin against Guy, for a time allowing Moslems to invade unimpeded through his territory. A new truce with Saladin came into force shortly after.

Reynald of Châtillon is credited with the single act that brought on the disaster of 1187, when in March that year he attacked a Moslem caravan bound for Cairo from Damascus, with which Saladin's own sister was travelling. Saladin demanded restitution, which Reynald refused, even when Saladin was now ready for the massed invasion and could only have been waiting for a pretext. Reynald had little respect for agreements with Moslems and would supply the required violation sooner or later. The caravan also had an armed guard, which in itself contravened the truce. Did Reynald expect the Sultan to invade anyway, and conduct his own war on the Moslem economy in the way he thought best?

King Guy was aware enough of how serious Saladin's campaign would become to take an unprecedented step. He ordered the *arrière-ban*, where every able-bodied male in the kingdom must come to its defence; a measure designated only for extreme crises. But then he gambled the entire defence on a single strategy, and Guy of Lusignan was no strategist.

Reynald cannot take all the blame for the defeat at the Horns of Hattin in July 1187; only part of it. Saladin was leading the Moslem army towards Jerusalem from the east, across a dry plain and through an arid mountain pass. Guy of Lusignan, leading the Frankish host in the field, now held a council of war with his commanders. Count Raymond of Tripoli advocated waiting for Saladin to come to them, knowing that crossing the dry plain of Hattin would weaken the invaders. Raymond's own wife was besieged in Galilee, and any delay would endanger her, but this waiting strategy made sense. He advocated that they abandon any attempt to relieve Tiberias, as the invaders would then march for Jerusalem.

If the Franks crossed the plain themselves, parched in the July heat and rationing the water, they would put themselves at a disadvantage, Raymond reasoned. Many of the *poulains*, as the Franks born in the East were known, also opposed this strategy, for they understood the terrain and climate. But the newcomers were all for riding forward to Tiberias, as if to attack was the more valiant and attractive option.

While deliberations went on, both Reynald and Gerard of Ridefort saw Guy in private and hectored him in favour of the strategy of advance. By the time they were through it sounded too much like cowardice for the king to delay, which made him reach his unfortunate decision. Soon the Frankish army was marching over the parched wilderness, bearing the True Cross (as it was believed to be) at its head.

Perhaps Guy remembered the accusations of cowardice in 1183, when he conducted his strategy of 'shadowing' Saladin's force. An experienced strategist would understand that the Moslem army would only last as long in the field as its supply train held, and that to simply hold firm in the same way could have saved the kingdom for the present, or at least gain a year's respite. But Guy had once lost his regency as a result of this policy, and he could ill afford such a reaction now, given how precariously he held onto his crown. Raymond had recently given Guy cause not to be trusted, and Reynald was a close associate. The Master of the Hospital, who might have balanced Gerard, had been killed in a Moslem attack the previous year. Added to this was the responsibility Guy had as overlord of Tiberias.

When they reached the Horns of Hattin, the twin mountains to the east of the Holy City, on 4 July 1187, they found the wells there poisoned, while the smoke of the brushwood that the enemy had fired stung their eyes and panicked their horses. When Saladin attacked much of the damage was already done. Again, Guy consulted Reynald and Gerard, and they advocated the army should stand and fight: it was too late to do much else. The Franks were at the exact disadvantage their enemies would have been, had they not moved forward.

Raymond of Tripoli led an attack on the enemy lines, which opened to let in the force and closed to surround them. Although most of this attacking force was massacred or taken prisoner, Raymond was one of the few prominent Franks to escape the battle. By the mid-afternoon all Franks who had neither fallen nor fled were forced to surrender. Saladin was pleased to see so many of the great of Jerusalem as his prisoners: King Guy himself, Gerard of Ridefort, Balian d'Ibelin – and Reynald de Châtillon.

Later that day Saladin himself came to speak to these prisoners, as they sat on the ground. They could all reasonably expect either captivity or ransom. In the event Guy and Gerard were later released and both repudiated their promises not to fight against Saladin again.

But on the day of the battle Reynald received his come-uppance. Saladin, genteel and magnanimous, gave a drink of water to the King of Jerusalem. Guy drank, and then gave the cup to Reynald sitting next to him, who took the remainder. Saladin was displeased, and reproached the king, saying he did not give drink to one he intended to kill.

Enacting long-awaiting retribution, Saladin killed Reynald personally, with a single blow of his sword. He struck off Reynald's arm at the shoulder, and the Frank bled to death. While the body was left to the dogs, Reynald's head was brought to Damascus to be dragged through the streets. There is an alternative version where Saladin gave Reynald a drink, and the Frank refused to accept it, and then behaved in a rude and disdainful manner. An angered Saladin then stabbed Reynald in the chest, his guard then beheading him. Either account could be correct, although the legend favours Saladin's personal vendetta ending at that moment by his own hand.

Guy had called up every man who could carry a weapon and taken most on the campaign. There was little resistance to the invasion after

Hattin and within the week Saladin entered Jerusalem in triumph. Soon almost the entire Frankish kingdom was conquered, only a few pockets of resistance fighting on. The city of Tyre held out and Saladin later lifted the siege, other matters more pressing. The Templars and Hospitallers held onto their strongholds including Krak des Chevaliers, Safad and Tortosa. Saladin was thus prevented from completing his conquest of the Frankish lands, and the Franks bought some vital time. Now the West was finally moved to a new crusade, the worst having happened.

The Third Crusade that finally arrived in 1191 had the most illustrious leadership of all. The German Emperor Frederick Barbarossa drowned in a river on the way, and King Philip Augustus returned to France fairly early, so it was King Richard the Lionheart of England who led the recovery of some of the territory lost after Hattin. He failed to retake Jerusalem itself, but at least saved some of the kingdom. He also added Cyprus to Frankish territory, which made it a useful source of supply. Saladin died soon after the crusade had returned to Europe, and his family fought over his empire.

Compared to the Frankish states of the mid-twelfth century, the total area recovered was pitifully small, but Outremer at least survived another century. Jerusalem was even regained for a time. Failure in the Moslem world to produce leadership against the Franks after Saladin accounts for this in part, and when the Mamluk sultans gained control over both Egypt and Syria after 1260, the end finally came.

While it cannot be denied that Reynald of Châtillon was aggressive, cruel, self-seeking and treacherous, from the First Crusade these qualities were common to many who ventured east. Christian charity was not the prime sentiment for those who vowed to beat back the Moslems with their swords, and who saw no dishonour in gathering wealth and lands in the process. Such sentiments were still encouraged in Europe by the time Reynald set out from France. But a second generation of Franks living in Outremer had the aggressive drive tempered by the realities of living with the Moslems and sought an accommodation; they understood that crusading was ephemeral in its nature.

By 1187 Reynald had already lived for a long time in the Frankish East, and although not a newcomer was of that aggressive mentality that many came with. He was hardly a young man, by then at least approaching fifty, and seems to have learned little in strategy and social skills for all those years. Even fifteen years in the dungeons of Aleppo had not slowed him down.

He was an upstart according to the *poulains,* and he gained position by twice seeking out heiresses; perhaps his face was his fortune. Reynald clearly had little patience with the established nobles, and he made many enemies among them. He appeared not to countenance any course but violence against the infidel and thought nothing of breaking promises made to non-Christians. But that was the mentality of the typical crusader, as the Church in Europe encouraged, and not the way of an established lord of Outremer.

If the Frankish states could have been saved from Saladin it could only have been in the period between 1174 and 1183, when he was seeking to unite Syria with Egypt and use the combined resources against the Franks. But this was the time of instability under Baldwin IV when no new crusade could be expected, and the two factions failed to produce any coherent strategy. Whether the Franks could have systematically frustrated Saladin by alliances with his enemies is questionable. Perhaps Reynald's policy of continual aggression was the best that could be followed at the time. Saladin was only awaiting a pretext when Reynald broke the truce in 1187 with his caravan raid. While this Frankish lord offended Saladin's sense of decent behaviour and was the object of the amir's personal hatred, Reynald was but a detail in his long-term plan to drive the Franks into the sea.

Although not a sympathetic figure, Reynald was a product of his time, and probably acted as he saw fit. The main problem was his role as a loose cannon, a nightmare for anyone trying to ensure the survival of Frankish Syria in such desperate times.

3

Enrico Dandolo, Doge of Venice

Despite Advanced Age and Blindness...

This is a tale of two cities and their attached empires, and of what is often described as the worst crime of the medieval epoch. It is also the story of a most remarkable man, in his eighties at least and allegedly blind, but energetic, astute and charismatic. The part Enrico Dandolo, the forty-first Doge of Venice, played in the diversion of the Fourth Crusade to the conquest of Constantinople has been the subject of serious debate, but while the evidence does not place the smoking gun undoubtedly in Dandolo's hand, his activities beg scrutiny.

Founded on a grouping of islands in a lagoon in the north-west corner of the Adriatic Sea, the Most Serene Republic of Venice was by 1200 long established as a trading centre for several worlds. Venetian ships sailed to Alexandria and elsewhere in the eastern Mediterranean and Black seas to return with silks, spices and precious metals. Close as it was to the Transalpine trade routes, the city could hardly fail to prosper. Spices were always in high demand, given the monotonous diets of many Europeans. Venetian merchants even stole the relics of St Mark from Alexandria in 828 as a means of bolstering their own city's prestige.

After Venice broke from Byzantine hegemony in the eighth century it developed its own aristocracy, eventually a cadre of forty wealthy mercantile families. Names such as Manin, Michiel, Mocenigo, Ziani appeared prominently in the affairs of the city throughout its history, as did the Dandoli. Down the centuries this oligarchy dominated the council, and through a multi-stage electoral system chose the Doge, the chief executive of the republic, from among their number. The title was related to that of duke and was a lifelong appointment.

The Byzantine Empire is in fact a modern name given to what remained of the Roman Empire of the East, which it still considered itself to be. After the original Roman Empire split into two and the western half collapsed in the fifth century under the weight of Germanic raiders and settlers, the East, its capital at Constantinople, would last another thousand years. At first it reconquered most of the former Roman Mediterranean, including Italy, and even Venice was for a time part of this resurgent empire. But soon the rise of Islam reduced its territories. Egypt, Syria and North Africa were lost in the seventh century and in the tenth the Turks colonized the eastern half of Anatolia. Slavs, Hungarians and Bulgars also grabbed lands in the Balkans while Spain and Italy also slipped away.

But the empire survived. At an early stage Greek replaced Latin as the language of government as much as of commerce and many institutions developed separately from the Roman models. The eastern Christian churches would not comply with assertions of supremacy from the Bishop of Rome and had long followed separate traditions. The Catholic Church saw the Orthodox as heretical, and vice versa. A long-running quarrel over the appearance of the word *filioque* in the Catholic Creed, whether the Holy Ghost proceeded from the Father or from the Father *and the son*, or rather whether Rome could decide on this insertion without consultation, was the principal cause for centuries of a serious schism.

The Franks, the western European Catholics, were as a whole far from in harmony with the Greeks. During the First Crusade there was unease when the Frankish host made its way to the Holy Land crossing to Asia Minor through Constantinople. The westerners came to see their Byzantine hosts as untrustworthy, their manner effete, and the Greeks considered the Franks boorish and predatory – as dangerous as the Moslems. There was even a real possibility at that early juncture of the crusading army turning on its Greek hosts.

As Venice rose as a commercial centre Byzantium became its most significant trading partner and its rival. There was a Venetian quarter at Constantinople and much commerce both ways. But there was always an underlying tension, especially as the Italians increasingly dominated the markets. The Greeks and Venetians were never far from confrontation.

Such resentment fuelled an incident in 1171 when a Greek mob stormed the quarters in Constantinople where the Italian merchants resided. The imperial government accused the Venetians of attacks on the Genoese, and ordered all those of Venice arrested and their property confiscated. Whole families were imprisoned and robbed, to the outrage of the Venetians when news reached the city. Doge Michiel took an armada on a punitive action to Constantinople, but this accomplished nothing. It took fourteen years before relations between Venice and Constantinople were normalised and many still remembered this incident in 1204.

In 1195 the Byzantine Emperor Isaac II Angelus was overthrown when his elder brother, soon to rule as Alexius III, defeated him in battle, ordered him deposed and then blinded. Alexius himself was not a competent ruler, and in Epirus and Nicaea on the edges of his empire Byzantine princes asserted their independence. The Bulgars also threatened. Many observers decided by 1200 that the Byzantine Empire had reached a state of near-collapse and was certainly at its weakest in centuries.

After the Third Crusade ended in 1192 Jerusalem was still lost to Christendom, and there was a widespread desire in Europe for a new crusade to regain it. The German Emperor Henry VI led a small expedition in 1197, but this accomplished nothing and he died soon afterwards. Henry had entertained ideas of the conquest of the Byzantine Empire, the submission of the Orthodox Church to Rome and the reconquest of the Levant all together. This was certainly a grandiose scheme, but not as wild as it might seem while Byzantium under the Angeloi was showing so many signs of fragmentation. Had he not died then Henry might have accomplished at least some of this, possibly to have gained a foothold in Greece. His brother Philip of Swabia also took a serious interest in an attack on Byzantium.

As it turned out there was otherwise in Europe little more than lip-service paid to completing the recovery of the Holy Land; the old story of calls for crusading without much action. Saladin had died in 1192, not long after making peace with Richard of England, and while the sultan's relatives were fighting over his empire between them the Franks of Outremer enjoyed some respite and preferred not to confront the Moslems at this time.

In 1198 this changed when Cardinal Lothario dei Conti di Segni became pope, taking on his elevation the ironic name of Innocent III. He is known to history as a reforming pontiff who worked from the outset to purge the Church of abuses and to renew the fight against heresy and Islam. Ignoring words of caution from the Patriarch of Antioch, the new pope ordered the preaching of a new crusade to finish the work left undone.

At this stage a successful preaching campaign could still raise a large army. The crusaders did not as in the previous venture include kings or emperors; Richard the Lionheart would have gone again but was killed in 1199, and the pope was loath to surrender the overall leadership of the crusade to kings. Those who came included Count Baldwin of Flanders, Louis de Blois, Hugh de St-Pol and Simon de Montfort, father of the Simon who later revolted against Henry III of England. There were also many ecclesiastics, notably the Cistercian Abbot of Les-Vaux-de-Cernay. Many barons, knights and footsoldiers also answered the call. Prominent, too, was Geoffrey de Villehardouin, Marshal of Champagne, who wrote a detailed account of the crusade.

Those who responded mostly came from northern France and the Low Countries. The Count of Champagne would have led the crusade, but died before it began and Boniface, Marquis of Montferrat reluctantly took over the leadership. Boniface had a claim through his family to the lordship of Thessalonika, but there is no evidence that this issue had entered the computations at this early stage.

During the initial discussion the land route through Asia Minor was definitely ruled out, drawing on the experience of the Emperor Frederick Barbarossa in the previous crusade when he lost many men fighting through the hostile region and then drowned while crossing a river. The plan that Richard of England had formulated during the previous crusade of invading the Nile Delta as the region that supplied the Moslem feudal warriors' resources was also discussed. Such an invasion would form the main strategy of the Fifth and Seventh Crusades and was certainly on the agenda early in the Fourth, as was the original plan to land in the Levant and attack Jerusalem directly.

To transport a vast army to either Acre or the Delta would require a large fleet of ships, and this problem was the crusade's undoing. Normally the Pisan and Genoese merchants would be all too ready to provide their own at a price, but these two maritime republics were then at war with each other. The crusaders therefore turned to Venice.

It was in Venice that the Papal legate Peter Capuano would encounter Enrico Dandolo, its formidable Doge. It was a business proposition that Peter had to place before him and his ducal council, which involved the building of eighty ships in addition to those they already had, to bring the estimated crusading army to its destination. It was a proposal of astronomical proportions which would turn the entire productive capacity of the city over to this purpose for at least a year. Dandolo saw the potentially huge income.

The year of Enrico Dandolo's birth is uncertain, given as early as 1108 and more likely as 1122, although even then his great age could have been exaggerated. His father Vitale Dandolo was a member of the ducal court and close advisor of the Doge, Vitale II Michiel, and had served as ambassador on occasions to Ferrara and Constantinople. An uncle, also named Enrico Dandolo, was Patriarch of Grado, the most senior ecclesiastic in Venice. The Dandoli produced four Doges, several admirals and many other prominent citizens in the history of the Serenissima.

His family was known for longevity. Perhaps this younger Enrico was overshadowed by his father and uncle for a large part of his life and had to wait for his own rise to prominence. He had many advantages coming from such an illustrious family, but it was only in later life that he could truly come into his own. He was married while Doge to Contessa, believed to be of the Minotto clan. He had one son, Ranier, who deputised for him when he sailed for Constantinople.

Enrico Dandolo's first prominent role was, ironically, to sail in the punitive 1171 naval expedition against Constantinople. After the Emperor had seized the goods of the Venetians, the Doge Michiel led a fleet in reprisal, but an attack of plague brought this campaign to naught and an angry mob lynched the Doge on its return. Dandolo, aging but very active, escaped blame for this failure, and in 1173 was appointed ambassador to Constantinople. He was later sent twice to the Court of King William II of Sicily, and then in 1183 again to Constantinople to negotiate the restoration of the Venetian quarter there.

How Dandolo came to be blind is uncertain. One story says that while he was in Constantinople the Emperor Manuel took exception to his arrogant and uncooperative manner and had him blinded with a burning glass. This is possible, as blinding was common in Byzantium, but has the feel of legend; there would have been an outcry in Venice had this happened to an envoy. Villehardouin the chronicler-crusader related how Dandolo had told him it was the result of a blow to the head, and there is a story of his injury in a brawl in Constantinople. It may have simply been due to advanced age. It is even possible that he was not completely blind, but acted as if he was for his own purposes.

On 1 January 1193 Enrico Dandolo took office as Doge. He was certainly in his seventies (some said his eighties) and reputedly blind, but still commanded awe for his obvious mental abilities. He was hale and even strong for his age. In his period of office his accomplishments were remarkable.

Dandolo's reform of the Venetian coinage had lasting effect. From the standard silver penny he produced a new coin, the *grosso*, which was worth 24 pennies. On one side it showed St Mark blessing the Doge himself, who is named on the edge. At that time there was no national currency in most countries and international trade was far from standardised, and this reform reduced Venice's dependence on Byzantine coinage. At a time when Byzantium's economy and politics were becoming unstable it was an astute move. The *bezant* had for centuries been the most stable currency but was losing that pre-eminence.

Almost at the beginning of his term in office, Dandolo turned his attentions to the problem of Zara. A city on the Dalmatian coast, Zara had long paid tribute to Venice, but this ended in 1186 when King Emeric of Hungary captured it. From 1193 Dandolo sent several expeditions to regain control of the city, at times with military aid from Genoa and Brindisi. He had not succeeded by 1202 and this matter would later figure in his dealings with the crusaders.

In April 1201 Dandolo and his counsellors heard the proposition the papal legate made on the crusade's behalf and agreed to it. Venice would provide transport for 4,500 knights with their horses, 9,000 squires and 20,000 soldiers, with food for nine months. The city would under a separate clause supply fifty galleys at its own expense in return for half the lands conquered. For the entire transport package, on the calculation of a payment of four marks per horse and two marks per man, the crusaders would pay the total sum of 85,000 marks in four instalments. The Venetians would immediately set about building their new ships and the fleet would sail a year from then.

The treaty was accordingly signed on this understanding and the crusade would rally in Venice at that appointed date. The Venetians knew at this point that Alexandria had been chosen as the destination but they voiced no opposition to this. Dandolo showed every sign of support for the crusade; this was a business venture although on a larger scale than any before and he treated the affair accordingly.

When the leadership of the crusade arrived in Venice in the spring of 1202 both they and the Venetians had cause for concern. Previous estimates of the size of the army were shown as unduly optimistic. As was usual when crusades were preached many in the west took the Cross, making solemn vows before church altars and wearing cloth crosses on their clothes. But when pressed for a date in which they would actually depart on crusade, far too many would find excuses for delay. To take the Cross allowed certain legally enforceable immunities, which some enjoyed without ever setting forth. There was forgiveness for previous sins for a crusader on swearing to venture on this divine mission.

Some had already made their own transport arrangements, despite the planned assembly at Venice. Part of the Flemish contingent had taken ship at Bruges, and many of the Burgundian and Provençal crusaders had gone from Marseilles, as both found it more convenient. On the whole, a far smaller number appeared in Venice than expected.

The Venetians expected payment for their efforts, while the plan for payment the crusaders had prepared now fell through; payments those assembled offered did not cover half of the agreed amount. The Venetians were not prepared to let a single ship sail, nor would they refund the amount already paid, having put so much toil and expense into the project. By September the crusade had little prospect of taking place. Some of the host were now making their own arrangements to press on to Acre while others were drifting back to their homelands, thinking the crusade over before it had begun.

It was Dandolo who offered a solution. There could be an agreement by which the payment would be delayed, in return for the crusaders doing a service for Venice. They would help capture Zara. This move was criticized as a serious departure from the parameters of the crusade. Zara was a Christian city and King Emeric had himself taken the Cross. On hearing of the plan in Rome, Innocent immediately denounced it and excommunicated the entire crusade. He later lifted this curse on the crusaders, although not on the Venetians.

Before departing for Zara the host assembled in the Church of San Marco, where Dandolo addressed all from the pulpit. 'I am myself old and feeble, and need rest,' he said, according to Villehardouin. 'My body is infirm. But I know that no man may lead you and govern you as I, your Lord, can do.' He then declared his intent to take the Cross himself and requested that his son Ranier deputise for him. The multitude clamoured for him to do so, and he swore the oath at the altar and had the Cross sewn to his hat. This expedition to Zara was hardly a crusade, but Dandolo remained at the forefront of the 'crusading' army from that day onwards. It is curious that in the tirade he made no reference to his blindness.

On 8 November 1202 the Venetians and Franks sailed together to Zara. At the head of the 480 or so ships sailed that of the Doge, painted vermilion with sails of the same colour, Dandolo himself stood in the prow bearing the banner of the winged lion of St Mark, the emblem of Venice. He never returned to his beloved city.

The campaign itself at Zara was no serious challenge. Laying siege with mangonels and other siege engines and attempting to undermine the walls by digging under them, the crusaders soon broke the citizens' will to resist. Zara surrendered after five days.

But as the siege began it was almost called off. The Zarans pleaded with the crusaders, saying that as they were Christians they should not have a crusading army besieging them. The pope had already forbidden this deviation from the crusade and the Franks had only agreed to it as they knew of no alternative. Even the Abbot of Vaux called for them to leave off this obvious travesty of crusading, as did Simon de Montfort and some French barons. Dandolo rounded on the leaders. 'My lords ... you have given me your promise to assist me in conquering it, and I now summon you to keep your word.' His insistence on this promise at least quelled the dissent long enough to gain the surrender. The crusaders and Venetians then quartered in the city and soon began brawling amongst themselves, mostly over division of the spoils.

It appears that it was only when the armies were obliged to winter in Zara that an expedition to Constantinople was first discussed. Alexius, son of the deposed Isaac II, had escaped imprisonment in 1201 and made haste via the Danube to the court of his sister Irene's husband, Philip of Swabia. Philip, as brother of the dead emperor Henry VI, had himself been frustrated in his own bid for the German Empire, and saw an opportunity to further his interests in the east, taking up where his brother had left off.

He sent envoys to Dandolo and Boniface at Zara on Alexius' behalf, suggesting the crusaders next apply their muscle to the restoration of Isaac as Byzantine Emperor. Alexius made free with promises: of large sums of money, of 10,000 soldiers for the crusade, of the union of the eastern and western churches and much else. In the context of the attack on Zara it all seemed more reasonable, and would have solved the financial problems, to say nothing of the needs of a dwindling crusader army. Dandolo agreed almost on the spot. His enthusiasm must have swayed the other leaders.

This did not seem a diversion of the crusade at this point. Many a knight's quest in medieval literature involved digressing on the way for adventures and military action. Richard of England had journeyed to the Third Crusade in just this fashion, when after taking time to campaign in Sicily he also stopped off to capture Cyprus from a Byzantine renegade, before reaching Acre and setting about the crusade in earnest. The crusade was presented with just one more stop on the way to engaging with the Saracens, one which would aid their efforts in the 'actual' crusade.

Again there was dissent over this new departure from the plan. Simon de Montfort made clear his own opposition, and subsequently set off for home in disgust, as did the Abbot of Vaux. Despite this, in early 1203 the Fourth Crusade set out from Zara, stopping to attack the island of Corfu, then held by the Greeks. Some of the army rebelled at this point, displeased at this turn of events. Dandolo and the leadership were again hard pressed to stop the crusade dispersing.

The seaborne crusaders reached the Bosphorus on 24 June 1203, at Chalcedon on the opposite side of the straits to Constantinople. From there they rapidly occupied the suburb of Galata, cutting the chain to the harbour of the Golden Horn. On 17 July they were attacking Constantinople itself by both land and sea.

The Varangian Guard, English and Danish mercenaries in the service of the Byzantine Emperor, fought doggedly and slowed down the Franks' progress, driving back the land attack, but the crusaders came again, using small assault craft. Once again Dandolo led the onslaught. Villehardouin related how in full armour this blind old man urged his craft towards the beach in the face of furious opposition from the Greeks, landing before the others. When he was first off the ship to plant the Banner of San Marco on the beach it spurred the others to surge forth, and the crusaders gained control of some twenty-five towers on the walls before the day was out. That night Alexius II the usurper lost his nerve and fled, leaving his wife and all but one of his children. The city surrendered.

This stage of the campaign thus ended quickly, and it appeared that the crusaders had accomplished the mission. They saw blind Isaac II restored to the imperial title and his son co-emperor as Alexius IV. It is not certain how many crusaders still believed that they would travel on to the lands of Islam.

Having fulfilled their undertaking to Alexius, the crusaders expected payment for their services. Alexius had made astronomical promises, all much easier to make than to deliver, and the imperial treasury was empty. The Greek nobility and intelligentsia resented how he had become emperor and the continued presence of this Frankish army at Galata was cause for concern, justly in the event. Alexius imposed new taxes and even ordered the melting down of church plate in an attempt to pay the Franks and this understandably brought further resentment. The Orthodox clergy were united in their opposition to the proposed union of the churches, which would have meant subjugation to Rome. When some Franks decided to burn down a mosque in the Moslem quarter, they started a fire that in two days levelled a large part of the city. By January 1204 tension between Franks and Greeks had come close to eruption.

Nine months after placing the two emperors on the throne the Franks were still waiting for their reward, but none was forthcoming. Dandolo was now changing his tune. He now advised the leadership that Constantinople should be taken once again by force. There was nothing to be gained from the Angeloi, he told them, and the only way was to take what they were owed and install a compliant ruler in the city.

Events inside the city itself precipitated this call to action, when the Greeks called an assembly which readily agreed to depose Alexius, but spent three days deliberating on who would succeed. Meanwhile Alexius was captured, imprisoned and later strangled. Isaac died soon after, probably by poison. Alexius Ducas Murtzuphlus, who staged the coup, now became Alexius V.

Now that it was obvious the Franks would not be paid for their efforts, Dandolo's advice was adopted. By March the crusaders were preparing to attack, becoming anxious when they saw the towers under repair at the new emperor's command. Boniface, many crusaders now felt, had been too close to the overthrown Alexius, and he accordingly lost prestige and influence. It looked more and more that Dandolo was directing the crusade, if 'crusade' was still an appropriate term. On 9 April 1204 the Franks attacked the city walls, lashing together their ships in the harbour so that they could make better use of the catapults mounted on them. Once they had occupied two towers and had broken down a gate the Greeks had little chance of resistance.

There followed a sickening chronicle of carnage and vandalism, followed by an orgy of looting and plunder. Everything of any value – gold, jewels, plate, religious relics and so much else – was taken. Many a common crusader left the city with a haul that made him wealthy for life. Monks were seen carrying several bodies of saints at one time. Many art treasures were destroyed. The *Quadriga,* the four brass horses which still adorn the façade of the Palazzo Ducale in Venice, were taken then from the Hippodrome.

Once the Franks had broken the remains of Byzantine resistance, they set about dismembering the empire and finding a new ruler for Constantinople. Dandolo declined this position; as he was Doge it would have posed constitutional issues. He adopted the parti-coloured stockings and scarlet buskin that the emperor had traditionally worn, and his successor as governor of the Venetian quarter also wore this outfit as regalia for his office. It was not difficult for the Venetians to block the election of Boniface of Montferrat, for all his efforts. The victors chose Baldwin of Flanders, a comparatively weak candidate the Venetians could easily control. The Latin Empire, as it is now known, began its short history from his coronation at Hagia Sophia on 16 May.

Dandolo and Venice, however, were the main beneficiaries of what is called the Fourth Crusade, when as agreed Venice received three-eighths of the territories. Dandolo laid claim to the district around Hagia Sophia and the Patriarch himself would be a Venetian. He also received many lands that would enhance Venetian seafaring strength: the western coast of the Greek mainland, the Thracian coast, the Ionian Islands, the Peloponnese, Naxos, Andros, Euboea, Gallipoli, Crete, and the city of Adrianople. He had also regained Zara. Once the other senior crusaders laid claim to other regions, Frankish Greece was at best a loose federation, unlikely to rival Venice in trade from the east. Dandolo's deal with the papal legate had paid well, several times over.

The Latin Emperor Baldwin I soon found that his material wealth fell far short of his titles. Most of the lands he received proved disappointing in terms of incomes gained and many territories named as his were more notional than real, occupied by other peoples. Byzantine rulers survived both in Nicaea in Anatolia, and in Epirus in western Greece, and sought to regain lands as the Frankish state sunk into decline. In addition, Karolyan, emperor of the Bulgars, posed as serious a threat to them as he had to the Angeloi. The Venetians in reality called the tune in the person of Dandolo, who remained in Constantinople for what would be the last year of his life. As the 'crusade' was now definitely over, the other Franks either carved out their various lordships in Greece or set off home, many bearing chests of loot with them.

In 1205, Dandolo, his energy seemingly unabated, once more led an army jointly with Baldwin against the Bulgars. The Franks were soundly defeated and Baldwin captured, and Dandolo led what was left of the force back to Constantinople. He died soon after his return.

It was surprising that Dandolo's body was not returned to Venice. He was interred in the great domed cathedral of Hagia Sophia, in the upper eastern gallery. The Turks destroyed the tomb centuries later on converting the building into a mosque, and the marker placed where it was believed to have stood dates from a later restoration.

In Venice Pietro Ziani became the new Doge. His predecessor's legacy had gained his office the additional title 'Lord of a quarter and half a quarter of the Roman Empire'. Venice now looked to a wider acquisition of territory, to a seaborne empire which Dandolo is credited with initiating. Ranier Dandolo was later killed in a war against Genoa over Crete. None of his family who later served Venice in prominent roles were Enrico Dandolo's direct descendant.

The conquest of Constantinople is the subject of a magnificent painting on a wall of the Palazzo Ducale in Venice, presented as a Venetian victory. Venice would see golden days in the centuries to come, but began a decline from the seventeenth century. Napoleon abolished the office of Doge in 1798, at the same time ending Venetian independence. First granted to Austria in 1815, Venice with its hinterland was finally incorporated into the unified Kingdom of Italy in 1866. In 1882 the Italian navy commissioned a warship named the *Enrico Dandolo* that figured significantly in naval activities for almost thirty years.

The Latin Empire lasted little more than half a century. Its emperors, poor and weak, lacked the resources and the power to rule effectively. Support from their Greek subjects, apart from the military aristocracy, was at best scant and often reluctant. Baldwin II even pawned the Crown of Thorns, the most revered relic, in order to maintain his empire in its last days. St Louis would later redeem the Crown and build the Sainte-Chapelle in Paris for its safekeeping.

The Byzantine resurgence threatened a dwindling Frankish Greece and the Nicene Despotate, its proximity to the Bosphorus granting it an advantage over the other survivor states, eventually regained Constantinople in 1261, making Michael I Palaeologus the first to rule a restored Byzantine Empire. But what had once been the Roman Empire of the East was seriously weakened by the dismemberment of 1204 and its story was one of decline from that time on. By the early fourteenth century, the Ottoman, or 'Osmanli' Turks had built an empire in Anatolia and would eventually swallow up all of Byzantium. Constantinople itself was the last city to fall in 1453 and the thousand-year empire ended. The Byzantine Empire was much weakened by the Fourth Crusade and the half-century of the Latin Empire and might otherwise have stood up better to the Ottoman onslaught in the fifteenth century, but there is no way of knowing. As Istanbul, the City of Constantine was capital of the Turkish empire until the twentieth century.

A crusade that set out to have liberated Jerusalem for Christendom and ended in the conquest and dismemberment of a Christian state was a sorry perversion of everything that crusading professed. But was

Dandolo to blame for it? It was a cynical act to serve the interests of the Venetian Republic as it developed, but to what extent, if at all did, Dandolo and the Venetians, or anybody for that matter, sit down in secret and plan the events as they came about, and how much of the results were foreseen?

Conspiracy theorists are divided on who was to blame, although more recently they believe it to have been Philip of Swabia in his plan to rule over the eastern and western empires. Boniface was believed to have colluded in this plot while pursuing his own agenda, but no conclusive evidence has been unearthed to support this. While it was clear that Venice was not exactly blameless in terms of using the crusade for its own ends, opinions vary as to whether Dandolo and his council manipulated the proceedings. At the early stage the Venetians were party to the agreement to attack Alexandria, a destination which, to avoid dissent at this early stage, was kept from most of the crusaders.

By the turn of the thirteenth century the crusade itself as an institution bore little resemblance to its ideals as an armed pilgrimage to further the cause of Christianity. While the acquisition of land and wealth was considered from the beginning a by-product of this holy endeavour, all manner of personal agendas were enacted with fewer genuine sentiments. Of those who took the Cross in 1200 and 1201, a proportion never even embarked on the crusade but enjoyed the practical benefits. The institution itself had been corrupted already and the Fourth Crusade was simply more blatant in its perversion of the ideal. Even more cynical travesties would follow in the coming century: crusades were proclaimed against the Catharist heresy in southern Franc, against the excommunicate emperor Frederick II and later against the Hussite heretics of Bohemia. The term 'crusade' has since covered many an endeavour; even the Reagan presidential campaign of 1980.

It was once believed that while the Venetians were preparing the crusade, they were negotiating a trade treaty with the Moslems in Alexandria. This cannot be proven, as the only known treaty of this nature is dated some years after these events. The initial strategy as agreed must certainly have been disconcerting to the Venetians. It was from Alexandria that many of their ships returned regularly laden with spices and other rich cargoes, which makes the suggestion of Venetian connivance in diverting the crusade more likely. Yet it could be said that the Venetians were as good Catholics as any, and many took part fighting the crusades. It must have posed a conflict of interest as the strategies were discussed, for it would have disrupted their most lucrative trade for years to come.

Venetians would gladly go crusading, or transporting crusaders, in Outremer itself. They were also happy to trade with Moslems at the same time: the trade routes from India and China crossed Moslem territory and the only safe road ran through Cairo and Alexandria. It is hard to believe that Venice would willingly kill the goose that laid the golden eggs. Perhaps they still believed they could continue trading after the crusade, possibly from a new foothold in Alexandria. Though it is far-fetched to conclude that Dandolo and his associates cooked up this elaborate plan to send the crusade where it would not harm their interests, given the switches in direction, it is more likely that as developments occurred the Venetians took advantage.

The undertaking to build an enormous fleet of ships shows that the Venetians were ready to place all their efforts into the crusade as planned, and the scale of it ensures they did not enter into the original matter lightly. They put up a fortune in building the ships and the whole of the city's available labour was channelled into the project. Rather than a desire to fight the good fight, this was business, but not incompatible with the crusading ideal. This was how the city survived. There was no reason at the beginning to fear that the crusaders would not come up with the payment. If the Venetians expected this, they could have discouraged Peter Capuano with a larger price, or simply declined the entire venture. They certainly expected to be paid enough to embark on such an ambitious enterprise.

Perhaps if the Venetians had decided to scupper the crusade against the Moslems, the best strategy would have been to turn down the crusaders' grandiose proposal from the beginning.

Crusades were essentially bursts of religious fervour, pious acts by men of coat-armour where killing Saracens was holy work. It was shown during the first of these that simply to walk off to the east and find Jerusalem somewhere down the road was far from viable. To transport armies and feed them while on campaign were concerns that faced all those who wished to go crusading; someone would need to pay for crusades, and charity was not a reliable source. Of course, crusaders saw little harm in acquiring plunder and lordships as perks of their righteous warfare, or perhaps as compensation.

Venice was confronted with the prospect of having invested time and money in this crusade and not being paid for it and faced financial ruin. That was certainly their most serious consideration. Dandolo was a businessman who wanted to recoup a poor investment.

The expedition to Constantinople did not arise from Venetian designs, it appears. That Dandolo had agreed to it because he had plans to dismember Byzantium is unlikely. The Venetians mostly hated the Greeks and Dandolo had reasons to do them harm in the interests of Venice. There is also a school of thought that says that given their previous behaviour towards the westerners, especially in 1171, Byzantium had it coming, and it was only a matter of time.

The Venetians certainly had an agenda of their own, and so did others, including Philip of Swabia and Boniface of Montferrat. But these two wished to restore Alexius IV and his father to the imperial throne, and it is unlikely that the Venetians had the same final aim as theirs. There are too many unplanned developments as one event followed another. Dandolo did not have the same final objective in 1204 when he sailed for Constantinople as when he set out for Zara, and certainly not when he authorised the original agreement with the crusaders. Even though the final result was what Venice would have long wished, far from a conspiracy to redirect the Fourth Crusade, the leadership changed direction as opportunity and necessity dictated. They simply ended where Dandolo would have wanted. When he called for the final act of turning on the Greeks altogether, it was not so much an abandonment of the previous strategy as the only possible way of making the best of a bad job.

For all Dandolo's cynical machinations he deserves some admiration for his acumen. He was one of the most astute of men in his time, and his achievements were considerable. Of course, for many Greeks it was a catastrophe: thousands were killed, mountains of valuables looted, churches raided and those remaining lived under masters of a different religion and culture. But this eventual conquest was no mean feat, and Dandolo was largely responsible for achieving it. His great age might have been exaggerated, but he showed incredible energy for one who was clearly older than almost everyone alive. His blindness, if he was blind, did not appear to impede him at all.

All that Enrico Dandolo did during the Fourth Crusade, he did for Venice. The destruction of the Byzantine Empire represented a new low in the distortion of the crusading ideal, a process that had already begun long before him. Above all else, he was a patriot who brought the republic wealth and overseas territory, even if he did so in such a terrible manner.

4

Eustace the Monk

Outlaw, Pirate and Reputed Sorcerer, but No Monastic

Eustace the Monk was a figure of legend, but despite such a soubriquet not for any pursuit of a religious nature. An outlaw, a reputed magician, his forte was piracy and intense naval warfare, both in the service of King John of England and later his enemy Philip of France.

Although Eustace was certainly a real person, he was also the subject of a French romance dated 1284 on its manuscript, anonymous but probably written by someone from Picardy, as some of the dialect within it suggests. It was based on legends that had grown around him, which mostly cannot be taken seriously. In this romance, Eustace is a sorcerer who sold his soul to the devil and who cast fantastic spells.

At least half of the tale of *Eustache the Monk* concerns a lengthy catalogue of merry pranks and practical jokes, some laced with magic. It resembles accounts of Till Eugenspiegel, Reynard the Fox, Bre'r Rabbit and Marlowe's Faustus, another credited with jolly japes. While a monk he magically caused his brethren to fast when they were to eat, to go barefoot where they should wear shoes, and so on. He put tar in the tarts at a feast. He disguised himself as a shepherd, a hay man, a coal man, once cross-dressing as a prostitute, and assumed various other identities. He was credited with shape-shifting, once as a nightingale. There are more sinister tales interspersed, involving cutting out the tongues of his enemies and hanging spies.

Such 'trickster' stories belong to an ancient storytelling tradition. While the occult was not so easily dismissed in those days, the magical acts ascribed to him could hardly be believed true. There is nevertheless a kernel of factual information in this romance.

Eustace Busquet was born at Course in the Boulogne region about the year 1170, a younger son of a lesser noble. He might have trained as a knight, and is said to have learned seamanship in Italy. The romance has him going to Spain to study black magic where he pledged his soul to Satan. What caused him to enter the monastery of St Vulmar at nearby Samer in early adulthood is not known.

The origins of monasticism date from the early days of Christianity. There were at first several established forms of living as a dedicated religious person, both individually and in groups, and these did not necessarily demand celibacy. It was only in the sixth century that the Rule of St Benedict laid down the fundamental practices by which a monk or nun would live, where those who wished for a religious life would forsake the world and all worldly goods and pursuits. Taking vows of chastity, poverty and obedience, they would live a life of prayer, specified work and religious observance, and such a lifestyle continues today. The period from the late eleventh century to the sixteenth saw a number of new monastic orders, each producing a rule where the practices varied from those of the Benedictines, but seldom by very much.

It was obvious that Eustace Busquet was not suited for such a life. He soon gained a reputation for using bad language and gambling, and his subsequent behaviour shows fairly convincingly that his temperament was not appropriate for a monastic lifestyle. His reasons for entering the cloister are not given, though entering the Church could be a route to the office of a senior prelate, a typical career path for a younger son of an aristocrat. A bishop would expect as much material wealth as an earl or count and could gain political power accordingly. This aspiration seems unlikely in Eustace's case, an opening as a secular cleric would have then been more appropriate than entering a monastery. Such a one once ordained as a priest might find an opening in the *familia* of a bishop and could progress through his patronage. It was still possible to rise from the monastic cloisters to a senior ecclesiastic role, but the secular route was increasingly the norm.

Eustace might have on the spur of the moment decided on this move as a personal vocation, divorced as it was from what was clearly his nature. Another possibility was a ploy to avoid an enemy: a monastery was not a place to be invaded lightly and many chose it as a place of safety. It was also the practice for a lord to confine an inconvenient person to a monastic house, to keep them from causing trouble. Charlemagne had Tassilo, the dispossessed Duke of Bavaria, so disposed of, and many a young girl, an heiress or one who could not be so easily married off would find herself in the convent and pressurised to take the veil. There is, however, no evidence that Eustace was coerced to become a monk.

Eustace only stayed in the convent for a year. His father was murdered and in about 1190 he promptly returned to the world to avenge him, and probably to claim his inheritance. He accused the local aristocrat Hainfrois de Heresinghen of the murder, and the two, according to their privilege as men of coat armour, elected to solve the matter by combat. This was still the accepted practice, that God allowed the just to win, although divine justice tended to favour the most skilful fighter.

In the event both parties named champions who fought it out on their behalf. When Hainfrois' nominee won he was declared innocent, and Eustace resolved not to let the matter rest. He never returned to the cloister and pursued his feud for some years. He had by now gained the nickname 'the Monk' and at times was known as 'The Black Monk'.

For over a decade Eustace conducted his vendetta, having resorted to brigandage and subterfuge. Then in 1204 Renaud, Count of Boulogne, took Eustace into his service, perhaps considering his talents useful. Eustace then served as his seneschal, but only for about a year. Sometime during that decade he reputedly acquired a wife and produced a daughter, as both are mentioned in the romance when he was in England. At the end of his buccaneering career there is mention of Eustace having brothers and an uncle in his service.

Eustace could not easily settle with any one master. Although he enjoyed titles, incomes and privilege as seneschal, he needed the Count's continued support. In the romance Hainfrois told false tales to the Count about Eustace, and relations soon deteriorated. It appears that Renaud summoned his seneschal to render account for his offices, and Eustace's resentment caused him to quarrel with his lord and then quit his service on the spot. The Count seized the lordships Eustace held as seneschal and burned the attached fields, for which Eustace then vowed vengeance. Again, this story was told much later, and may or may not have been true.

The same romance relates how soon after Eustace burned two mills belonging to the Count and was accordingly outlawed. The events that followed were probably true, in that Eustace conducted his guerrilla war with as much ferocity as he had against Hainfrois, and the romance relates a series of audacious pranks and some sinister acts of cruelty as described earlier. We may gather from it that Eustace was resourceful, and often gained advantage over his former patron without winning much from his efforts. Eustace lived on his wits thereafter, probably only a step ahead of capture and execution part of the time.

Outlawry was not unusual in all medieval Europe. It was often imposed after one was summoned to answer criminal charges and did not appear. It involved withdrawal of all legal protection and rendered the outlaw liable to be killed by any without redress. 'Let him bear the wolf's head,' ran an Anglo-Saxon law code. An outlaw was to be hunted down like an animal; none could give him shelter or sustenance, and anyone who brought him dead or alive to the authorities would be rewarded.

One variation of this status was common practice in Iceland in earlier times. When a family feud escalated beyond proportion and the death toll exceeded an accepted level, the one responsible would be ordered into outlawry for a number of years. This was usually an easy option; he would take ship and spend the time either as a Viking or a mercenary, away from Iceland until the period was over. Eric the Red spent this enforced absence colonising Greenland. Anyone who remained at home while outlawed was declared *nithing* ('nothing'), ostracised and killed as a matter of course, as the saga of *Burnt Njal* testifies.

In popular culture there is now an air of romanticism concerning the outlaw. We might see up to three different television series at any one time concerning the exploits of Robin Hood and at least one film is made every decade retelling his story. All perpetuate the myth of the good man driven from his lands by a tyrant, who fights a guerrilla war to protect the needy against Norman oppression. Such legends appeared even in later medieval times in popular ballads extolling this people's champion.

To place Robin Hood in Nottinghamshire at the turn of the thirteenth century was a fairly recent development. The original stories and ballads name his county as Yorkshire and the king is often an Edward. There is also folklore that blurs the outlaw with the 'little people' of the woods, the fairies, and also hints at pagan cults. One television series emphasised these possible pre-Christian origins of the legend and had the Saxon forest god Herne the Hunter (or a shaman in this role) as Robin's mentor.

In recent centuries the characters of Jesse James and Billy the Kid have acquired the status of popular icons. American outlaws, from these to Bonnie and Clyde were popular in their time and afterwards, often portrayed as heroes. People love outlaws, as much as they resent overbearing authority, and whoever gets the better of a tyrant is often popular. Charlie Chaplin consistently played this theme, to his own success and later his downfall. But not even his biographer claimed that Eustace the Monk robbed from the rich and gave to the poor. He was not known to have championed any cause other than his own desire for revenge. Some of the stories in the romance show that he was no jolly outlaw but cruel and predatory. In this he was typical of real outlaws, who were forced to live by robbery and seldom gave quarter.

Eustace apparently did not live for long. He was known in 1205, the same year of his outlawry, to have crossed the Channel and presented himself to King John of England. From 1154 the House of Anjou, the Plantagenet kings of England, had also been rulers of the western half of France from the Normandy coast to the Pyrenees, as John's father Henry II had gained by inheritance and marriage. John's brother Richard I had spent his ten-year reign away on the Third Crusade and afterwards fighting King Philip Augustus of France over his continental possessions, and only came to England twice in that time for a total of nine months. When Richard was killed in 1199 he had no legitimate issue and it was John, the least able of the Angevins, who inherited the empire. Early in his reign John lost most of the lands in France.

John must have seen how useful rogues and hell-raisers such as Eustace could be when Philip had already taken Normandy early the previous year using a feudal convention as a pretext and invading the duchy. John had imprudently offended some of his powerful vassals and suffered the consequences when they did not rally to his defence. Now the French had brought their front line to the Channel. Eustace's new incarnation as a privateer admiral, a soldier in the King of England's service and part-time pirate was easily preferable to hiding in the forests of the Boulannais. It did not involve so much of a change in activities.

John was concerned over what was now a French threat to England itself. Normandy and other French provinces were now lost, all long ruled by his family. Poitou, the northernmost county of Aquitaine, was now under threat. He could only transport armies to his remaining French possessions by sailing around the Breton peninsula, whereas Philip now held the Norman ports and could mount attacks on England itself. Eustace, ruthless fighter and expert seaman, was a useful lieutenant.

King John is credited with the formation of the Royal Navy, although his two predecessors owned ships and even King Alfred was known to commission some into his service. There were a number that the king owned, mostly transport vessels. It eventually became the practice to tie the royal ships at the wharf of the Tower of London, and the suffix 'of the Tower' in a ship's name denoted that it belonged to the king.

There were agreements with a federation of Channel towns, known as the Cinque Ports, which despite the name eventually comprised thirty-five member towns. The burghers of Dover, Sandwich, Deal, Romney, Winchelsea and Hythe, along with many smaller places, had certain privileges in return for rendering a number of ships to the king's service according to varying requirements.

Naval warfare was still in a primitive stage of development, and mostly comprised of floating platforms on which armies fought. Archers would fire at the enemy ship, and once the other vessel could be secured with grappling hooks the soldiers would fight as on land, boarding one ship or the other. To facilitate this warfare a ship would often have a castle-shaped structure, sometimes both fore and aft. The forecastle (or fo'scle) is still a feature of naval architecture.

Eustace's royal patron now sent him to secure the Channel Islands, the only part of William the Conqueror's continental domain that had not been taken by Philip in 1204. The French had invaded Jersey, by which they threatened English interests in Aquitaine, Having lost Normandy, Anjou, Maine and Touraine and consequently influence over Brittany, John was faced with troublesome access to Aquitaine, the large province on the south-east of France; all that remained now of the Angevin possessions. Further military activities, and certainly trade with the region, were under threat when ships now rounded the Breton peninsula, and piracy would become an escalating problem, as would attacks from French shipping.

The Channel Islands, Jersey, Guernsey, Sark, Herm and Jethou, with Alderney a little north of the group, had long been appendages of Normandy but were invaded and occupied by Philip's men just after mainland Normandy fell. John sought to at least salvage the islands from this disaster and in 1205 he sent Eustace and his flotilla to recover them.

A lack of reliable records makes it difficult to tell what happened there. The Romance has Eustace and his men retaking the Channel Islands, which is questionable. Eustace reached Jersey in September, and his invasion made a difference, but he did not succeed in re-establishing Angevin rule there. John apparently believed that Eustace by the 19th held not only Jersey but also Guernsey and Alderney. The writ he issued soon after making appointments there does not appear to have been sent, but it was clear that Eustace had not retrieved nearly as much. John then sent another force, which accomplished much more.

Eustace then took a fancy to the smaller island of Sark and set up a base there for his activities. Piracy was far from uncommon in the Channel, and many a merchant vessel was forced to defend itself or yield. Eustace the Monk acquired much wealth by this method. John did not express any objection while Eustace was an effective presence for his interests in this sensitive area. As late as 1216, when the papal legate Cardinal Bicchieri requested safe conduct from Philip for his passage to England the French king could not guarantee his safety crossing the Channel while Eustace and other pirates had free rein. Eustace, again according to the romance, had a large house built in London. He was not short of money, it seemed. Able to combine royal service with outright piracy, he had gained wealth and esteem, a fair achievement for an outlaw. In 1209 he served as John's ambassador to Boulogne.

Eustace did not settle in John's service either. What went wrong is not certain: the romance says that his old enemy Renaud Count of Boulogne appeared in London as a refugee, and Eustace resented him being granted shelter. In 1214 Eustace certainly was expelled from the Channel Islands, whose Warden Philip de Aubigné apparently decided that the Monk's presence was not desirable. The romance states that John burned and mutilated Eustace's daughter, although it is known that Eustace plundered some coastal villages in England, for which John outlawed him. For a time Eustace occupied Castle Cornet on Guernsey.

Eustace was not an consistent follower of anyone, as his previous record suggests. At the same time, John was not the most astute manager of men. His hold over Aquitaine had suffered when he alienated the powerful Lusignan family of Poitou, who afterwards lent Philip their assistance; John had failed to absorb important lessons about maintaining a following. Eustace travelled to Paris and offered his services to King Philip of France. Soon the Black Monk was terrorising English shipping, and Philip found him as useful as John had. Two years later the French planned an invasion of England, for Philip now decided on an attempt on the crown of England itself.

This was a perfect time for it. John had faced a serious rebellion from his own nobles and had been forced into making serious concessions. The sealing of what later became Magna Carta and the effect on English constitutional monarchy is widely known, though not so well remembered is how soon John repudiated it. Civil war ensued. The French invaded in 1216, and the Dauphin Louis could command enough credibility to set himself up as an alternative king of England. He crossed the Channel in Eustace's own ship.

Even London expressed loyalty to 'King Louis,' as did the majority of the English barons already fighting John. The story of how serious it really was for John to have lost his baggage carts in the Wash has been contested, and whether this really included his treasure. John was already plagued by ill health, and this new disaster could have been a final blow. He died a week later on 16 October 1216, and in the name of the nine-year-old Henry III most of the barons rallied to the Plantagenet monarchy. Loyal ships, probably of the Cinque Ports, drove back the French convoy bringing reinforcements and Louis was subsequently forced to withdraw. The 'reign' of the forgotten king of England was over.

But the matter was not quite at an end, and Louis set about a new invasion in 1217. Once again Eustace participated in a naval convoy attacking the Kent coast. When the ships reached Sandwich the English fell upon them, and the invasion was repulsed. It was in this engagement that Eustace's luck ran out, or else his tactics failed him. The English boarded his ship and Eustace was captured.

According to the romance the English attacked Eustace's ship in rowboats, firing bows and crossbows as they came. Eustace's men fought back with arrows and everything they could throw at the attackers. They then produced pots filled with lime to throw at the enemy, but the wind was against them and blew it into their own eyes and the English boarded. This graphic but suspect account has Eustace himself lashing out with an oar, many an enemy going down around him. There were too many, and he was finally disarmed. There is also the account that had Eustace hiding in the bilges when his enemies found him. He offered large sums for his life, but this was ignored by those who had suffered from his depredations.

Eustace was beheaded before the day was out on his own deck and his head was taken to England for display. About this time the French threat subsided. The Dauphin succeeded as King Louis VIII of France the following year, and it was some time before the French attacked the English coast again.

As is clear from this account, the unknown author of the 1284 romance mixes extreme fantasy and 'merry trickster' storytelling with the facts, and the truth can barely be extracted from the result. The romance can only be approached with caution. In all that is written of him Eustace does not appear a sympathetic character. He emerges from all accounts as cruel, ferocious in his hatred and self-serving. He was resourceful and certainly able, and his apprenticeship fighting Hainfrois and then Renaud made him an ideal commander. Perhaps his time seeking in vain the justice he felt himself denied led him to a harsh and violent disposition. If a reliable detailed account of his activities as a pirate sailing from Sark could be found, it would almost certainly have made unpleasant reading. He cannot be reproached as harshly for changing sides so easily, for many did so in the wars between John and Philip. Eustace was a mercenary who ultimately served none but himself. He took whatever side suited him best at the time

'No man who spends his days doing evil can live a long life,' runs the epilogue to the romance. Eustace was certainly self-centred and obsessed with personal revenge. Before he reached fifty some of his enemies caught up with him, and the result was exactly as expected.

The story of his life shows rather than a bad man who gained his just deserts Eustace was a player of harsh and dangerous games, who finally lost. It also shows us that we should not expect outlaws to be the good guys.

5

King Mindaugas of Lithuania

The Last Apostate King

Traditional narratives on the early expansion of Christianity often catalogue the conversion of various peoples, usually *en masse*. The standard formula talks of a determined monk who sets forth and brings one nation or another into the Christian fold by preaching the True Word to the heathen. So impressed are the rulers with his preaching and example that they resolve to forsake their vile pagan ways and follow the precepts of Christ, promptly accepting baptism from this missionary's hands, and their people soon follow into the new faith.

Such is the stuff of saints' lives, as written by later ecclesiastics. As just one example, early in the sixth century St Remegius guided Clovis the Merovingian to the font, as a consequence bringing his people the Franks into recognition by Rome as Christians and a king's crown for Clovis himself. Besides the pagans surrounding Christendom, the early Catholic Church of the time also contended with the Arian heresy, strong among the Germanic tribes, and later with Orthodox Christianity, inspired by the Greeks and gaining ground among the Slavonic peoples. That the Franks were first drawn to Arianism has been suggested, and if so it might have made the transition to Catholicism easier.

The Venerable Bede told how Pope Gregory the Great sent St Augustine the Less, the 'Apostle of England', at the head of a mission to the English in 597, who soon converted the Kingdom of Kent. There follows a list of saints such as Birinus, Chad, Cedd, Paulinus, Patrick, Aidan, Columba, Ninian and Mungo who converted the various Saxon and Celtic peoples, eventually refounding the

Christian religion in the British Isles to the almost complete exclusion of any other belief; a story told as the advance and triumph of the True Faith. Such a picture is in fact very simplistic.

The reality of the spread of Christianity involved instances of apostasy, where the converted, often in the second generation, turned back to paganism, or at least to a partial tolerance of the older religion. Or else conversion was often far from sincere. King Aethelbert of Kent who received the 597 mission was married to a Christian Frankish princess and was certainly aware of the advantages that Christianity could bring from this link with the Continent. Bede spoke scathingly of King Raedwald of the East Angles, who in the mid-seventh century kept heathen idols in his temple next to the Altar of Christ and sacrificed to them while professing Christianity. In many cases the acceptance of this new religion had serious political ramifications. It meant alliances with other Christian rulers, dynastic marriages, cultural links with Rome and Christian nations, literacy and administrative reforms. On the other hand, it could mean making enemies and antagonizing one's own powerful nobles; consequences that disturbing the status quo often brought.

Many a king of early medieval Europe would be drawn to baptism more often for pragmatic considerations than personal conviction. In seventh-century England, Penda of Mercia told the monks that he would not be a hypocrite and while allowing them to preach in his kingdom declined conversion for himself. As the usual strategy involved converting the king and working downwards, the brethren made little headway while Penda lived and only succeeded when his successor accepted baptism.

Before the first millennium of Christianity was complete, most of Europe practised one of the two versions of Christianity, and even in Scandinavia the process of conversion was under way. By the thirteenth century the frontier of the Christian faith coincided in north-eastern Europe with the limits of German territory while the peoples of the eastern Baltic Sea adhered to older religions.

At that time also the state of Lithuania rose from practically nothing to a formidable power in its region and still followed paganism for centuries after. Such a state was to an extent the achievement of Mindaugas, the only king of Lithuania, who did eventually accept Christianity but not for long. Lithuania appears as a recognizable entity around the turn of the first millennium, but only just. It could not be easily said that there was a Lithuanian people at the turn of the thirteenth century. There were a number of tribes, with little unity among them. It was in reality many separate regions, each dominated by a tribe: the territory of the Samogitians in the north-east had a short coastline. The Lettgallians, the Semgallians and the Yatvingians held areas to the south and west. The Lithuanian language, together with Latvian and the now-extinct Old Prussian, are said to have descended from the prehistoric Indo-European language just as most other European tongues but changed far less from the original. There are striking similarities of these languages with Sanskrit and those of northern India.

The Lithuanian tribes made good use of their resources and utilized whatever land could be cultivated, despite much of their region being forest and swamp. The horses the region bred were much prized. Fishing, hunting and apiculture allowed them adequate means to survive and develop political systems, and a free peasantry supported a religious elite and a warrior caste. Yet government was far from centralized as local rulers, or *kunigai,* (plural *kunigaisciai)* which the chroniclers translate as dukes, ruled over areas of a few hundred square miles at the most. In the early thirteenth century, it was possible for the dukes to cooperate, and the concept of a Grand Duke, or at least one first in seniority over the others, was at least thinkable.

The Balts were surrounded by Slavonic peoples. The Poles lived to the south and west, Roman Catholics who were mirrored in the east and north-east by the Orthodox *Rus,* of which several principalities centred on Kiev and occupied some of the modern Ukraine. There was constant threat of invasion on all sides. In 1222 the first Mongol forays threatened Russian principalities, and only the death of Genghis Khan in 1227 halted their outright conquest. The German people, in the form of two monastic military orders, posed an acute problem throughout this period.

The Teutonic Knights, or the German Order (*Deutsche Orden*) were warrior monks who in the style of the Templars and Hospitallers performed the religious duty of incessant warring against the enemies of Christianity. Founded in Palestine in 1192 during the Third Crusade, they soon chose a different theatre of war. As the heathens lived on the doorstep of the German empire itself, they reasoned that their efforts would be more effectively applied in bringing Christianity to these eastern lands by the sword. There had been 'crusades' or military campaigns against non-Christians conducted against pagan Slavs in the twelfth century. In 1193 Pope Celestine III proclaimed what would be an ongoing crusade against the north-eastern pagans, and the Teutonic Knights took the lead. German settlers often followed.

The *Drang nach Osten*, or push to the east, would rank highly in the German psyche in coming centuries. It was revived by the Nazis, who sought to imitate the Teutonic Order, and even used its principal fortress at Marienburg as a school for the concept of eastward expansion. There is a celebrated propaganda poster showing Hitler riding in the armour of a Teutonic Knight and many a Nazi pageant featured riders in armour and the Order's regalia.

In 1228, Duke Konrad of Mazovia in eastern Poland granted the land of Kulm to the Teutonic Order, urging them to conquer the Prussians with an understanding that the Order would keep the lands it won.

At the same time another order, the Knights of the Sword (*Orden der Schwertbrüder*), or the Livonian Order as it was also called, were threatening the Lithuanians from the north. Founded in 1202 by individual knights from the German Empire, this would fight its way into the Lettgallian and Zemgallian regions. At the same time German colonists were appearing in the Baltic, founding towns and ports. There was an Archbishop of Riga from 1199 and Livonia, the region north of Lithuania, was settled and converted.

The Balts' religious beliefs were similar to those all over pre-Christian Europe; pagan cults firmly rooted in nature worship. The Lithuanian gods were of the elements, of fertility and the bounty of the earth. Their lands and waters were populated by spirits, wood elves, mermaids and ghosts. While they acknowledged the Supreme Being, named Dievas, whom they identified with the sky, there was a large and diverse pantheon of deities, important to every aspect of their lives. The Goddess Lada was the Mother of all, identified with the Earth. The most immediately powerful god was Perkunas, or Thunder. Similar to Thor or possibly even Shiva in other cultures, Perkunas was the patron of fertility, of justice and morality, whose anger would bring retribution by his hurling of bolts of lightning. Perkunas is often presented in a trinity with Patrimpas, who presided over agriculture and brought abundance and peace, and with Pikuolis, otherwise called Pikulas, god of the dead and the underworld.

The moon god Menulis and the sun goddess Saule head a separate group, with the planets as their children.

There were many others, the gods of the farm, the field and the home figuring highly. The snake was sacred to Lithuanians, and many thought it lucky if one lived in their homes. The gods might have different names according to tribe and region and might rank differently or change gender by region and timespan, but for a pagan religion it was surprisingly well organised by some accounts. A high priest (*Krivu Krivaikis*) maintained seniority over all the priests of every tribe. At a temple at Vilnius, on a stone altar the sacred flame to Perkunas always burned, tended by a company of priestesses. There was also a fairly standard litany. Later assessments have considered this view of a united pagan religion as simplistic and perhaps there was more diversity than believed.

Romuva, the modern name for the old religion of the Baltic lands, even saw a revival in the twentieth century. It flourished from the 1920s during the Baltic States' brief independence, suffered under the Soviet occupation, and has achieved a comeback in more recent times. From 1988 it was officially tolerated. As throughout pagan Europe, the winter solstice was the chief festival, where rites and celebration would go on for twelve days, and where the supreme god was chiefly addressed. There were other rites commemorating the changes of the year. Ancestors and the dead were honoured. Romuva was in fact little removed from the pagan cults in Britain, Germany and Rome before Christianity took hold.

The Christians readily equated pagan religions with devil-worship and wrote their history as the progress of the conversion of peoples from their idolatrous ways. The custom of cremating the dead was one practice that Christians abhorred. The early Church either hijacked pagan institutions – they turned Christmas, Easter and Halloween into Christian festivals and built shrines in pagan groves – or else they forbade pagan practices altogether. The English monk Winfrith, later known as St Boniface, began his mission to the Germans early in the eighth century by personally cutting down the Sacred Oak at Geismar, and when the Germans saw no retribution from their gods, they were moved to accept baptism, or so the story went. But pagan practices continued in many places, somewhat discreetly and often disguised, or else as custom. Evidence for this is abundant in England, from the Green Men depicted in churches to Midsummer Eve romps in the woods, to hot-cross buns and egg-rolling at Easter and even to the modern practice of touching wood for luck.

In the earlier decades of the thirteenth century the Lithuanian dukes fought the Romanov rulers of Halych and Volhynia over Black Ruthenia, a region of the upper Neman River. In 1219, the two sides agreed to a peace treaty; an act showing the nature of Lithuanian governance at that time. Twenty-one dukes signed, of which the seniority of five were recognised by the other sixteen. These five, between them ruling the region known as Aukstaitija, or Upper Lithuania, included Mindaugas and his brother Dausprungas. The remaining dukes of the coastal region of Zemaitija had allied with the five. Although these had recognised a kind of precedence this was hardly an acceptance of sovereignty, and in any case this confederation only comprised about half the Lithuanian territories.

Mindaugas then ruled a region in southern Lithuania between the Neman and Neris Rivers, and having inherited this he gradually asserted his own authority. His father Ringaudas had begun this process, as had Dausprungas, who died in 1238. Mindaugas' career thereafter featured intrigues, military campaigns, murder and treachery in the gradual elimination of his opponents.

His presence in that confederation as a senior duke indicates a standing he probably inherited. He was said to have been born in 1203, which would have made him sixteen in 1219, which makes it likely that he and his brother inherited their positions. It was still a fair starting point for Mindaugas to begin his rise to supremacy. He had much to contend with, for within this vague alliance there were enemies and to the west other Lithuanians, not even involved in this grouping, were potential enemies too. Slavs, Russians to the east and Poles to the south, threatened independence, as did the two German orders. As could be expected, the other dukes were suspicious and some intrigued with the enemies without.

Over the next few years Mindaugas eliminated several dukes, seizing their lands and often driving them into exile. It was a gradual process but soon his leadership was needed, for Rome had become interested in the Baltic region. In 1228 the Papal Legate brought about the creation of the Livonian Confederation, comprising the Knights of the Sword, the Archbishopric of Riga and three bishoprics. After a dispute over who would hold the lands the Order had conquered, the Confederation was drawn up as a compromise, creating a feudal settlement between the knights and the bishops. Despite this agreement, tensions between the members would continue, but the arrangement continued until abolished in 1560.

In 1236 Pope Gregory IX announced a crusade against the Lithuanians, and in September that year the Lithuanians repulsed an army led by the Knights of the Sword. At the Battle of Siaulai, (or the

Battle of the Sun) Volkwin, Master of the Order and forty-eight knights were killed. Mindaugas's cavalry copied Mongol methods, using spears and swords instead of bows, while his infantry had crossbows and all wore coats of mail. The Lithuanian lands thus escaped the fate that befell their neighbours. The following year the pope ordered the union of the Livonian Order with the Teutonic Knights, although the former retained some autonomy.

Whether or not Mindaugas was personally responsible for the defeat of the Germans, from that time he had achieved recognition as the supreme ruler of upper Lithuania, and the title of Grand Duke appeared from that time. Perhaps the dukes were realists, recognizing the need for an overall command for their defence, but Mindaugas was still in reality head of a loose confederation, although he had eliminated some of his opponents within. There had been other contenders for the most powerful of dukes, but Mindaugas's efforts over two decades had gained this much for him.

Although Russia to us is a vast expanse across the north of Europe and Asia, this is fairly recent, and at the time the area just east of Moscow was a number of small principalities including what we now call the Ukraine and Belarus. The Golden Horde, a Mongol (or Tatar) khanate, conducted aggressive policies towards all the Slavonic and Baltic states. From 1239 Mindaugas renewed the drive to capture Black Ruthenia. This would have strengthened his position, for to give the dukes work to do and promise them rewards could bind them further to his cause. The Russians had recently had the Tatars to contend with, and could not stand up to the Lithuanians so easily. In 1248 Mindaugas had gained control of the region and put it under the governance of his son Vaišvilkas, who made his capital at the castle of Novogrudok. He had also in recent years won Polovsk, Pskov and other lands from the Belorussians. In 1249, Mindaugas prepared a new offensive against Smolensk, and appointed three of his relatives to conduct the campaign. Tautvilas and Gedivydas, sons of Mindaugas's brother, were joined by their maternal uncle Vykintas. The campaign began with a success, Duke Michael of Moscow was defeated and killed near Protva, but the dukes of Suzdal defeated the Lithuanians at Zubtsov soon after. Mindaugas's prompt decision to expel the three dukes from Lithuania may seem ungrateful, but he had never been overly loyal to family members. He might have sent them on campaign so that he could grab their lands in their absence, as was the nature of his political intriguing, but it was a poor manoeuvre, uncharacteristic of Mindaugas, and caused him trouble at least in the short term.

For by the next year Tautvilas, Gedivydas and Vykintas had fled to the court of Daniel, Duke of Volhynia, who was married to the sister of the first two, and who had reasons of his own to put a stop to Mindaugas. He organised a coalition of the Grand Duke's enemies, including Duke Vasiko of Halych, and the Livonian Order. Daniel told the Poles 'Now is the time to go and fight the pagans, for they are warring among themselves.' Although alliances between Christians and pagans were not unheard of, there would often be some dissent over it. Tautvilas journeyed to Riga and accepted baptism from the archbishop.

The Russian dukes attacked and occupied Black Ruthenia, while the Lithuanian exiles bribed the Yatvingians and half of the Samogitians, who threw off their vassalage to Mindaugas. The Order attacked Nalša land and also the domains of Mindaugas and those parts of Samogitia that still supported him.

This state of affairs could have been the end of the Lithuanian state, but Mindaugas was no ordinary ruler. He exploited conflicts between the Knights of the Sword and Albert, Archbishop of Riga, and made agreements with the Master of the Order, Andreas von Stierland, which he sweetened with bribery. Andreas still had an axe to grind over Vykintas for his actions in the Battle of Siaulai.

Mindaugas survived this coalition's onslaught. He agreed to cede some lands to the Order in western Lithuania. He also agreed to become a Christian, and to be crowned as king as a concession. This split the coalition, and Tautvilas, who probably expected to take Mindaugas's place, was soundly defeated when he attacked his uncle at Voruta. Tautvilas was forced eventually to return to Daniel's court. Vykintas died in about 1252 and Daniel made peace with Mindaugas in 1254, although he kept Black Ruthenia where his son Roman was installed as ruler. Tautvilas recognised Mindaugas' superiority and ruled over Polatsk as his vassal. Vaišvilkas, who had converted to Orthodox Christianity, decided to retire to a monastery.

The 6th of July is celebrated as 'Statehood Day' in modern Lithuania, the date when Mindaugas and his wife Morta were crowned in 1253. The actual date has since been disputed, but it was certainly in the summer of that year. Pope Innocent IV had sanctioned this, glad that a new nation had joined the Catholic fold.

There is no doubt that Mindaugas's conversion was motivated by other sentiments than a sincere desire to forsake his wicked heathen ways for the paths of Christian righteousness. The Church of the time may have spoken of similar conversions in such a manner, but probably had few illusions. Mindaugas simply wanted to remain sovereign, and his conversion now obliged the Sword to support him rather than attempt to overthrow him. As the Church claimed the power to appoint kings by divine assent, Mindaugas had gained further credibility for his assertion of authority.

For the eight years Mindaugas was king, he showed remarkable ability as he modernised his little kingdom. He created a court on the European model with all the appurtenances of medieval monarchy. He established an administrative system, with royal charters verified by his own seal and also a diplomatic service. He created a monetary system with a silver coinage. It was likely that he had the help of Christian officials, either from the Order or from Riga, but the king was all too willing to learn statecraft.

Now at peace with the Catholics, he expanded his influence eastwards, but without much warfare. His influence over Black Ruthenia increased, despite losing direct control, and Polovsk. He married his daughter to Svarn, son of Daniel of Halych, and made peace with Halych-Volhynia. These eight years saw peace and stability for Lithuania.

But he was beholden to the Livonian Order. As soon as he was crowned, he granted by charter the lands he had promised to the Brethren. There are other documents making further grants, although it has been suggested that some of these were falsified later, as lands mentioned were not in his jurisdiction at the time. Still, the Order and the Church as a whole gained from this conversion.

Soon after the coronation Archbishop Albert consecrated a member of the Order called Christian as Bishop of Lithuania, the name surely signifying that he was also a convert. There was a dispute between archbishop and Order over the oath that the archbishop had extracted, and Mindaugas and the Order successfully petitioned the pope to cancel the oath. Christian was consecrated again, but now directly subordinate to the pope.

The reign of Mindaugas did not turn Lithuania into a Christian country. The remains of a Christian church dating from the time of Mindaugas have been found in Vilnius. A pagan temple was built upon the site after this church was burned down and its ruins covered in sand. While churches were built and missionary work went on with royal patronage in the 1250s, it would take considerable resources and personnel to convert the subjects of Mindaugas. Romuva was in fact a developed religion in its own right, and there was opposition to the new faith. Christianity had few supporters to begin with and Mindaugas was far from completely in control of his kingdom.

Perhaps the Christians failed to understand that while the addition of Christianity to the lives of pagans was comparatively easy to accomplish, an attack on the existing gods and practices was a more serious proposition. Pagans could countenance more than one religious observance at the same time. Only a long war against paganism and intensive missionary activity could hope to succeed in eradicating Romuva, and none of this took place given the later turn of events. Nor was the king's support for such a campaign in evidence. It was said that even during this period Mindaugas himself was known to sacrifice to the pagan gods and observe their festivals. It would not be surprising if in reality he had, as Raedwald and many other convert kings did, simply added one more god to his pantheon. His reasons for conversion were shallow and he was certainly aware that to support a drive to replace Romuva with Christianity in Lithuania would have risked making many enemies. He was a Christian by convenience as much as many other kings had been.

'This Christening was only for appearances,' wrote the unimpressed author of the Galician Chronicle.

> Secretly he made sacrifices to the gods – to Nenadey, Telyavel, Diveriks the hare-god, and Meiden. When Mindaugas rode out into the field, and a hare ran across his path, then he would not go into the grove, nor would he break a twig. He made sacrifices to his god, burned corpses and conducted pagan rituals in public.

Mindaugas was obviously a pragmatic Christian, but one could wonder if he was still a sincere pagan.

The Sword had plans of its own, and before the 1250s had ended there were new developments. The Knights still sought to gain control over the lands of the Samogitians who were still pagan and their designated prey. But the Samogitians were not so easy to subjugate as they showed by effectively defending their territory, enough to gain a two-year truce in 1257.

When hostilities resumed in 1259, they defeated the Order at the Battle of Skuodas. In 1260 they followed this up by a more spectacular victory at Durbe, where the Land Masters of Livonia and Prussia were killed, as were 150 of their knights. Such a defeat encouraged the Prussians, themselves long under the thumb of the Teutonic Order, to rise in revolt. It was around this time that Mindaugas would abandon the alliance that had brought him success.

It appears that his nephew Treniota encouraged him to join the revolt. Since he had placed himself under the tutelage of the Livonian Order out of necessity, perhaps Mindaugas had decided that it was time to break their hold over him. It certainly looked like it, given the reverses they were suffering. In doing so he lost all the diplomatic successes of the previous eight years. Mindaugas had always shown an effective grasp on diplomacy and strategy, but this was not his best decision. Perhaps his advanced age had impaired his abilities. As it later unfolded, Treniota had his own agenda and might have manipulated him into this to prepare his own accession. Thus Mindaugas broke peace with the Order and renewed his drive for conquest. The chroniclers state that as Mindaugas repudiated the alliance, he returned to paganism. This is disputed, although his baptism was half-hearted in the first place and there was no need to maintain any such pretence now.

Treniota first took an army to Cēsis, now in Latvia, and eventually reached the Estonian Coast. He then fought the German orders at Mazovia, now Polish territory. He called for an alliance of the Baltic peoples against the Germans under Lithuanian leadership. At the same time, Mindaugas was concentrating on his campaigns in Ruthenia. It became obvious that Mindaugas and Treniota had different priorities, while Treniota was growing in stature and influence. Mindaugas was probably uneasy over this and became openly critical of his nephew's failure to rally the support of the Balts. Perhaps this was the inevitable confrontation when a new man seeks increased influence while the established ruler resists him. Treniota was certainly planning to overthrow his uncle.

About this time Queen Morta died, and Mindaugas was said to have planned to marry her sister, the wife of Duke Daumantas of Nalšia. He apparently refused to let her leave after she visited and declaring that Morta had wanted him to marry her, for she did not want anyone else to raise her children. However true this was, Daumantas joined in Treniota's plotting.

Perhaps even his outward profession of Christianity had provoked opposition to Mindaugas. The Livonian Rhymed Chronicle had Treniota tell the king in 1261 that the Samogitians were unhappy about his forsaking the old gods. This is suspect, as Mindaugas did not appear to insist on conversion for his subjects, and still clearly acted like a pagan some of the time. But to be Christian meant accord with the Livonian Order, which many Lithuanians thought a big mistake in the longer term.

In September 1263 Mindaugas was assassinated on the orders of Treniota and Daumantas. The legend says that the king had sent his army to fight at Bryansk and kept only a small escort, when his party was surprised by troops led by the two in person at Aglona. Two of his sons, Ruklys and Rupeikis, were also murdered in this attack. It was said that Mindaugas was buried with eighteen horses, the custom established before Christianity. While it does not necessarily affirm his paganism it shows no desire to abandon this pagan-rooted practice and suggests that the king's paganism prevailed in the end. Mindaugas's final resting place is not known.

Treniota then declared himself Grand Duke. It is significant that he did not call himself king, which may have been an attempt to dissociate himself from his predecessor's previous pro-Christian stance. The Lithuanians as a whole now showed themselves as confirmed pagans and Treniota still hoped to unite them against the Christians. Treniota himself only lasted six months: he was murdered in the bath-house by some of Mindaugas's servants in the spring of 1264.

Vaišalgas was now lured from his monastery and elevated as Grand Duke. With the help of his brother-in-law Duke Svarn of Volhnyia he suppressed the resistance in Lithuania and regained Black Ruthenia. Daumantas, who had run to Pskov, was baptised in the Orthodox persuasion and elected Duke, where he reigned until 1299. He was later canonised for his pious acts. In 1267 Vaišalgas returned to the cloister and Svarn was now Grand Duke of Lithuania. Neither of these Christian rulers made much attempt to renew the conversion of the Lithuanians. Over the following decades a much-disputed succession did Lithuania little good. A revolt of the Balts against the German Orders begun in 1259 went on until 1272. There was much fighting between factions and the Knights attacked Lithuania several times. It was only on the accession of Vytenis in 1295 that stability was restored.

But for all the reverses after Mindaugas's death, Lithuania remained a 'modern' state that retained its new institutions and returned to an expansionist policy. In the time of Grand Duke Gediminas (1315-1341), a cousin of Vytenis, Lithuania began a major expansion to the east, and by the reign of his son Akgirdas (1341-1377) the Grand

Duchy was a gigantic state stretching from the Baltic to the Black Sea, comprising thousands of Belorussian and Ukrainian subjects. There were new attempts to convert these peoples to Christianity: Gediminas wrote to the pope in 1322, offering the conversion of his subjects, although this was again a means to thwart the Teutonic Order's plans and he thought better of it when the powerful pagan elements protested. Akgirdas also flirted with the idea of baptism, again as a diplomatic ploy, but talks broke down when the Order did not agree to terms. The enlarged state now had many Christians, both Catholic and Orthodox and there was a degree of religious tolerance, but the rulers still worshipped at the altar of Perkunas, as did most Lithuanians. Both forms of Christianity grew slowly.

Finally, in 1386 Grand Duke Jogailo sought to marry Queen Jadwiga of Poland. To do so he agreed not only to accept baptism, but to bring all his people to Christianity. This finally confirmed Catholicism in the country, at least in outward practice. Jogailo, also known as King Wladyslaw II of Poland, linked the two lands, although the formal union would only come about in 1569. But Lithuania itself was the junior partner and its sovereignty gradually became absorbed into the Polish kingdom and later, with Poland, into the Russian empire.

That Lithuania was now Christian did not deter the Teutonic Knights from their plans to subjugate its territories. In 1410, a combined Polish and Lithuanian army fought the Order at Tannenberg as it sought to conquer Samogitia. This heavy defeat of the German Order meant that it was never again a serious threat in the region.

There was in fact one more attempt at producing a king for Lithuania. In 1918 the Germans, having wrested the Baltic States from Russia at Brest-Litovsk, produced as their candidate Wilhelm Duke of Urach and Count of Württemberg. The Council of Lithuania agreed to him, at least in default of any other option. He took the name Mindaugas II but was never crowned. He remained at his home near Stuttgart throughout until the victory of the Entente powers ended his hundred-day reign and the state on second thoughts became an independent republic.

Twice in the last hundred years Lithuania became independent, first between the wars, from the 1919 peace settlement until occupied from 1939 by the Nazis and then the Soviets, and since 1991 as one of the first republics to break from the Soviet Union. The Lithuanians are proud of their history, and Mindaugas is revered as a founder of the nation, which he in part deserves.

When Mindaugas was a child, Lithuania was at best a vagueness. The tribes remained pagan when those around had converted one way or another, following a standardised pagan practice, and spoke close enough to the same language, but that was as far as unity went. Mindaugas was as ruthless and ambitious as the other dukes, but more politically able, so that he emerged as Grand Duke. His domain did not even include the lands of the Lithuanians to the south-west, and his conquests brought many Slavs under his rule. Yet by the end of his life there was a recognisable state called Lithuania that could maintain itself against its neighbours. If it did not represent the Lithuanian people as a whole, it provided a framework and Mindaugas began a road to establishing his country.

It was a fairly 'modern' state by the standards of the time. Mindaugas's ambivalence towards Christianity did not prevent him from importing the institutions of Christian Europe, and his kingdom was much better governed than most in the region. He made good use of the Livonian Order alliance. He also provided the basis for a Lithuania that dwarfed its neighbours. From his own conquests came the gigantic state of the fourteenth century.

His address to the new religion did not follow the expected pattern, and from late in his reign Lithuania was as pagan as it had been. It contradicted the image of Christianity as an essential component of the march of civilisation. Mindaugas treated Christianity as a political device, and he was more conspicuous in his lack of sincerity than most.

6

Peter of Morrone, Pope Celestine V

Too Good to Be Pope?

The papacy has long been the subject of negative criticism on many counts and by the yardstick of a simple Christian morality many of the popes could easily be found wanting. Once the Bishop of Rome claimed primacy over all Christians in the third century and when elements of political power and doctrinal supremacy entered the computations, his successors stood accused of every possible crime and transgression against Christian teachings.

By the second Christian millennium, election to the primacy of the Catholic Church was achieved through politics and driven by personal ambition, as the office had become worldly in its nature and dealt in wealth and power as much as in spiritual issues, so much so that many felt it did not fit with the example of Christ himself or the ideals of the Christian life. Popes not only lived in extreme luxury like the richest of princes but were secular rulers of most of central Italy and actively engaged in the politics of the nation. Even while in this postion of wealth and power a small number of popes could be commended for their pursuit of the Christian mission and reform of what the Church had become. Some, such as Gregory VII and Innocent III, laboured to correct the abuses that had grown about the Church and to reaffirm Christian values, but the majority of the 265 or so men who have occupied the papal throne were at best time-servers and often too mindful of temporal matters. Some were known for their duplicity and cruelty, and their lust for worldly gain.

In very recent times the Catholic world was rocked by a pope who voluntarily resigned the office of the papacy. Although this had happened before in papal history, the example of Pope Benedict XVI in February 2013 was shocking to many. It was tradition alone that has whoever attained the papal throne remaining there until death, but to leave it of his own free will is considered an extraordinary and some say a blasphemous act. It was equally so in the thirteenth century.

The pontificate of Pietro di Angeleri, known as Peter of Morrone (or Murrone) and as Pope Celestine V, ran very much against this trend. His time in office is known to history as one of the shortest, and he was often named as the only one to resign the papacy voluntarily, which is not strictly true. He was one of the most unsuitable popes ever consecrated, known for a complete lack of any political or administrative understanding whatsoever, nor any worldly comprehension. He was also, according to all known accounts, one of the most sincere, devout and venerable men ever to hold this office. Until immediately before his elevation, Peter of Morrone was a hermit.

Peter's earlier life is sketchy, and much of the information comes from a hagiography written much later. He was born at Isernia in the Abruzzi Mountains 200 kilometres east of Rome, about the year 1214. He came of peasant stock, eleventh of twelve children, and entered the Benedictine monastery at Abruzzo at the age of seventeen. He must have remained in the monastery for some time, long enough to be ordained priest. Eventually, his own love for solitude and the contemplative life took him to live as a hermit on the slopes of nearby Monte Morrone. He later moved to Monte Majella in the same region, which was even more remote, but his name recalled his association with the former mountain thereafter.

When exactly he began this solitary lifestyle is not known, but it was certainly long before 1264, when he was about fifty. If he was ordained priest at thirty, the traditional age, it was some time from the mid-1240s onwards. There could easily have been ten years leeway in dating his departure from the cloister to the mountains.

Hermits occasionally figure in stories of medieval times. They are often shown as solitaries in remote areas and might appear in tales giving shelter to injured knights, as did Naciens in Malory's Arthurian epic. While some such as Peter did live alone in wild country, the picture varied. A hermit might share with another or live in a modest house in a town. In the fifteenth century a hermit lived in one of the disused towers on London Wall. Women, known as anchoresses, also followed this way of life. In more recent decades Sister Wendy Beckett combined her eremitical lifestyle with presenting television programmes on art appreciation.

There was even in the earlier centuries of Christianity a sub-category of hermit known as Stylites, or Pillar Saints, who lived for years on the top of stone pillars, usually those of Roman ruins, determined never to come down. Simeon the Stylite died in 460 after living for thirty-seven years atop different pillars in Syria, each one higher and narrower than the last. His contemporary Daniel the Stylite of Constantinople was another who survived thirty-three years on a column in Thrace. This was a serious undertaking, and the elements were seldom kind. Daniel was almost blown off several times. Others appeared in the centuries that followed who emulated this lifestyle.

There was also a practice of permanently walling up hermits at their own request. Such cells existed in cathedrals where their entrance would be bricked up after them until their deaths. With little more than a water supply, a drainage trench and a small window, incumbents would live out their lives in this manner, their food passed through the aperture and pilgrims might come to seek their blessing.

Peter of Morrone showed a determination for self-mortification and strict devotion, going further than most. He wore a form of hair shirt reinforced with knots and a chain about his body. He fasted every day except Sunday, kept four 'Lents' each year, living on bread and water, and spent each day and part of the night in prayer. John the Baptist, who had also lived in the wilderness, was his model.

It is surprising that he lived so long on such a regime. Various forms of self-harm are not uncommon throughout the Catholic Church, even to the present day. Fasting, hair shirts that cut at the flesh, chains about the body and self-flagellation were always fairly common self-impositions, and some of these are still practised by monks, nuns and lay members of *Opus Dei,* it is said. Many Catholics might still forgo at least one pleasure for Lent. In the modern age unduly harsh treatment of oneself cannot be understood so easily, but one can respect the will-power and dedication required to do this incessantly for years at a time, even without agreeing with the need for it. Peter spent at least half of his eighty-two years in this way of life, and there is no evidence that he once forsook it before his fateful summons to Rome.

Paradoxically, he did not remain alone. Others were impressed by his example and sought to emulate him; soon a community in the mountains of hermits recognised Peter as their mentor. He would not produce a rule but gave them guidance. In Peter's lifetime there were said to be thirty-six 'monasteries', a total of 600 men and women who followed his example. Pope Urban IV approved the order in 1264, and it later came to be known as the Celestini after Peter's papal name. Having commenced as a Benedictine, Peter did not sever his link with this order and the Celestini were considered a subsidiary of the Benedictines.

Peter was no administrator and being considered head of a religious community gave him responsibilities he could not easily bear, for a following of that size would require organisation sooner or later. In 1284 he appointed one Robert as his vicar and set out alone once again into the wilderness. He was now in his seventieth year and hardly suited at his age to such a life. Peter had done much by this time and might otherwise have been canonised in due course as founders of religious orders usually were. The events that followed a decade later would allow him to do little good and to suffer considerably.

A conclave of cardinals elects the popes, usually from among their number, but sometimes they name an outsider. They would meet in closed session nine days after a pope's death and remain so until this was accomplished. Many cardinals represented the aristocracy of Rome, or the princely families of Italy and ecclesiastics of other countries who often maintained their links with their princes. The pope was secular ruler of much of central Italy and elections ran on political lines, for not only were many cardinals personally ambitious but they often represented the interests of secular rulers. A decisive vote of one more than two-thirds of the conclave was needed before any election was valid, and this could be difficult to achieve.

When Pope Nicholas IV died on 4 April 1292 the election of his successor became a farrago of intrigue and stalemate. There had been eleven popes in the previous thirty years and several long periods of vacancy. At this time only twelve cardinals formed the conclave at Perugia in the Papal States, each with a different agenda. Six were of Rome, four more came from other Italian cities and two were French. Italy was divided between Guelph and Ghibelline political factions, and Rome itself between their affiliates, the Orsini and Colonna. Cardinal Benedetto Gaetani of the Colonna was certainly the most able candidate but could not find the required nine votes given such a divided conclave. Twenty-seven months after the cardinals first gathered, they had reached no decision, and unease among the faithful was growing.

Early in 1294, King Charles II of Naples appeared in Perugia with an agenda of his own. He was son of Charles of Anjou, a brother of

King Louis IX of France, who had built a Mediterranean empire. The revolt of the Sicilian Vespers in 1270 had lost Sicily to the Kingdom of Aragon and now Charles II needed papal support to regain it. The pressure he put on the conclave probably forced the issue.

Apparently, Cardinal Latino of the Orsini faction 'revealed' a message sent from God himself to a 'saintly hermit' he did not name that the Almighty would visit his wrath on the Church if a new pope were not elected within four months. In reality, the entire conclave was exhausted by these two years of indecision, and the hermit to whom the revelation was erroneously attributed, which they all decided was Peter of Morrone, captured the assembly's imagination. Someone claimed that a previous pope had seen Peter hang his cowl on a sunbeam. They were at this point ready to elect almost anyone and on 5 July 1294, the Sacred College unanimously declared Peter their choice.

Peter was dismayed when the three emissaries from the College finally found him in the mountains and he immediately declined the papacy. A multitude of lay people and minor ecclesiastics had followed the mission up the mountain and now implored him to accept the elevation. Faced with the admonition that it was for the good of the Church, and after a short prayer, Peter tearfully agreed to be pope. He took the name Celestine V.

There were other considerations that the cardinals had been aware of. As their choice was at least eighty years of age, he was certainly chosen as a stop-gap pope. This was far from unusual when elections were deadlocked, and they hoped the stalemate would ease during Peter's short pontificate. Perhaps the factions could bolster their own support with new cardinals in that time. The cardinals may have believed they could control the papacy while this innocent held the office, but even if they could have followed a coherent policy between them, they had picked the wrong innocent. Celestine believed he could make his own decisions independent of them.

The most cunning of Machiavellians would have had difficulty navigating through papal politics. Peter, now Pope Celestine, had no idea of how such politics worked, but his election was widely acclaimed as a return to true Christian values. As the Franciscans were then split over practices and values, the faction known as the Spirituals, then calling for a back-to-basics reassertion of their founder's ideals, hailed this new pope as their ally. Prophecies that righteous monks would take back control of the Church became fashionable.

Charles of Anjou quickly pressed his advantage. The new pontiff was his subject, and he came in person to do homage, but in reality the king took control over Celestine and dictated his own desires. When the cardinals requested that the Pope come to Perugia for his coronation they soon received a reply that they should meet him in Aquila instead. Charles knew that once Celestine had gone to the Papal States he would fall under the control of this body and Aquila was on the frontier of Neapolitan territory. The cardinals journeyed there, with a bad grace in ones and twos, Gaetani the last to arrive. Celestine then arrived, riding on a donkey led by Charles and his son, the titular king of Hungary. On 29 August, when only three cardinals had arrived, Charles ordered the coronation to go ahead, even though it was repeated a few days later for the benefit of the later arrivals.

For the five months Celestine V was Pope, many of his actions were among the most ill-conceived that could possibly occur. Charles won the tug-of-war with the cardinals by having the Papal Curia move to Naples. At a stroke, the new pope doubled the College itself by creating twelve new cardinals. Seven of these were French, and the rest, except possibly one, Neapolitans; certainly Charles' nominees. Cardinal Latino sickened and died soon after the Aquila gathering. Of course, Charles was bent on breaking the power of the cardinals and Celestine did as he was told. He even had the pope appoint his son Louis, a layman just come of age, as Archbishop of Lyon. What appeared as papal endorsement boosted Charles' struggle with Aragon.

Celestine also acted independently – and ineptly. He ordered that Monte Cassino adopt the Celestini style of hermit-monks when he stayed there. They apparently humoured him until he moved on. He created the Bishop of Benevento a cardinal, ignoring traditional procedures. Making free with many benefices, he was known to grant the same one to at least three rival claimants. It appears he could not say no to anyone. We do not even know the full extent of his misjudgements, as some of his actions were stricken from the record by his successor. Celestine did not even understand Latin, which placed him at a disadvantage within the Curia.

Celestine granted many privileges to the order he had founded. Abbot Humfrey had drawn up a rule for the Celestini, which the pope approved, although perhaps it lost its spontaneity as it turned from a quasi-anarchistic grouping of hermits to a monastic order. He also recognised a Franciscan congregation of Celestini, who lived under the rule of St Francis while acting as hermits.

In his palace at Naples Celestine had a replica of his hut in the Abruzzi built and lived there. He wearied of his papal duties, fearing they took him too much from his devotions and worried that he was imperilling his soul. As a temporal prince as much as head of the western Church his responsibilities did not sit easily with him. He rarely consulted the cardinals, to their annoyance. Perhaps he sensed their hostility, or he might have realised that their ways were not what he expected of religious men. Gaetani, who still saw himself as pope-in-waiting, was hardly a supporter of this pontificate.

Who first called for Celestine to abdicate is not stated. The cardinals certainly soon regretted choosing him in the first place, and it was not difficult for even the new cardinals to become frustrated with the pope's chaotic behaviour. Harder as it was for him, and torn between his responsibility and misgivings over his personal dedication, he could have considered resignation fairly early. He first requested more time for his own devotions, offering to leave the management of papal affairs in the hands of three cardinals. This was rejected: either because the cardinals did not trust each other or because they wished to maintain pressure on him to resign. But now a serious legal issue came under discussion: *could* a pope resign? When this was raised some maintained that the pope was subordinate to no-one on Earth and none could authorise his resignation. It was also held that the pope was God's choice and could not shirk his obligation, no matter how unworthy he felt himself.

The part that Gaetani played in the resignation was probably decisive. A trained canonist and scholar, he very obligingly came up with a precedent. Yes, popes *had* resigned before, he said, naming Clement I, a little-known Christian leader in Rome in the first century. In reality Pontian and Marcellinus (who apostatized) had given up the office, but both were in fact leaders of the Church before the office of the papacy as now understood had come about. Silverius, another early pope, had been forced to abdicate. Benedict IX in the tenth century was deposed and reinstated twice and then finally resigned in the course of his conflict with the emperor. There were several rival papacies both before and after this time. Popes *could* resign, although Celestine was one of the few to do so of his own free will. Gaetani later claimed that the abdication was valid because Celestine did so in consultation with the cardinals, himself included. He also denied persuading him to resign, claiming to have originally opposed it. There is no secret that Gaetani wanted the papacy for himself, and it is difficult to believe that he did not at least subtly encourage Celestine in this course, in the manner of a medieval Francis Urqhuart.

There is a legend that Celestine, alone in his replica cabin, heard the disembodied voice of an angel exhorting him to abdicate. The voice according to the story belonged to Gaetani with the aid of a concealed speaking tube, and this made the pope's mind up for him. This story cannot be taken as fact but is not inconsistent with the general atmosphere of intrigue and dirty tricks that permeated the Curia. Nor was the faking of miracles and of divine intervention unusual throughout the history of the Catholic Church.

As word of the pope considering abdication spread, many were far from pleased. Charles for one, who had used Celestine much to his own advantage, did all he could to dissuade him and stirred up a popular opposition. To many of the common people Celestine was the godliest pope who ever took office and thousands came to Naples to implore him to remain in office. A procession of priests and monks walked around the papal residence. Under pressure from both sides, Celestine gave a non-committal answer. The crowd sang the *Te Deum* and dispersed.

On 13 December 1294, it was over. Celestine announced his firm decision to resign to the College. He divested himself of his ring, tiara and other papal regalia, and put on once again the brown habit of a hermit, announcing that he would return to his hut in the Abruzzi. In the last he was being over-optimistic.

The conclave assembled according to custom nine days later, and the next day, on the third ballot, Cardinal Gaetani was elected. Taking the name Boniface VIII, Gaetani immediately revoked many of the acts of his predecessor. He was logically the most likely candidate, given the nature of the papacy. Besides a scholar and accomplished curialist, Gaetani was also an experienced diplomat and able administrator. He set about reforming the Curial archives and cataloguing the papal library, and also further codified canon law. Unlike Celestine, he was astute and cunning – and also unlike Celestine, he was heartless.

Boniface insisted always on the supremacy of the pontiff in both temporal and spiritual affairs, and even had a second circlet placed on the papal tiara as a symbol of his secular authority. He was the scourge of kings, Philip IV of France included, although his long conflict with Philip over his taxing the clergy gained him little in the end. Later he came to conflict with the cardinals of his own faction, the Colonna. He died in 1303, soon after a term imprisoned at the orders of Philip.

Before the abdicating Pope Celestine could get through the door so to speak, in 1292 Boniface had him arrested and kept under close guard, for the new man was not about to allow Charles or anyone else to set him up as a restored rival pope. Celestine wished for no more than to go home to his mountain, but this would not have prevented him being used as he had been before.

Celestine escaped when his successor took him to the Papal States, slipping away at San Germano and appearing by surprise among his own monks at Majella. Boniface sent his troops to arrest him and Celestine took off again, wandering through the mountains for months evading capture. His supporters arranged his passage to Greece, but a severe storm drove the ship back. He was finally taken at the foot of Mount Gargano and sent back to the pope.

Boniface had him confined to a small room in the tower of the castle of Fumone, near Anagni. His guards were contemptuous, but he did not suffer much from his captivity. Two of his monks attended him, and the former pope spent his time in fasting and prayer as he had done while in the Abruzzi. He did not complain. 'I wanted nothing but a cell,' he was reported to have said, 'and a cell they have given me.'

Celestine V died on 19 May 1296, nine months into his confinement. There is no evidence that, as believed by some, Boniface had him murdered: it is remarkable that he reached such an age, the way he had lived most of his life. He was buried at Ferrentino but was not forgotten. Other popes soon followed Boniface, some better disposed to his predecessor and Clement V had Celestine canonised in 1313. His relics were brought to a Celestine monastery at Aquila and are still the object of pilgrimage.

From Boniface's time onwards the hold of the papacy over the minds of secular rulers declined. The French cardinals that Celestine had appointed increased the influence of the king of France and were in part responsible for a French pope decamping to Avignon in 1305. This 'Babylonian Captivity', as the Avignon period was named, did not end until 1377 when Pope Gregory XI returned to Rome, but soon the 'Great Schism' followed, where until 1417 rival popes in Rome and Avignon divided Europe's ecclesiastical allegiances.

The College of Cardinals has since grown and contracted several times in size, and many papal elections were disputed, although few for as long as for Celestine. There were misgivings in 2005 when it was revealed that Pope John Paul II had arranged votes in the conclave for a limited number of nominated cardinals, who would elect a successor as conservative as himself.

Until the present century only one other pope after Celestine abdicated. Gregory XII agreed to step aside when the Council of Constance chose a new pope and thereby end the Great Schism in 1417. His rival Benedict III refused to resign, but at Constance Martin V was chosen as the universally recognised pope and any further schism did not survive Benedict.

The resignation of Pope Benedict XVI in 2013, allegedly without external pressure, was a major departure from the tradition since Celestine. Conspiracy theories apart, Benedict XVI was said to claim ill-health, even though popes would never allow this to divest them of the title before.

Celestine V contributed nothing to the development of the medieval papacy. He should never have been pope, and only a cynical act by a deadlocked conclave placed him in the Chair of St Peter. He would have had an easier time if he had simply allowed the cardinals to rule in his name, and it was his tragedy that Charles gained control of him first. Gaetani was only waiting for a more viable balance of cardinals and did not expect to wait long after agreeing to elevate an octogenarian.

Many continued to question whether Peter should have voluntarily relinquished the papacy. Dante, writing about 1310, told of one soul in the first circle of Hell that he recognised as

The Coward spirit of the man who made
The Great Refusal...

This is believed to have been Celestine. Dante blamed Boniface VIII for the ills of the Church, and thus castigated Celestine for resigning. Popes are considered immune to damnation, but Dante also had Boniface further down in Hell among the simoniacs. How many others blamed Celestine for 'il Gran Rifiuto' is not certain.

The simple and devout manner in which Celestine lived made such an impression that many were moved to emulate him. The Celestine order continued to flourish after his demise, until its extinction in the eighteenth century. Although this non-Catholic writer cannot easily understand his preoccupation with self-mortification, such a total commitment to his personal quest is impressive, and this hermit knowingly did no harm to anyone else. He was known during his brief pontificate as *papa angelica*, the angelic pope, and many laid hopes on him for a church truer to its founder's ideals. He was truly a devout and saintly man according to Christian criteria, but as pope this made him the proverbial lamb among wolves. He was still much loved: the Colonna later wanted to put Boniface on trial for his alleged part in Celestine's abdication.

Peter, or Celestine, never wanted anything other than to continue his life of solitary devotion, and it was a cruel turn of fate that the conclave decided to use him for their own ends. Celestine V was a godlier man than the cardinals for all his shortage of worldly insight, and his unsuitability for the office of pope represents an indictment of the papacy itself at that time.

7

Jacob van Artevelde

Burgher, Demagogue and Reputed Social Climber

Across a century and a half, Marxist historians have expended gallons of ink on the relationship between capitalism and feudalism. While the maxim of the inevitability of one system supplanting another is by no means accepted nowadays, the clash of the two politico-economic systems was crucial to the society of Flanders in the fourteenth century, and to international events in which Jacob van Artevelde, known as 'The Wise Man of Ghent', became a decisive player.

Feudal society was rigidly circumscribed, where everyone knew their place and their obligations. Its solid foundation was an agrarian economy where a multitude of peasants worked the land to render material support to a military ruling class who in theory at least would protect them from harm. Not only did this provide wealth to emperors, kings, nobles, knights and gentry but also the Church, its bishoprics, monasteries and various clergy. This was the understanding of society that Europeans knew from the eighth century until the rise of capital over a thousand years later.

Those whose livelihood depended on making goods and trading in commodities did not fit well into this model. The medieval centuries saw the development of the urban centre and the economy of the merchant and craftsman. As the towns and their activities involved a small proportion of the total population, this did not interfere unduly with the feudal system, and in fact complemented it. Someone had to make both the swords and the ploughshares, and trade in the corn and wool the peasants produced. But medieval townsmen expected different treatment from that of peasants and the towns strove for self-government, to know no overlord but the king.

A medieval town anywhere in Europe has unmistakeable features to the eyes of modern-day visitors. Each would have at least one market place, surrounded by a haphazard arrangement of winding streets and might still have some of its city walls standing. Sometimes the streets were extensions of the markets: Bread Street, Milk Street and Poultry in the City of London are close to its principal market, Cheapside. Whole streets might hold a number of the same craftsmen, whose homes had their workshop and retail outlet on the ground floor. A town was effectively a trading centre that had attracted a permanent population engaged in commerce and manufacturing. Many townsmen grew wealthy and sought to win privileges and degrees of autonomy for their home towns. 'Town air is free air' they would claim.

The Low Countries, now Belgium and the Netherlands, had a large concentration of such towns. The land was often of poor quality – much of it the result of reclamation from the sea and marshland – and the economy of the region depended heavily on the weaving of cloth. Flanders and much as its neighbouring regions became an important centre for the skilful production of cloth, lace, tapestries and other textile products, and its towns grew large and prosperous, Bruges, Ypres and Ghent the most successful. When Chaucer spoke of his Wife of Bath's skill at weaving, that she 'passed hem of Ypres and of Gaunt' was his hyperbole. Close as it was to the most densely populated area in Europe and with easy access to the great fairs of Champagne, a vigorous market for Flemish textiles was long-established by the middle of the fourteenth century.

This burgeoning textile industry required large amounts of wool, far more than local flocks could supply. The traffic in wool from England to the Low Countries accordingly grew with this economy, a trade that flourished for centuries, during which wars between France and England caused a conflict of interest. While in feudal terms the ruler was Louis de Dampierre, Count of Flanders, a loyal vassal of the King of France, the economy of the Flemish towns linked them strongly with England.

The towns were not always as independent as they hoped to be; they may still have paid the local lord's taxes. In Ghent, the Castle of the Counts overlooked the town; complete with garrison, dungeon and torture chamber, it provided a stark reminder as to who was ultimately in charge there.

Jacob van Artevelde (also James or Jacques) was a burgher of Ghent. Events over the last two centuries in his land have inflated his image into a forerunner of Belgian nationalism, but this is erroneous. He was born about 1290 or possibly as early as 1285 into a mercantile family of Ghent and was destined through his wealth, business acumen and family connections to succeed as a burgher in his turn. His father was Willem van Artevelde, a successful cloth merchant and dignitary of the city.

Popular legend has the young Jacob accompanying Charles de Valois, brother to King Philip IV, on his expedition of 1301 to Italy, Greece and Rhodes. This story is thought to have appeared in the nineteenth century out of a refusal to believe that the Belgian hero did nothing of note before reaching his forties. Jacob would have been between eleven and sixteen if his birth year was within those stated, and while this is a possible age for a page, there was no firm evidence that the boy was ever in Charles's party. He was also believed to have served in the household of Count Louis of Evreux, but again, this is not verified by evidence.

In the absence of reason to believe otherwise, Jacob van Artevelde grew up in his father's house in the Kalandenberg, in the affluent centre of the town. He was sent to school to acquire at least an elementary education, and almost certainly had some secondary schooling where he learned Latin and French, important languages when his native tongue was Flemish. Three letters he wrote survive, all in French. He was afterwards apprenticed where he learned his trade, either under his father or one of his father's associates. On reaching manhood he dealt in the buying and selling of cloth and in due course inherited his father's lands and business. Such was a typical background of those born into the urban mercantile class.

Besides his cloth business, Artevelde traded in cattle, fish, wine and silver. He owned several polders, or land reclamations: it was not at all unusual for such merchants to diversify. He married twice, the first of his wives by 1320 who is not named in the sources, and who owned a brewing business that Artevelde took over. They had one daughter who would marry the Lord of Erpe in 1341. His second wife, Kathleen De Koster, took an active part in his business ventures, and at times voyaged to England representing him. Thus Artevelde prospered, although before 1338 he held no civic position apart from tax collector.

While the merchant grew up and established himself, political upheaval affected his world. The death in 1314 of Philip IV 'the Fair' of France, believed divine retribution for his recent harsh suppression of the Templars, heralded a phase of high mortality in the ruling house of Capet and no less than four kings, sons and grandson of Philip, reigned in the next fourteen years. The death of the last Capetian king in 1328 initiated a succession controversy between Philip IV's brother's son and his daughter Isabella. The latter had been Queen of England as wife of Edward II, until she had forced his abdication the year before and had Edward murdered in September 1327. Now Isabella with her lover Earl Roger Mortimer ruled in England in the minority of her son, Edward III. She sent delegates to Paris who eloquently argued her case for the succession, but her sex, if not her imperious manner as Queen of England, counted against her. Her rival the Count of Valois was crowned as King Philip VI.

When in 1330 young Edward III finally overthrew his mother and took the reins of his kingdom he had more to concern himself with than the French succession. In 1336 he gave shelter to the banished French noble Robert of Artois, and when Philip retorted with an attempt to confiscate the lordships Edward held in France that Edward was moved to act. The conflict escalated to a major war, where Edward would eventually see fit to claim the crown of France for himself and the two nations fought over this matter intermittently for over a century. The term 'Hundred Years War' is not strictly accurate as the English and French did not fight anywhere near all the time until 1453, which was in the end longer than a hundred years.

Flemish society was long divided almost from top to bottom between the *Klauwwerts* and the *Leliards*, the 'Claw' and the 'Lily'. The names had a heraldic basis. Those of the Claw supported the Counts of Flanders, whose coat of arms featured a rampant lion, while their opponents adhered to the King of France, symbolised by the Lilies. This division persisted down the generations. It is believed that Willem van Artevelde was one prominent Klauwwert who supported the Count in the 1302 revolt.

In 1337, the feudal obligations of the Flemings collided headlong with their economic realities. Supporting Philip in the war with England, the Count of Flanders imposed an embargo on English wool and the weavers of the region all but halted production for lack of raw material. Whatever their loyalties, the burghers could not countenance financial ruin, and Ghent was the first town to rebel.

On 28 December 1337, a massed meeting of the rich and poor of Ghent gathered at the open space known as the Bijloke, where Jacob van Artevelde addressed them. The looms of Ghent had been idle for too long, and everyone knew the anxiety that this economic disaster was causing. When Artevelde advocated revolt against the Count and making an accord with Edward of England, his words struck home with the multitude.

Six days later, on 3 January 1338, the town appointed a 'revolutionary council' of five captains, which was an old office long in abeyance. Besides Artevelde, two other cloth merchants, Willem van Vaernewijc and Gelnoot van Lens, shared power with the leading weaver Willem van Huse and one Peter van den Hovene whose background is unknown. Artevelde, elected to the captaincy of the parish of St John and traditionally the most senior, was given a larger salary for this office and allowed a larger bodyguard. The council itself endorsed his almost dictatorial powers, although he was exceeding the traditional brief.

Artevelde in his role as *Hoofdman* (or Captain) set about securing his city from financial ruin. In 1338 he negotiated a treaty with England that normalised trading relations and declared Ghent neutral in the rising dispute between the English and French kings. Other towns of Flanders followed Ghent's lead and commercial concerns won over feudal politics. Soon Ghent, mostly on Artevelde's initiative, created the *Driestedenbestand,* the Alliance of Three Towns, with Ypres and Bruges. The three had similar agendas, and after the Count fled to Paris this grouping dominated what was for a time a virtually independent Flanders, with Artevelde among the most influential individuals.

Once the embargo was bypassed the towns of Flanders could breathe more easily and the economy revived. But Artevelde, now with a new mandate from his success, could assert Flemish independence further. He made new overtures to the king of England.

Edward III had launched a campaign in the Low Countries in which he planned to take the pressure off Gascony. Mostly by buying support, he built a string of alliances that included the Holy Roman Emperor Louis IV, who made him Imperial Vicar General of the Low Countries, and the Duke of Brabant. But this campaign of 1339 accomplished little, for while the naval battle at Sluys that year dealt the French a severe blow, the land war gained little ground, advantage, or booty. When Edward returned to Flanders in 1340, he found the going even tougher and met more military failures. His influence had diminished and the emperor had revoked his appointment.

It was also at this time that the English king decided to cultivate the support of the towns of Flanders. Now that Artevelde was virtual dictator of Ghent and a leading light of the new confederation, he was one that Edward could ally with. Rebels against such a powerful prince as the king of France needed powerful allies, and it suited this *de facto* republic based on clothmaking to maintain the protection of the country that supplied their raw materials.

Edward remained for a while in Ghent in 1340. Heavily in debt from his campaign, he relied on loans raised from the town's merchants. When he moved on he agreed to leave his pregnant Queen Isabella and two of his children as surety. His fourth son was born there that year and known thereafter as John of Gaunt. There is no doubt that Artevelde made himself useful to Edward while the king was there, keeping Flanders on-side.

It was in Ghent in 1340 that King Edward III announced that he was the true king of France. The House of Valois had usurped his rightful succession to the throne, he declared, citing the dispute of 1328, and this war was fought to gain his second crown to which he felt entitled. His reasons for doing so have long been debated, and it was almost certainly a propaganda ploy, at least at that early stage. The war had hitherto been fought over a vassalage dispute and Edward was claiming the kingship in order to attract disaffected elements in France, which would be a successful policy throughout the French wars. Yet Edward and then his successors came to take this claim to the French throne more seriously as time went on. He would use this claim as a bargaining counter in negotiations and almost relinquished it for peace in 1360, but there was plenty of evidence that he and the sovereigns after him at least believed themselves kings of France.

Edward took the dramatic step of quartering his own royal arms, those of the Three Lions of England which his predecessors since Richard I had borne, with the Lilies of France, the arms of the French kings (see plates, p. 5). Heraldry, the display of regalia and individual colours and designs, was a precise science in the Middle Ages, with a terminology and exact rules that could be used to make political statements. Splitting the Royal Arms into quarters meant binding the two blazons into one personage; the King of England represented as King of France too. In heraldic terminology *quarterly first and fourth, azure, semée of fleur-de-lys or, second and third gules, on three lions passant guardant or,* accordingly became the arms of the Plantagenet and then the Tudor monarchs. Although the Stuarts and Hanoverians produced revisions of the Arms the Lilies remained in at least one quarter until 1806, removed after the English kings had finally renounced their claim to the French monarchy.

There is a legend, although without any documentary basis, that it was Jacob van Artevelde himself who persuaded Edward to claim the French throne. He was said to point out that Ghent and its confederate cities would both be committing treason and would break their oaths of fealty to rise against the king of France, and if Edward would simply claim it as his own, Flanders would affirm their allegiance to him. While it may seem unlikely that Edward would act so quickly on such a vague strategy, it must be remembered that he was in need of support while his campaign in the Low Countries went so badly and as his hold over the region was slipping. It is beside the point whether it was Artevelde's own idea. Artevelde would end up out of his depth playing diplomatic games with the English while he pursued his own agenda for Ghent and Flanders. Froissart told of the Flemings encouraging Edward's assumption of the title. The pope ordered Artevelde to abandon the English allegiance, but this had little effect.

Having gained the assent of the *Driestedenbestand* to recognise Edward as their king Artevelde raised an army of some sixty thousand from Flanders and marched against the French Duke of Normandy. The *Hoofdman* showed his skills as a commander in war. It was remarked that his standard bearer was a woman who dressed as a man.

There is no doubt that to grant Artevelde his powers was beneficial to Ghent. He organised a scheme to widen the River Lieve in crucial places so that ships could sail to the sea more easily. Those who held land on the banks were compensated. He also set up neighbourhood militias in the 250 districts of Ghent, each with a commander. Many other measures would ensure a standard amount of corn brought to the city and generally encouraged commerce.

Once the *Driestedenbestand* had replaced the Count in the supremacy in Flanders, the smaller towns resented the increase in power and trade that the three members now enjoyed. The Count and his supporters probably exploited this discontent as they tried to regain the county, and there were still many Leliard supporters throughout the region. Late in 1342 Artevelde arrived in the township of Ardenberg with his private army and killed one Peter Lammens, apparently a leading Leliard, at his own front door.

This was not the only act of its kind of which Artevelde was accused. It brings to mind many a revolutionary leader who resorted to eliminating opponents he decided were enemies of the revolution. Such acts reached industrial proportions during the French Revolution and under the Bolsheviks. Had he been allowed to, would Artevelde have become another Stalin? It is consistent with criticisms of his dictatorial disposition, but his draconian methods were successful; Count Louis soon withdrew from Flanders.

He did incur opposition within Ghent. Soon after this incident, early in 1343 Jan de Steenbeke accused him of overreaching his authority, and called his own supporters to arms against Artevelde. But soon sixteen of the craft guilds affirmed their support for the *Hoofdman* and others came from other towns prepared to fight for him. The magistrates, fearing Leliard involvement, acted to halt what could have turned into a civil war and had both Artevelde and Steenbeke confined while they deliberated the accusations. Finding in Artevelde's favour they ordered Steenbeke and some of his associates banished from Ghent for fifty years.

Artevelde always claimed, as he did during this affair, that he held his position purely by the consent of the people. The magistrates of the city had appointed him *Hoofdman*, and most had confidence in him to further the interests of Ghent. This definition of a political mandate is in fact a more 'modern' concept. In the Middle Ages people usually deferred to one of higher social rank for leadership; common people obeyed a knight, knights looked to nobles, and all to the king. A town had a more flexible approach, although as in all towns Ghent had a social hierarchy of which Artevelde was of the elite. His popular following was the basis of his political power, for many of the guilds, particularly those connected with the textile industries, supported him as their saviour. His mandate was legally conferred, if perhaps he exceeded what was envisaged. He even in 1342 resigned his captaincy and stood successfully for re-election.

In Artevelde's time there was a clearer definition of the guild hierarchy and their place in the civic framework. Guilds (sometimes written gilds) were formal associations of the same craft or trade, although their membership may be organised on different lines. They acted to protect the interests of their business, to maintain standards of workmanship and of the training of apprentices, to look to their members' welfare and often to act as political pressure groups. In most towns no newcomer could practice a trade without sanction from its appropriate guild.

According to the economy of each town there was usually one or a few guilds that dominated civic affairs, and in Ghent it was logically the weavers. There were also 'lesser' guilds or *neringhen*, who often sought greater political power, and who often favoured the Leliard cause. While the weavers mostly supported Artevelde's leadership, he took great pains to enlist these lesser organisations. Citing his ownership of a brewing business he enrolled in the brewers' guild and was soon elected its *deken,* or doyen. He was eventually deken of 52 guilds.

For the next few years that the English fought in Normandy, Flanders saw less interference in its economy. Artevelde acted in the best interests of his town and the region. He made the much-favoured change of issuing official documents in Flemish as well as in French. He was almost certainly considered dictatorial in his manner; Froissart talked of a bodyguard of ruffians who accompanied him. But even though the Claw and Lily division was far from dead, many of the merchants were glad to see the constraints that the Dampierre counts imposed removed by Artevelde's actions.

Many must have wondered how long this defiance of the Valois kings could last. The affairs of the nobles were dangerous to take part in, and their agendas might not always coincide with those of townsmen. Artevelde was pursuing a grand design that involved abolishing the Dampierre suzerainty in favour of an English Count of Flanders, and this was an explosive proposition.

Some successful burghers did become involved with the national politics of their time. London merchants such as Nicholas Brembre in the reign of Richard II and Richard Whittington in that of Henry V were two prominent examples. The role of moneylender to kings and nobles often gave such men leverage. The London Mayor Edmund Shaw gave decisive support to the accession of Richard III in 1483, his brother a friar who preached the just succession of this king through his interpretation of canon law.

It was also possible in England for a merchant to advance to the gentry and even to the nobility. The de la Pole family, earls and then dukes of Suffolk by the fifteenth century, had once been merchants 'of the pool' in Hull. Wealth gained by trade and industry could buy land outside of a city, and knighthoods were granted to London merchants increasingly from the fourteenth century for services to the crown. There was an element of upward mobility a townsman could look to, even in an age of social rigidity.

Ghent under Artevelde's leadership was far from content in these years. Resentment between the weavers and the fullers, an old animosity, became more pronounced, and words were said on the quiet concerning Artevelde's dictatorial manner. The direction he was taking Ghent and Flanders was disquieting to some, who expected reprisals. The feeling was growing that Edward could not deliver as he had promised, and Artevelde's insistence on supporting the English was now harming his standing. Like almost any politician, he had made enemies. It was not known how much resentment there really was until the final crisis.

There was less harmony between the guilds than before. Artevelde had nothing to do either way with the demands of the fullers for their promised higher wages from the weavers, which erupted into violence in 1345, not long before the fall of Artevelde. On 'Bad Monday' the two guilds fought a pitched battle, ending only when the priests intervened, and many fullers were killed.

Although the Marxist picture of feudalism at odds with capitalism is simplistic, there was much scope for conflict of interest between townsmen and nobles. The story so far has shown what could happen when one party fights a war and the other is trying to earn a living, but we have also seen how the two could cooperate. Yet there was an element of suspicion that burghers harboured for the aristocracy. For all Artevelde had championed the cause of Ghent and its industries, there was a creeping suspicion among its citizens that he was associating too much with princes and nobles.

The discounted tales of Artevelde's early life as page in the households of the great come to mind. Also as *Hoofdman*, essentially a military command, he might have fancied himself on a par with the aristocratic captains who fought in the wars. He had married his daughter to a nobleman. Although Artevelde might have entertained ideas of social climbing there is no evidence that he was acting other than in a pragmatic manner. It suited the towns of Flanders to support the English claim to the French throne and Artevelde was making use of the conflict to gain the best advantage for Ghent and its confederate towns. Whether he understood that Edward was making use of him in a similar way was not known.

His plan to have the Count of Flanders replaced with Edward's heir, the Edward later known as the Black Prince, was in keeping with this policy. Ghent's problems lay with the pro-Valois Louis Dampierre and even if Edward did not become king of France that year or next, to have his heir as their prince assured Ghent's economic interests. This was still a drastic act and many of the influential burghers of Flanders had misgivings, for it smacked of meddling in the matters of the great.

Much of what we understand of the following events comes from the writings of the Hainaulter Jean Froissart. While acting as official historian in the service of Edward's Queen Philippa he produced a chronicle of the recent past, in particular of Edward's activities in the French wars. Froissart in his anecdotal and somewhat gossipy narrative tells how early in July 1345 Artevelde, together with other delegates from Ghent and also from Bruges and Ypres, journeyed to Sluys where the English king rested with his fleet. There was a conference aboard Edward's flagship the *Catherine,* where the business of deposing Count Louis was raised. On the 17th, Artevelde himself called for action, and for the Black Prince to take the Count's place.

But there was understandably some unease among the other delegates. It was a step with huge implications, even for those with major grievances. The delegates, under pressure from Edward and Artevelde and faced with the prospect of an action they suspected they would regret, resorted to a formula they obviously hoped would kill the project, or at least absolve themselves of the blame. The Flemish burghers declared that they could not make any such undertaking without a mandate from their cities. Despite further urging from Artevelde, they gave their answer that they would return in a month after receiving instructions.

It was obvious to Artevelde that his grand project was in danger of falling apart. He still resolved to gain this agreement at least in Ghent. During a consultation with Edward when the gathering dispersed he talked as if he could rally his home city. Perhaps he was trying to keep Edward interested and was buying time, or he might have grown fatally over-confident of his popularity. His big mistake was to tarry at Sluys assuring Edward that he could deliver Flanders. The other delegates had returned to Ghent ahead of him and convened a meeting in the marketplace, where they denounced the proposal in no uncertain terms.

Hours later, when Artevelde himself entered Ghent, he was dismayed at his icy reception from its citizens. Many he saluted turned away as he rode along the streets or ran for their houses, including those he counted as friends and supporters. The townsmen had been inflamed by his opposing delegates over his intent of displacing a 'natural lord in favour of a stranger' and Artevelde had thus been demonized at the meeting. Froissart had them saying as Artevelde arrived: 'Here comes one who is too much the master. And wanted to rule Flanders according to his own will and pleasure, which must not be longer borne.' He talks of them 'putting heads under one hood', which was his way of decribing them huddling in conspiratorial groups.

Besides popular opinion branding Artevelde as a control freak, a rumour had appeared that morning that Artevelde had collected revenues for the previous nine years and not rendered them to the Count. He had according to this tale been living sumptuously on the taxes he had collected from them. True or false, this rumour was shocking and the popular burgher was rapidly becoming a figure of hate. Perturbed, Artevelde proceeded to his house, ordering the doors bolted.

But within an hour or so he had cause to wish he had left the town instead. The Kalandenberg was soon filled with an unruly mob who sought to break down his doors. Gerard Denijs, master of the weavers, (although Froissart described him as a saddler) was apparently ringleader. Artevelde appeared at an upstairs window requesting to parley with the mob and was greeted with demands for the accounts of his revenue gathering. Artevelde replied that he did not have such records to hand, and he would gladly show them if they all returned the next day. But the mob would not be held off and renewed their attempts to break down the door.

Artevelde knew his life was in danger and left the house by the back door and through the stable, where he tried to gain refuge in a nearby church. But Denijs and some of the mob were already round the corner in anticipation, and on a backstreet behind his house called the Paddenhoe they killed Jacob van Artevelde. Another chronicle supplies different details of the confrontation between the townspeople and their former leader, saying a cobbler who lived in this backstreet and whose father Artevelde had killed waylaid Artevelde as he ran out and drove an axe into his skull.

There were other issues raised by this second chronicler. He reinforces the view that Artevelde's co-deputies stirred up misinformation and hatred against him. One reminded the crowd that he once said that if he ever mixed with nobles or acted like a noble, none should trust him. This he said applied in particular if he married his daughters into the nobility, which he had done. This pledge he may have made was ill-conceived, as he was now hobnobbing with kings and apparently acting in a manner above his station. Although this is not a story of class war, there is a strong element of the uneasy relationship of the burgher with the noble. Artevelde's intentions were easily interpreted with suspicion.

After the end of Artevelde and his plan, the English found new theatres of war. A year later Edward invaded via Normandy, and this campaign in Picardy and victory at Crécy are legendary. Count Louis of Flanders was among the French dead. Edward subsequently laid siege to the town of Calais, which was physically the closest port to England, and which took him almost a year to capture. From the 1360s until the French regained the town in 1558 the Wool Staple was located at Calais, where all wool exported from England with few exemptions would be shipped for resale. This did not fully solve the problems of Flanders, for later wars did disrupt the trade, but the wool supply was now standardised.

The spectacular fall of Artevelde did not in itself harm English influence in Flanders. The Flemish towns soon after reaffirmed their allegiance to King Edward. There was later a suggestion that his son Edward the Black Prince should marry Margaret de Dampierre, daughter of Louis II of Flanders, who inherited the County in 1346 from his father. This was a more acceptable expedient than Artevelde's grand plan and would have eventually assured the pro-English status quo. The new Count favoured the English and was far from keen on his heiress marrying a Frenchman. If Artevelde had delayed his action a year, he might have gained his objectives in due course, and survived. In the event, in 1369, Margaret married Philip of Valois, a son of the next French King John II, known as Philip the Bold, who had been granted the dukedom of Burgundy. When this Philip added Flanders to his possessions in 1384, he began a century of rule by the Valois Dukes of Burgundy over the Low Countries, which his heirs expanded. His successors were not strictly loyal to the Valois monarchy and even fought in civil wars against it.

While still waiting to inherit his father-in-law's estates Philip the Bold helped him to suppress a reprise of the Flemish revolt. Once again, in 1381 the weavers of Ghent led their revolt against their noble masters, and this time their *Hoofdman* was Philip van Artevelde. With English support this fourth son of Jacob van Artevelde, named after Edward III's Queen Philippa, was the focus for armed rebellion. After initial successes occupying Bruges and controlling most of Flanders Philip met with troops loyal to Louis and Philip. This younger Artevelde was defeated and killed at Rozebeke in 1382.

Jacob van Artevelde was neither a Belgian nationalist leader nor a champion of capitalism against feudalism. He was a businessman and burgher whose prime concern was his city, in many ways typical of the cloth merchants of Ghent and other Flemish towns. As a result, his agenda conflicted with that of the French monarchy and nobles and he was drawn into extreme intriguing. In this Artevelde was fairly successful, and for a time accomplished what he wished. But this was an order of politics traditionally reserved for the nobility where a burgher could easily swim out of his depth.

It is unlikely that Edward would have gone ahead with Artevelde's plan. There is a letter the English king wrote to the Flanders towns at the time where he exhorted them to accept Louis as their count. There were only certain circumstances in which an overlord could deprive his vassal of his estates, and to interfere with what was considered a hereditary right would bring him more opposition from the French nobles than any support he could hope for. Artevelde probably did not understand this, his background not tied down to such considerations and himself of a radical frame of mind. Artevelde was a useful ally to Edward of England and exploited this understanding to further his own schemes. Needless to say, if this alliance became a liability the English would drop it quickly enough.

Since 1863 a sculptor's interpretation of Jacob van Artevelde has looked over the Friday Market of Ghent (see plates, p. 5). It shows a moustachioed warrior somewhat reminiscent of the Dark Ages in mail armour and bearing a sword and shield. This is hardly a typical depiction of a burgher, and again reminds the viewer of a burgher who took up arms and might have aspired to nobility. But this is the statue of the Belgian hero that Artevelde was not. About the plinth scenes of his achievements are shown. In full colour the heraldic devices of the various craft and trade guilds are also placed about the base, which is closer to accuracy.

The tales of Artevelde associating with princes and nobles in his youth have been discounted for lack of evidence, but his behaviour, where his readiness to comport himself as a noble and walk in their world caused concern among his fellow burghers, gives a ring to such stories. In an age where the concept of equality of opportunity is widely accepted the constraints of feudal society are not so easily taken into account.

This is yet another story of the greasy pole of politics. Those who rose as champions at the head of the multitude could for a time count on serious political power, but the mood of such a public can change, quickly and radically. Artevelde might have taken more care over his own power base before he engaged in the politics of the great, and he might have tried not to appear as high-handed in his actions.

8

William of Ockham

Razor-wielding Thinker

The histories of medieval universities, the development of religious thought and the rise of the Friars are all interlinked, although each is a fascinating study in itself which would take (and has taken) entire volumes. From the thirteenth century onwards a line of theologians, mostly friars, challenged fundamental issues of faith and reason, William of Ockham was the last significant one of this number, distinct in the way he dismantled most of what was already accepted at once. We have all heard of Occam's Razor, but our perception has suffered from the over-use of the term.

We know little of William of Ockham's early life and background. He was born around the year 1285, and his name identifies his birthplace in Surrey; the village of Ockham is close by Guildford. His parentage and social status are unknown, but he certainly went to school. It is said that he entered the Franciscan Order at a fairly early age and probably received his training at Greyfriars in London, before going up to study at Oxford. He might have been sent to Paris to study, as every Franciscan province could choose a quota of brothers for this, but no evidence survives.

In addition to other kinds of ecclesiastics, Friars had by 1300 been an established feature in everyday life for nearly a century and four large orders were established: the Franciscans, known as the Grey Friars for their simple habits, the Dominicans, or Black Friars; the Carmelites or White Friars; and the Austin Friars. Each was an international organisation exempt from the Church establishment, distinct in role and outlook from the many monastic orders. A few smaller orders appeared, such as the Friars of the Sack, the Crutched (or Crossed) Friars, so named for the crosses they wore on their backs, and the Beating Friars, or Flagellants, who whipped each other and themselves for the sins of the world, but these lesser foundations were never numerous or lasting.

Although they had long shed most of their simple ways by the fourteenth century, the Franciscans had begun as a radical challenge at the turn on the thirteenth, as an anarchistic and somewhat simplistic version of living a Christian life. Giovanni Bernadone, 'Francesco' or 'Francis' to his friends for his 'French' manner, lived the life of a hedonistic youth and pseudo-noble until a religious experience as he rode to war in 1205 altered the course of his entire life. His father, a cloth-merchant of Assisi in northern Italy, had been pleased to fund his son's excesses as it furthered his own interests for the youth to associate with young nobles, but eventually disowned him when Francis took the word of the Gospel literally. 'If thou would be perfect, go, sell what you possess and give to the poor, and you will have treasure in heaven, and come, follow me.' (Matthew 19: 21.) Francis did exactly that, even handing his clothes over to his father. Keeping nothing but the cast-off garments he had been given, he lived in a hovel of branches and devoted his time to begging for food and preaching a simple Christian message. Others joined him in this, and a community soon developed a lifestyle and later a rule. They owned almost nothing and would allow no thought for the morrow, not even as to where their breakfast would come from.

Few who met Francis failed to be impressed with his example, whatever they thought of his ideas. He was strict in his interpretation of the Gospel and Pope Innocent III gave tacit encouragement to what became the Order of Friars Minor or 'Little Brothers of Christ'. Perhaps he was impressed by Francis's argument that whereas the Church as a mirror of secular society had its princes and nobles, the friars were its poor; so Francis was therefore unwilling to challenge the wealth and lifestyle of the established Church. The Waldensian sect, who also made a radical stand on material issues, had been condemned as heretics.

Francis died in 1226 and was canonised two years later, but soon his brethren discovered ways of making compromises with their founder's strict ideals. They still owned nothing, claimed Bonaventura, who succeeded Francis in the leadership, but they would have the 'use' of facilities that lay associates officially owned. A friar would be glad of the 'use' of a donkey to transport him where he would preach. He might benefit from the 'use' of a warm, dry friary to lay his head at night, preferable to the shelters made of foliage that Francis and his first followers made do with, and he would certainly benefit from being fed adequately. Any other material needs could be similarly justified, but this reasoning was hardly the way Francis had lived. Of course this logic could be applied to any possessions the original Friars would disdain to own, and it became easier for a Franciscan to live in modest comfort.

Few had the resolve that Francis displayed, and it was simply too easy to opt for some minor compromise given the choice. At the same time, common sense could be a factor. A Friar might ask himself how effectively he could do good works when half-starved, tired from long journeys on foot and ill from sleeping in the rain. Francis sallied forth propelled by his own inspiration, but those who came later found themselves dogged by practical considerations that could not be surmounted by this simple faith.

Many sincere men were still attracted to the Order, but the Friars were often criticized as having abandoned their founders' principles entirely. Chaucer's Friar, obviously a caricature, appears an amoral, moneygrubbing lecher. Christopher Marlowe had Dr Faustus insist that Mephistopheles appear in the form of a Franciscan Friar, for 'that holy shape becomes a devil best,' which was perhaps a comment on the Friars' hypocrisy. Francis's example was extremely difficult to live up to. It drove him to an early death and his followers could not be blamed for seeking an accommodation with their most basic needs.

It was inevitable that some planning and organisation was needed as the Franciscans grew in numbers and spread throughout Christendom. They learned quite early to ensure that missions to other countries must include at least one brother who knew the language. They also saw that to preach the Gospel effectively required some learning, and their appearance in the universities resulted from this understanding.

The first Franciscan mission came to England in 1224 and established itself quickly in London The Friars set up headquarters in the Shambles near Newgate where the butchers slaughtered animals. Their Friary would enjoy international standing as a school of learning until the Dissolution. Place-names in the City still testify to where the various orders of Friars resided; Blackfriars Station occupies the site of the first Baynard's Castle, which Henry III gave to the Dominicans. If, as believed, William of Ockham undertook his training as a novice at Greyfriars, it is then certain that he was encouraged to take up studies at Oxford. Given his evident academic ability he would be of use to the mission as a teacher and theologian.

From as early as the sixth century BC some have been moved to ask serious questions about the world, the universe and one's part in it, including how to behave. Thales and two other Milesians were the earliest known, and a long list of Greeks – Pythagoras, Plato, Socrates, Aristotle – and a multiplicity of schools of thought follow, all at least identifiable in the consciousness of western society. The Classical world yielded up a number of such thinkers and although a detailed account of philosophy cannot be presented here, philosophers have continued their enquiries over the centuries to the present day and many have studied their works. The teachings of Aristotle took on a new relevance in the Middle Ages.

The Christian era defined the parameters of the universe. From the early centuries Christians were obliged to believe in a heaven, earth and hell, a supreme creator and a human race born to sin from which Jesus Christ was set to redeem it. Such a picture emerged as the doctrine of the prevailing faction of Christianity and belief in this model was enforced, few daring to question it. Yet the search for understanding continued, although within this framework, and the philosophers were usually clerics. Arguably, Christian dogma restricted this quest.

In the thirteenth and fourteenth centuries the 'schoolmen', the learned clergy, attempted to reconcile the Christian cosmology with the analytical rigour of Aristotle. Up to the time of William of Ockham the debate was lively and much was deliberated on. Knowledge of many areas of learning emerged and the work of medieval thinkers is much underestimated.

There have always been scholars; those who sought available knowledge and then worked to further it. Unlike in the present day such learning was only available to a minority, when comparatively few children even gained an elementary education. Higher knowledge required an advanced command of Latin, and learning from the writings of classical Greeks was even more limited when so few knew the language. There were schools established throughout England by 1300, although an education was hardly available to all, but the need for literacy and numeracy among merchants, stewards and town officials among others had become acute by the thirteenth century. There appeared, or were re-founded, cathedral schools, charitable foundations and private establishments. Sometimes a parish priest doubled as a schoolmaster. They all at least offered a basic education to those who could attend.

Having gained a grounding in the 3 Rs older boys might attend a grammar school and undertake rigorous learning in Latin, in the hope that some at least would train for the priesthood. There was almost no provision for educating girls, except at home or in nunneries. While elementary education in some form was fairly widespread by the thirteenth century, grammar schools were few; in London there were only three by 1450, shortly before restrictions on licensing such establishments were lifted.

Foreigners often remark upon the exclusivity of the public schools of England. Eton, Rugby and Harrow and others not as well-known were founded in medieval and Tudor times, initially with the brief of teaching a number of poor boys, although from an early stage the sons of the wealthy could also be taught for a fee, and this category of pupils eventually made these schools exclusive. These foundations were intended to promote literacy in Latin, usually to make a career in the Church possible for some.

A few young men in every generation would be attracted to the life of the scholar, as distinct from, but not always exclusive of, Holy Orders. This life involved a kind of vagabondage, the medieval scholar would often travel on foot to where he could hear one teacher or another. By the twelfth century it was widely known that at Bologna the best instruction in Law could be found, for Theology it was Paris and Toledo for Medicine. Poverty was the lot of many such scholars, although the patronage of the wealthy and powerful could provide the means for sustenance. As the university system developed into the form we recognise, bursaries became available.

A large amount of learning inherited from Roman times was never quite forgotten. At the turn of the ninth century, the English monk Alcuin promoted the value of learning at the court of the Emperor Charlemagne. He not only ran the cathedral school at Aachen but made use of whatever written material could be found, and the copying and study of classical texts became established within this court culture. Charlemagne himself could read but not write, but he saw the value of education. Some of this written material survives to the present day and even such limited resources made some learning possible.

Although such writings were valued they represented a small amount of scholarship garnered from the classical world and it took the efforts of Petrarch, Boccaccio and others from the fourteenth century to recover more texts from those times. It was only from the late fifteenth century that a much wider range of ancient learning was accessible, when the western scholars discovered the wealth of writings in Greek. The capture of Constantinople by the Ottoman

Turks in 1453 and the subsequent exodus of Greek scholars with their rescued texts is popularly believed to have been the cause of learning that brought about the Renaissance, but this was in reality only part of the process beginning the love affair of western Europe with Greek and Latin literature. By the sixteenth century Classical knowledge had spurred the development of many branches of learning: science, philosophy, literature, even the theatre.

The study of Classics, still a strong and essential subject within living memory, has been in decline in Britain these past fifty years, but there is no doubt of the mark such studies have left. The terminologies of almost every field of knowledge, from Athletics to Zoology, were drawn from Greek and Latin. Latin is still taught in the equivalents of some grammar schools in the UK and on the continent.

A further dimension in the search for ancient knowledge lay in the culture of Islam. As the Arabs first conquered the Near and Middle East in the seventh century, they took it upon themselves to absorb the Greek masters such as Pythagoras, Euclid and others, eventually translating them into Arabic. Moslem scholars over the centuries advanced this knowledge and from the twelfth century it was possible for Christians to attend classes in Spain and Sicily in Mathematics, Geometry and Medicine.

It was thus the practice of those who loved knowledge to journey far and wide throughout the period. In the early twelfth century a scholar might hear the sharp analysis of Peter Abelard on the Left Bank of the Seine. Over two centuries later, students from Bohemia listened to John Wycliffe at Oxford as he questioned fundamental Church teachings. From 1512 at the University of Wittenberg in Saxony many heard the verbal duel between the academics Martin Luther and Johann Eck over matters of religious observance.

Oxford University had its humble beginnings in the late twelfth century. Scholars were known to teach there in 1096, but when Henry II forbade English students from studying in Paris in 1167, word spread that accomplished academics took on students in what was then the market town of Oxford. By the 1170s scholars would sit on the floor in a Master's lodgings in this town to hear him impart the fruits of his learning. By the time the restrictions on travel had ended, Oxford was established as a place where teachers could be found; an alternative to Paris or at least a stop on a scholar's itinerary.

Oxford was still a commercial centre, too, and division between the traditional 'town' and 'gown' elements of the city that emerged almost at the beginning has never since ended. There were violent riots in 1209 when a student murdered a local girl who was then his mistress. Such violence between the students and the townspeople continued and disrupted the teaching and it was the intervention by the papal legate five years later that restored safe conditions for the scholars. This re-establishment in 1216 formalized the university, appointing its first chancellor and laying the foundations for more organization. Some of the academics who had fled the town after the riots set up at Cambridge instead.

The practice of founding 'halls' or simply dormitories in response to the rising number of scholars had begun by the end of the twelfth century. These might be owned by an established teacher or could be provided as a venue for masters to teach. The colleges as we now know them first appeared around the middle of the thirteenth. Balliol, University and Merton colleges each still claim to have been founded first, but all were developments of the hall system, only with a more formalized membership and teaching structure.

The influence of the established Church cannot be overestimated in the universities. A student was tonsured on entry, taking minor Holy Orders as a matter of course. Chaucer referred to his student as a 'Clerke', which is the name of the lowest grade for those aspiring to the priesthood. Students might progress through the minor orders as doorkeeper, lector, exorcist and acolyte without the need to commit to the religious life, but they had the option of becoming a deacon and then a priest with all the attached possibilities and constraints. Scholars did not often marry, and the difference between the academic and the religious lifestyles was blurred. But scholarship developed over the centuries, and by the fifteenth century the university was not entirely a training ground for the Church: Margery Paston wrote to her son studying at Oxford at that time and implored him not to be drawn to the priesthood.

The curriculum taught in the universities was based on the classical model of the Seven Liberal Arts, divided into the *Trivium* and the *Quadrivium*. It would be a mistake to see the division as between arts and sciences, or literate and numerate disciplines, as they were in themselves a progression of understanding and the application of understanding. The *trivium* consisted of Grammar, Logic and Rhetoric, while the *quadrivium* was Arithmetic, Geometry, Music and Astronomy. The study of Music was purely theoretical, concerning the laws of harmony. Astronomy was mostly Astrology. Students progressed through such studies and gained their degrees of bachelor and master through disputation. A few gained doctorates in the faculties of Law, Medicine and Divinity.

The thirteenth century saw a renewed interest in the classical philosopher Aristotle. In the third century BC, Aristotle, for a time tutor to Alexander the Great as a boy, promoted a decidedly analytical approach. His drive for definitions more or less began the many disciplines of Biology, Physics, Metaphysics, Politics, Ethics, Poetics, Zoology and certainly Logic, which had a profound effect on learning for many centuries. He also wrote on Philosophy, Economics and Drama among many other subjects, each significantly with a name of Greek origin. 'Everything is either A or not A' and 'Man is a social and political animal' are but two of his maxims that he presented to his students at the Lyceum in Athens.

Although Aristotle's wealth of surviving writings translated into Latin were much valued in the Middle Ages, he was still a pagan and the church banned their study for a long time, apart from Logic, which was a prized discipline. This ban ended in Paris about 1245, and soon Oxford was a thriving centre for studying the works of Aristotle.

Also in the mid-thirteenth century, the Friars appeared at the seats of learning. Francis had never envisaged his following to take such a route, but it made sense to those who followed to acquire learning in order to preach. The Dominicans, whose main concern was orthodoxy in religious thought, also embraced the university system and soon the most acclaimed thinkers and academics were Friars of these two orders.

In the early thirteenth century Robert Grosseteste began this tradition of scholastic philosophy. Not a member of either order, he was eventually Bishop of Lincoln. There followed in turn two Dominicans, Albertus Magnus and Thomas Aquinas, and afterwards three Franciscans; Roger Bacon, Duns Scotus and eventually, William of Ockham. Each had their period of pre-eminence as teachers from the early thirteenth century to the mid-fourteenth.

The interest some had in what we now term scientific research began this discipline as a by-product of their teaching. 'Science' in that time simply meant 'knowledge,' and had no distinction from other areas of learning. Grosseteste conducted much research on Optics and Astronomy. Bacon is credited as the 'first scientist', but this is misleading. He may have suggested that different-shaped glass lenses could correct defective vision, but never tried this out. Similarly, he suggested the mix of ingredients that produced gunpowder, but others put it into practice much later. He anticipated hydraulics, steam power and powered flight, and was the first to recognise the visible spectrum in a glass of water, but as he refrained from practical experiments on his ideas, the benefits of this deliberation did not appear for centuries after him.

William is on record as ordained as a subdeacon by the Archbishop of Canterbury in 1306. It appears that after some years studying he became known as a teacher of Logic. He lectured from 1317 to 1319 on the *Sentences* of Peter Lombard, a theological work of the previous century that examined the fundamental issues of faith and the analysis thereof. At this time, too, he was licensed to hear confessions. From 1321 to 1324 William was lecturing in logic and natural philosophy, at the time writing his *Summa Logica*. This was when he met with huge controversy.

It was the norm for academics to dispute issues as part of the process eventually leading to their doctoral thesis. The core of the polemic was the reconciliation of the disciplines of Philosophy, which included Logic, with that of Theology. The Aristotelean concepts were too sound to be ignored, but the core of belief in Christian doctrine could not be denied. While this account cannot deal with medieval philosophy in any great detail, it is relevant to understand the main concepts debated in the early fourteenth century.

By the time Ockham was at Oxford there was a serious debate over the concept of *universals*. There was much said on the relationship of the concept of anything and its counterpart in reality, and on different classifications. In the thirteenth century, Thomas Aquinas produced a synthesis of philosophy with theology, which produced further problems where the nature of God could not easily fit into the model of logical analysis. The Thomist stance, that presented by Thomas Aquinas, still had many adherents by 1300, but there was dissent. John Duns Scotus was the most influential thinker when William was first at Oxford. Before his death in 1308 he had led the attempts to define the main issues, but he and his contemporaries tended to speculate heavily, and qualifying factors complicated the deliberations.

The first principle of William of Ockham's own thesis concerned God as transcendent and distinct from the universe and all else, which breaks with the Platonic model. One cannot use logic to define God, he said, and no application of reason could access such knowledge.

The laws of nature were decided on by God and by His will only and whether humans in a state of grace were not rewarded or wrongdoers were not punished was His prerogative and His observance of the laws of nature was His choice alone.

A modern reader might find this all bewildering and may wonder what the point of it all is. Whatever philosophical thought that goes on today does not exist within such a framework; it even questions whether God exists or not and if He does, can we expect any divine intervention in the universe or human life? It must be understood that this was the apex of discovery for those of the time. How can we humans understand the truth and answer important questions? A small minority sought answers. They had writings dating from Ancient Greece onward to act as points of reference; but one major constraint, Christian thought and the tenets of the Catholic Church, dictated the limits of enquiry. Medieval thought was first of all Christian thought, and this could not be denied.

Perhaps Duns Scotus and William of Ockham began the process of cutting philosophy loose from theology. Unlike the Thomist model, logic concerned itself with the material world and philosophy with God. This at least prevented the one interfering with the other. It is not that William denied the Christian view, but he altered the perspective in a more comprehensible manner.

Of course, William of Ockham is best known for what is known as 'Occam's Razor'. Our understanding of this is diluted and debased by over-familiarization, but this created a stir that rocked the entire academic community. In fact, it was not revolutionary, and others had thought along similar lines. By this time speculation over universals had become rife, and all kinds of definitions had emerged and were debated on, that created complicated arguments and in the long term did not solve much. Ockham simply stated that if an assumption or hypothesis is not necessary, one should reserve judgment on it: *Pluralitas non est ponenda sine necessitate*, although those precise words are not in fact found in his writings.

This has often been interpreted as the modern KISS principle ('Keep It Simple, Stupid') but the core directive is not to automatically endorse entities for which there is no reason to believe exist. Many certainly saw this as a welcome return to a clearer focus, without unnecessarily multiplying entities. However, it rendered much of the scholarship of the previous century redundant and it is not difficult to see what discontent it aroused among the academics of the time. It is often the case today that academics can be territorial about their areas of interest and unreasonable when they consider them invaded.

Ockham's influence on political thought would later have far-reaching influence. Partially initiated by his preoccupation with logic and partially by a growing quarrel the Franciscan order had with the papacy itself, William produced an understanding that put him at odds with the pope. John XXII had shown his dislike for the ideals of poverty by which the Friars maintained their core doctrines and William stated that the pope had 'erred' in this action. There was also a point where John had said that the blessed did not enjoy the vision of the divine presence until the Day of Judgment. Ockham then interpreted the papacy in a strongly Franciscan manner, that it enjoyed material wealth by way of holding the 'use' of it, but this did not entail legal ownership.

Later critics would raise these points. Christ founded the papacy, William said, but scriptural truth was the overriding authority. He looked at previous attempts at conciliarism, where the best minds of the Church would resolve disputes in conference. His views were similar to that of his contemporary Marsilius of Padua, with whom he would later associate, and who advocated a model where the papacy would be the supreme authority in spiritual matters but secular matters were the province of rulers, both separate and neither claiming supremacy over the other.

Certain issues in Ockham's teaching clearly contradict the tenets of the Catholic Church, where the doctrine of Papal infallibility trumps all. Ockham acknowledged the supremacy of Holy Writ rather than this, and he supported his order's advocacy of clerical poverty. Such ideals as he presented were later raised in the Hussite heresies later that century and were still present in the thinking of the Reformation.

This did not do Ockham much good at the time. Thomas Aquinas was canonised, and Duns Scotus later beatified, but no such honours came William's way. He never obtained his doctorate, and was prevented, after four years' disputation and lecturing, from admission to the Master's degree. Several of the previous teachers had gained distinctive titles: Roger Bacon was known as *doctor mirabilis*, the Amazing Teacher, and similarly Aquinas, the Angelic Teacher, while Duns Scotus was the Subtle Teacher, and those who were recognised as meaningful theologians also gained such recognition as doctors of the Church. But Ockham was only known as *inceptor venerabilis*, sometimes translated as the Venerable Innovator but was more likely to have meant the Venerable Postulant, showing what he did not attain. Events before he would have completed his Master of Theology qualification changed the course of his life.

In 1323 the provincial chapter of his order called on him to explain the thirteen proposals he had produced in his commentary on the *Sentences*. No further action came of this, but the following year William received a similar summons, this time to the Papal Curia. This was not to Rome but to Avignon. In 1309 civil unrest in the Eternal City had caused Pope Clement V to decamp to Avignon, where he could avail himself of the protection of Philip IV of France. This relocation lasted until 1378, when on the urging of the visionary Catherine of Siena, Pope Gregory XI returned to Rome, but this only began a new controversy. There were soon two popes, in Rome and in Avignon, and neither recognised the other. For decades, until the Council of Constance in 1414, western Christendom was split by the rival papacies and the Church was far less effective.

On reaching Avignon, Ockham was probably not too surprised to see John Lutterell at the Curia, almost certainly his main accuser. A Dominican and a canon of Salisbury Cathedral, Lutterell had been Chancellor of Oxford for five years. Described as an 'over-enthusiastic Thomist' he had been expelled from his office in 1322 after a serious academic controversy. The following year he had made his way to Avignon to further his career. It is not known if he had clashed with Ockham in his time at Oxford, but it is not inconceivable. Aside from the latter's rejection of Thomism, the division between the two mendicant orders often produced friction. Armed with what he declared were fifty-six philosophical and theological statements from the commentary on the *Sentences* that were 'in error' Lutterell called for enquiry into Ockham's 'false teaching.'

Although it might have been difficult for Lutterell to have Ockham condemned as a heretic, he made a case for his work being in error, but this was not universally accepted. A commission of prelates and prelates-elect first threw seven of Lutterell's points out, and then debated with William on his ideas. Lutterell tried to refute Ockham using Thomist arguments, but among the commissioners there were some who defended Ockham's ideas. Eventually, the commission rendered no formal condemnation, although Ockham was held under house arrest.

Pope John XXII was at the time in conflict with the Franciscans, who were then declaring their beliefs that the Church should not be so materially wealthy; their founder's insistence that while they remained poor the 'princes' of the Church need not was forgotten, by the look of it. The Spirituals, a back-to-basics movement within the order, were causing this trouble. That they stated that Christ and the Apostles lived in poverty themselves the pope declared heretical. It was an unfortunate situation that Ockham had stumbled into at Avignon and he found himself caught in the crossfire. Other Franciscans were similarly caught on the wrong side of the argument.

In 1328 Ockham, with two brothers, Michele da Cesena, General of the Order, and Bonagratia da Bergamo, slipped away to the port of Aigues Mortes and took ship to Genoa, eventually arriving at Pisa, where the court of Emperor Louis of Bavaria was then in residence. John had them excommunicated and ordered their arrest, but the last act was impracticable. The emperor was then in conflict with the pope and welcomed Ockham, and he remained with the court for the rest of his life.

Louis (or Ludwig) IV had a serious quarrel with the papacy; he was excommunicate and had been crowned emperor in Rome by a layman shortly before this meeting. He welcomed the Franciscans, particularly William, as he probably saw his value as an aid to advancing his cause. Marsilius of Padua was also in his service by this time and it is likely that he and Ockham had much discussion once they met. While at Pisa the friars attended a ceremony in the cathedral where a straw effigy of Pope John in papal regalia was declared condemned of heresy. William went with the court in the spring of 1329 to Munich, to where Louis had established the Alter Hof, the first permanent residence of the Holy Roman Emperors.

William of Ockham spent the rest of his life adding to his political writings. The politics of the time were mostly tied up with the relationship between the pope and emperor; not a new political theme. Louis died suddenly in 1347 and William was without a protector. Excommunicate and with no means of support he prepared a petition of repentance, seeking to be received again into divine grace. If this act was intended to restore his forgiveness in the afterlife, as the Church believed it did, it was sent too late. William of Ockham died in 1349 in a convent at Munich. It was said that he was one of those struck down by the Black Death as it found its way into southern Germany, but this is not certain. William was over sixty by that time and could have died by other causes.

Ockham was the last of the important 'schoolmen' and his influence persisted for some time. There were many known as 'Ockhamites' who had various theories not always closely related to the teachings of Ockham. Perhaps Ockham popularised skepticism as a viable standpoint; nothing should be taken at face value. The next important development at Oxford was theological, when John Wycliffe radically challenged Catholic doctrine. A little later the conciliar movement thought again of Ockham when they sought to solve the Great Schism. Before new ideas that appeared first in the Renaissance and the Reformation the debates continued, but they were still tightly enmeshed in Christian tenets.

William and his kind can only be commended. They gave serious thought to the fundamental issues of the universe as they understood it and tried to make sense of it. Such thinking became dangerous for William once the politics of the papacy, empire and between the mendicant orders reached a critical moment.

9

King John of Bohemia

An Excess of Chivalry?

Narratives on the Battle of Crécy in 1346 usually tell of a minor incident concerning King John of Bohemia. It is the legend of the king who took part in the battle although he was completely blind, commanding his following to guide him into the thick of the fight so that he could engage the enemy. This act of such conspicuous valour understandably brought him his death, and as the legend has it, so impressed the Black Prince that he adopted his fallen enemy's plumed badge and his motto.

This much is often said of the king, mostly from Froissart's account of this action, but John of Bohemia was in truth a more complex person and his fame spread far. He lived in more than one medieval world; a flamboyant figure whose career blazed from central Europe and the Baltic to that fateful field in Picardy. He was in fact only blind in his last few years. Was it his tragedy that he believed in chivalry too strongly?

John of Bohemia, also known as John of Luxemburg and as John the Blind, was born the eldest son of the future Holy Roman Emperor Henry VII on 10 August 1296; his father then Count of Luxembourg and his mother Margaret, daughter of the Duke of Brabant.

The title of Holy Roman Emperor would last almost a millennium and is shrouded in myths and misunderstandings. Despite what is commonly believed, the Holy Roman Empire was *not* that founded by Charlemagne. While Charlemagne, or rather Charles the Great, King of the Franks, built a massive state uniting continental western Europe in the eighth century and was crowned Emperor on Christmas Day 800, this empire did not survive his grandsons. By the tenth century there was a loose association of tribal duchies in

central Europe and northern Italy, the eastern regions of the former
Carolingian Empire, who took to electing one of their princes to
the imperial title. This German Empire developed its mythology,
particularly when the Emperor Frederick Barbarossa claimed in the
twelfth century to be the heir, not only of Charlemagne but of the
Christian emperors of Rome, a spurious claim in both cases. Even
then, the title of Holy Roman Emperor that he then assumed was
not officially recognised for centuries. In theory at least, some of
the princes had the power to elect one of the German rulers initially
as King of the Romans, who would assume the imperial title when
crowned by the pope. This could take years to accomplish in full,
if at all. Since the death of Frederick II in 1250 the title of emperor
had been vacant, and Henry of Luxemburg would be the first in half
a century to resume it.

There were several dynasties of emperors; from Otto of Saxony,
the first emperor in 962, through the Salians of Franconia, the Staufer
(or Hohenstaufen) dynasty of Swabia began by Frederick Barbarossa,
to the House of Luxemburg that Henry VII founded. There were
several intervening emperors of other regal families in this time, but
succession mostly passed from the head of the reigning house to his
heir. From 1440 to the end, the emperor was always the head of the
House of Habsburg. It was always debatable as to how much power
the Holy Roman Emperors really held, but it generally waned as time
went on. In the eighteenth century, Voltaire commented that this body
was neither holy, nor Roman, nor an empire. When Napoleon ordered
an end to the title in 1806 it was little more than that: a title.

John of Luxemburg grew up expecting to succeed as emperor
himself. From an early age his education resembled that of most
aristocratic males and he was sent to Paris to learn. Apart from
some book-learning he served as page and then squire. Training as a
knight began around the age of twelve, where a boy learned the arts
of horsemanship; in particular how to stay on a horse in combat.
Training in the use of the sword, lance and shield followed as a matter
of course, and by early manhood he could expect some practical
experience of warfare.

Much like the tank in modern warfare, the knight was a formidable
fighting machine. Protected by armour, mounted on a powerful horse,
equipped with the best close combat weapons of the time with which
he trained to a high degree of proficiency, he was the most effective
player in the game of war. Although a knight may not be supreme in

every situation, when a host of knights charged together at the right moment on the field of battle there was little chance of resisting them.

The education of such a young man would also include total immersion in the culture of what we call chivalry. The term has since acquired a vague interpretation and the debate on its nature, origins and significance goes on still. It essentially envisaged an international fraternity open only to those born into the military class. Peasants could hardly be chivalrous and whoever was dubbed a knight was distinct from common men.

A knight's education, including the many manuals and the vast body of literature of the period, stressed high standards of behaviour and a litany of virtues. A hybrid of martial and Christian moralities, a knight should not only be terrible in war but gentle and affable in peace. He should render devotion to God, Christ, the Virgin and the Saints, fighting the good fight at the same time. He should be the protector of the weak and righter of wrongs, and in particular he should be the defender and upholder of women. His inspirations would be the *Chansons de Geste* and the quests of King Arthur and his Knights. Chaucer has his 'verray parfit, gentil knyght' at the head of his gathering of pilgrims, an idealised figure around whom the author explores the concepts of love and chivalry.

A modern tendency towards cynicism colours our perception of such an ideal. Being human we naturally wonder about placing our trust so easily, and expect that others would act pragmatically where it suited their own agendas. Cervantes created Don Quixote when such values were no longer taken as seriously, a caricature of a time when to ride forth and bring good to a wicked world was believed a genuine option.

A chivalrous knight nevertheless gave his word of honour and kept it, we are told. The institution of safe conduct, including the understanding that enemies coming to parley would depart in safety whatever the outcome, has been an essential feature in war and diplomacy ever since. The Marquis of Queensberry Rules, Scout's Honour and all such codes of behaviour have their beginnings in such ideals.

One of the two mistakes many of the knightly class made was to believe themselves automatically chivalrous by virtue of their social backgrounds, for such ideals require a conscious commitment to maintain them. The other error was denying that those of lower social orders were capable of such chivalry themselves. The term 'villain' once meant an unfree peasant, the lowest in the social scale, so believed to be the most morally inferior. We can also observe the use Shakespeare made of such terms as 'slave,' 'base-born' and even 'base football-player' as aspersions on character. Even today the term 'bastard' is used as an epithet of bad character, regardless of one's parents' marital status.

As to how well and how effectively the medieval knight practised this code of behaviour, there is much debate. Of course, it was breached countless times, and many were called 'false knight' for doing so. The traitor Ganelon lured Roland and Oliver to their deaths and Mordred destroyed the Round Table by setting its knights against each other. A false knight might have his spurs cut off and his shield besmirched as a ritual degradation.

The Hundred Years War in particular showed events that indicate how seriously this code of behaviour was taken. King John II of France, captured at Poitiers and released from imprisonment in England while his ransom was still to be settled, returned to England when his son, then standing hostage, escaped captivity. In Brittany in 1351, rather than violate a truce, English and Breton knights settled a dispute by appointing thirty knights each and fighting it out as a tournament, using an alleged slight on a lady as a pretext. The Combat of the Thirty as it was called was as much a bloodbath as any battle, but it at least did not break the truce. There were so many instances of chivalric exchange between the two sides in the whole of the wars, ranging from the stirring and honourable to the frankly ridiculous. It was a tournament culture, where to be seen to do the right thing was all-important.

This was John of Luxembourg's education and how he lived his life; he would be perceived in his lifetime as an exemplar of chivalric virtues. As his education neared completion his father, then Count of Luxemburg, became an important player in imperial affairs. The turn of the fourteenth century saw a vicious conflict between the supporters of Pope Boniface VIII and those of the incumbent King of the Romans, Albert I of Habsburg.

Albert, who had never gained the imperial crown, was murdered in 1308 by a relative and once again the succession was up for debate, particularly while many powerful elements wished to prevent the founding of a Habsburg dynasty. As tradition dictated, the election would be decided by a collective composed of the Archbishops of Trier, Mainz and Cologne, the Count Palatine of the Rhine, the Duke of Saxony, the Margrave of Prussia and the King of Bohemia, and thus a list of candidates was drawn up. Archbishop Baldwin of Trier was Henry's brother who raised the support of other powerful elements, and Henry of Luxemburg was created King of the Romans. It was only in 1312 that the pope crowned him emperor; a marked achievement as the role had been vacant for over half a century and might have eventually lapsed.

For his son every possibility opened. John was himself made Count of Luxemburg in 1309 and could reasonably aspire to succeed his father as emperor in due course. Very soon after this, Henry had a new role for him in Bohemia. In his mid-teens John was crowned as a king – but did not know this would be the highest he would go. Bohemia, an area now covered by most of the present-day Czech Republic, had long been the Slavonic fringe of the Holy Roman Empire, although its native ruling dynasty, the Přemyslids, who styled themselves kings of Bohemia from the twelfth century, had long lost its vigour. Some of the line also held the crowns of Poland, Hungary and Carinthia at different times and planned a 'personal union' of Poland and Hungary with Bohemia.

Following the death of Wenceslaus III in 1306, there was a drawn-out succession controversy in Bohemia. The Habsburgs had imposed their candidate, the young Rudolph, by force, but Rudolph was not accepted by the Bohemian nobles and died the following year. When the murder of Albert of Habsburg followed, it was easier for Wenceslaus's brother-in-law Henry of Carinthia to usurp the Bohemian throne, but his short reign was disappointing. His support came from the towns, mostly populated by Germans, but the Czech nobles were not pleased with his mostly ineffective rulership. As Henry of Luxemburg was now King of the Romans, they thought it politic to offer the crown to his son John, and in return for his father's assistance in removing the usurper, John would marry the heiress Elizabeth and gain the throne. John's father saw this as an ideal opportunity to buttress the House of Luxemburg's hold on the empire by making his son one of the electors.

It was not as easy as it seemed: Elizabeth had to be kidnapped from a castle of a pro-Carinthian noble and was not herself initially sold on the marriage. Only after Abbot Konrad of Königsaal persuaded her did she agree, and she and John were married at Speyer in September 1310. John then rode at the head of an army that drove Henry of Carinthia from Prague and on 7 February 1311 was himself crowned there. It is unlikely that John, then fourteen, was in command of this host personally, but it certainly presented his image in a positive manner. He now also had claims to the crowns of both Poland and Hungary.

At first the Bohemians were pleased with their new dynamic young king, but soon they had cause to doubt his commitment. A precocious young man, brought up in the values of grand and chivalrous deeds, he was clearly in his element when grandiose projects and military campaigns were happening, but showed himself unsuited to the daily duties expected of a ruler. He was an alien king who hankered for the excesses of court life he had known in France. His reign saw high taxation, much of it to fund his lavish lifestyle. He had gained a dispensation from the pope enabling him to tax the clergy of Bohemia, which he used, causing inevitable discontent.

He and Elisabeth had seven children, of which five survived. As they were born between 1313 and 1323, it is certain that he spent at least some of his time with his wife in Bohemia for the first ten years of his reign. But for most of the time he left the running of Bohemia to officials and regent and was conspicuous in his absence, living a sumptuous and active life elsewhere in Europe, usually returning to Prague only when he needed more money. He named his eldest son Wenceslaus, obviously after his father-in-law, but later changed his name to Charles and sent him to France for his education. John's children were mostly brought up in monasteries and he apparently saw little of Elizabeth after begetting the last child. She died of tuberculosis in 1330.

One achievement of John as King of Bohemia was the acquisition of Silesia. At that time the region was a number of petty lordships, mostly ruled over by Polish collaterals. In 1335, John made an agreement with the King of Poland by which he gained suzerainty and where in return he renounced the claim that he had inherited to the Polish crown. This only began the integration of Silesia into Bohemia, but it made a difference.

The young king brought new glamour to Bohemia. He set up a series of tournaments where the sons of the Czech nobles jousted, and he took part himself. Once he fell from his horse and almost died. There was much concern for the succession at this point and he obliged on his recovery by producing another child, his son John Henry, named after the Luxemburg succession.

As king, John made many enemies. His activities raised an alliance of Austria, Brandenburg, Bavaria and the Palatinate against him. It is surprising that he remained king for the rest of his life, given that he offended so many and spent so little time in his kingdom.

At first, as emperor-in-waiting as he thought himself, John supported his father in a new offensive in Italy. Henry VII only held the full imperial title for a year and was clashing with Pope Clement V and Robert of Naples as he sought to re-establish control in parts of Italy. On 24 August 1313, while King John of Bohemia was leading an army across the Alps to join his father on campaign in Tuscany, Henry suddenly died.

His father's death may have been a shock to John, but a new reverse soon followed when the imperial succession was deliberated, and he learned early in the proceedings that he was not to be the next Holy Roman Emperor. The House of Luxemburg itself had no dynastic claim to the succession, as this was by nature elective. Previous emperors had arranged to perpetuate their dynasties by securing control over the elective process and Henry VII had himself begun this by making John King of Bohemia, which gave the young man a voice in the election. But Henry was not emperor long enough to consolidate his hold. The electors wanted to resist the Habsburgs' bid to regain the title, but they did not think John was ready to fill the role. He was only seventeen, and imperial politics required a shrewd and seasoned intellect, something John had not then exhibited. Even his two committed supporters, the Archbishops of Mainz and Trier, had to admit that they could not sway the election for him and persuaded John to support the candidacy of Louis (or Ludwig) of Wittelsbach, Duke of Bavaria, instead. Louis finally gained five of the seven votes and was acclaimed king and later emperor.

It was by no means the end of the House of Luxemburg as emperors, nor that of Habsburg, but a new controversy arose when Frederick the Handsome, the Habsburg Duke of Austria, immediately disputed the election. Frederick received the support of Henry of Carinthia, who still claimed to be king of Bohemia. When he and a rival claimant to Saxony declared for him, Frederick claimed to have had four of the seven votes. It was most irregular, but who could say what was lawful, when so much was based on tradition?

While Louis was crowned in Aachen, Frederick received the crown from the Archbishop of Cologne in his cathedral and there followed eight years of civil war over who really was King of the Romans. In this early stage John supported the Wittelsbach succession and took part in the campaigning, including the Battle of Mühldorf on 28 September 1322, where Frederick and many of his supporters were taken prisoner. Louis kept him in custody for three years, releasing him after Frederick publicly recognised Louis as emperor.

Louis was also concerned when John of Bohemia withdrew from the alliance along with others. For the rest of this time John alternated between support and opposition towards Louis as emperor, still believing that he could be emperor himself. There were also territorial disputes and as John became increasingly friendly with both the King of France and the pope, relations with Louis soon became strained.

John showed some awareness of statecraft where Henry of Carinthia was concerned, although without success. At times John was obliged to negotiate with his rival and offered Henry the hand in marriage of his sister Marie in return for renouncing his claim to the crown of Bohemia. John also suggested reinforcing this with the marriage of Henry's only daughter to John's heir. The plan fell through when Marie herself objected to the marriage – she declared that she did not want to marry a barbarian. He also planned the marriage of another sister Margaret to the son of Otto of Bavaria, but she was too young at the time and this marriage did not come about either. John did eventually gain control over the Tirol by marrying his son John Henry to its heiress.

No doubt disappointed at not being emperor, John soon resumed his wanderings and was seen in almost every capital in western Europe. He came often to Paris, as it seems the King of France's court was his true home. His sister Marie was finally married to King Charles IV of France.

While in France, John received a message from some of the Bohemian nobles that a plot to overthrow him in his absence was under way. John quickly returned to Prague, where his chancellor, John of Viserhad, a bastard son of Wenceslaus II, was intriguing with Queen Elizabeth. The king quickly threw the regent into prison; but having suppressed the plot he did not appear to learn the lesson that long absences could undermine his position.

John was aware of the Přemyslid claim to the kingdom of Poland, which he had inherited through his marriage. He was also astute enough to realise that it would take an ambitious campaign to contest this claim against the reigning Ladislaus Lotietek and would ultimately do the Habsburg cause more good than his. He would eventually renounce the claim, but it is likely that his activities in Lithuania were in part designed to give this claim credence.

During his long career John was also involved in other conflicts. He did make considerable efforts to make himself King of Lombardy. This also came with the territory of Holy Roman Emperor and he inherited this project from his father, as it would further his unforgotten ambitions for the imperial throne. Both his parents had died on campaign in Italy and there was an element of seeking revenge in his own campaigning. In 1331 John took a small army across the Alps again on the invitation of the dignitaries of Brescia. He received the homage of some of the towns, but soon found his army too small to defend this position. He also made alliances with the kings of Hungary and Poland against Louis and his allies.

As John was also Count of Luxemburg, he had issues that demanded his attention there. He sought to extend this principality, and campaigned at times against Metz, against Duke John of Brabant and the Archbishop of Cologne. In reality, he felt that Bohemia was too much of a drain on his attention and once suggested to the new emperor that he exchange it for the Palatinate. Bohemia was now becoming unstable once again and John's attitude did little to reverse the trend.

For many years, John was ensconced in the court of Charles IV of France. Although afforded the respect of a king, he lived the life of a courtier, and became close to the new king. John became well-known in the tournaments and other courtly events, the hero of many a knightly deed and a respected member of Charles' court. He sent his seven-year-old heir to Paris for his education, which did the future emperor much good, and he grew up highly educated and multilingual.

For a time, John had one of the most prestigious poets of the age in his service. Guillaume de Machaut, famed for both his writings and musical compositions, was his household chaplain and secretary. Although he eventually left for a canonry at Rheims, Guillaume followed John everywhere for some years, to Prague and to Lithuania. One of his best-known works was *The Judgement of the King of Bohemia,* a long lyric poem on a complicated theme of courtly love, in which he has John of Bohemia pronouncing the final judgment. Of course, Guillaume was flattering his patron; John obviously liked being presented as an authority on *courtoisie.* After John's death, Guillaume had other patrons. His work influenced Chaucer, Christine de Pisan and many other writers of the following generations.

Charles had plans for a new crusade. Of course, this was the expected intention of any chivalrous king, even though the Holy Land had long been lost to Islam. Yet although as before many voiced such an intention, or even took the Cross as Charles did in 1323, no action came of it. In this case problems arose over the pope sanctioning the funding, as he thought Charles would have redirected the money to domestic use. Charles also had considered intervention in Byzantine affairs; an expedition that had echoes of the 1204 'crusade' but died before he could take action. No doubt John of Bohemia was enthusiastic about accompanying him on such military operations. As these failed to materialise, he did go on crusade himself several times to the northern frontier of Christianity, where a knight could still fight the good fight against the heathen.

Lithuania had since the days of Mindaugas been as steadfast a pagan state as before his flirtation with Christianity, and had recently gained a hold over Samogitia, among other territories. Early in the fourteenth century, Grand Duke Gediminas had showed himself as much a reformer as Mindaugas had a half-century before; he had introduced a feudal system and exerted his influence over Minsk, Kiev and Polotsk. Despite the tales the west heard, he had shown no opposition to Christian missions in his territory and many of his subjects and new vassals were Christians to begin with. But the Lithuanians generally remained decidedly pagan, and those who sought to convert by persuasion had made little headway. The Teutonic Knights still waged war to spread the faith, even though they had less justification than ever.

In a way, crusading in central Europe and the Baltic region was another endeavour that came with the territory of being a prince of the Holy Roman Empire. John, using the influence of his uncle the Archbishop of Trier, pledged his support for the Knights' cause and in February 1329 he brought an army and large amounts of money to Königsberg. That year he was one of the commanders at the taking of the Lithuanian fort at Medewagen. But the Knights observed that his support had a price-tag. Having taken the fort they would have massacred the garrison after it surrendered, as they often did, but John opposed this.

Even though chivalry did not usually apply to peasants and certainly not to heathen enemies, John insisted on quarter for them as the laws of war demanded. The Grand Master and he finally agreed that those who accepted baptism would be spared. Over six thousand did, most obviously to save their lives. The crusading army took four forts in all on that campaign. On the same expedition a Lithuanian leader named Margalis was captured. John spared him and tried to induce him to accept baptism, which he refused, even when the Bohemian king sent theologians to debate with him.

There is a story, possibly fabricated but sounding too much like a tacky imitation of the courtly love tradition to be without some foundation, that John tried a more carnal method of guiding him to the font. A young girl, daughter of one of John's knightly following and present on the campaign, was sent into the garden where Margalis often walked. Her singing soon gained his attention, and she showed herself eager to return his love, if only he would accept baptism. Margalis was smitten by this pretty maiden but told her solemnly that he could not betray his own faith. Despite this, he proposed marriage to her, but she declared that she would rather be burned alive than marry him while a pagan. The story goes that just before John and his following left the region, he had the girl sat opposite him at dinner and she repeatedly exhorted Margalis to convert. Margalis could not, even for her, and soon after she left with John's entourage, the chief sickened and died.

This story has elements that remind the reader of similar tales of courtly love and may have come from that storytelling tradition. But it certainly did not end in the usual way. If John indeed used this ruse, based as it was on the values he understood at the French court, he must have been surprised at Margalis's failure to take the bait.

John crusaded against the Lithuanian pagans three times in all. His main contribution was to promote the ideals of taking arms and riding to this eastern frontier of Christendom. With his encouragement many knights gave their services and revived the long haul the Teutonic Knights had set themselves to. Gautier de Brienne, Count of Lecce and titular Duke of Athens, rode with him in 1329. Later that century, Henry Bolingbroke spent some time on this ongoing crusade. Chaucer had his knight, an idealised figure rather than a real person, returning from crusade in the Baltic. It was a more attractive option to many nobles than seeking to reconquer the Levant after it had been long lost, and especially now that the Mamluks were its defenders.

John still had designs on the crown of Poland. He may have taken up the crusade as a chivalrous knight should, but it is clear that he was seeking to enlist the Teutonic Knights' support for his claim. At one point he and the Knights were considering an attack on Ladislaus at Kracow. Nothing came of this plan, and John would eventually use his claim as a bargaining counter, trading it for Silesia.

There were other times that John was occupied with affairs of the French court and its wars. In 1328 Charles IV of France died, and with him ended the ruling house of Capet. The Salic Law as recognised prevented the succession of his existing and posthumous daughters or his sister Isabella, and his cousin Philip of Valois accordingly became Philip VI. The claim of Isabella's son Edward III of England would later bring war to the fields of France. John of Bohemia showed himself both a close supporter of the new Valois monarchy and an active player in the coming wars. John married his son Charles to Marie de Valois and his daughter Bonne to Philip's son, the future King John the Good.

John retained the crown of Bohemia when Elizabeth died in 1330 and he remarried to Beatrix, daughter of the French Duke Louis of Bourbon. They had two children: Wenceslaus, born in Prague in 1337, and Bonne, a daughter with the same name as her half-sister. To give this son a decidedly Bohemian name might have been a gesture to placate the Czechs.

John's position at the French court took him to fighting in the wars with the English. In 1338 Philip decided to attack the English presence in the south-west and made John commander of the army and his governor of the Languedoc. Edward III was then campaigning in the Low Countries and Philip struck at the region where the Garonne, Lot and Gironde met, close by Bordeaux.

John again showed himself a competent commander, and under his leadership some towns and castles were taken. He did not succeed in driving the English out of Guyenne, although this would have taken a much larger and longer campaign than could then be mounted. John was often considered too chivalrous in his manner. Of course, a true knight was expected to observe a high standard of behaviour, even when dealing with his enemies. Yet one might wonder how much one had to compromise such ideals when there was a war to fight, and to run a military campaign like a tournament tended to limit options. While such conventions as guarantee of safe conduct and offering quarter in return for surrender were essential to proceeding with war, too strict an adherence to the many rules could frustrate both sides. Such a code of practice required all parties to be equally chivalrous, and the one who broke (or bent) the rules often won the fight. Even those held as examples of chivalrous knights must have tempered their principles with at least a little pragmatism.

In 1340, John accompanied Philip on a campaign to the Low Countries. The French clashed with English forces reinforced with the town levies Jacob van Artevelde had raised, and it was not a campaign where either side gained much. When Philip took Lille he was of a mind to execute the Earls of Suffolk and Salisbury who were captured there. It was John of Bohemia who saved them, reminding the king that certain protocols concerning the exchange of prisoners applied in these circumstances. The English earls may have been grateful that John gave Philip such counsel.

John's son Charles was now rising to a position of significance and his time in France had prepared him for his adult role. Under his tutor, the Benedictine Peter Roger, later Pope Clement VI, Charles had grown up highly educated and politically astute. His father had created him Landgrave of Moravia and Charles now acted as his regent in Bohemia, preparing to inherit his throne. In due course he succeeded in becoming Holy Roman Emperor where his father never did and resumed his family's ambitions in Italy, but he never forgot that he was King of Bohemia, too. His efforts to manage the kingdom, in particular the building projects that brought French architectural styles to Bohemia and the founding of the University of Prague, were far more substantial than his father's concerns with the country; activities that John really should have considered while king.

Once the English threat to France subsided for a time, John decided to go once again to Lithuania. His personal prestige did the cause much good. As Dietrich von Altenburg, Grand Master of the Teutonic Knights, lay dying in 1341, he considered placing the Order under John of Bohemia's protection. John was no longer as effective: he now had little money left and only a small personal following, but his name was still held in high regard.

On this last crusade, it was clear by 1344 that John had a new problem: he was going blind. He contracted ophthalmia after a cold settled in one eye and it became inflamed. When he returned to Bohemia he had lost the sight of that eye and the blindness was spreading to the other. John saw a doctor in Breslau whose poor treatment only made it worse, and he had the doctor drowned in anger: it seems that chivalry did not apply to unsuccessful physicians any more than it did to commoners. John then attended an Arab doctor in Montpelier and when this did no good was treated by Guy de Chauliac, the most accomplished physician then living, again without success. By his last years John's eyesight had probably gone completely. It did not seem to slow him down, for his mind remained as active as ever, even though his attendants now led him about and described everything to him.

In 1346, the electors of the Holy Roman Empire gathered again. Louis of Bavaria had angered John further by voiding the marriage of Margaret Maultasche, heiress of Tyrol, to John Henry of Luxemburg, and marrying her to his own son. Louis had made many enemies, and the alliance John of Bohemia made with the pope proved more effective than any previous intriguing. Pope Clement VI declared Louis a schismatic, a heretic and everything else he could plausibly accuse him of being; in reality, the pope was annoyed at Louis' interference in Lombardy. Louis had also conferred the counties of Holland, Hainault, Zeeland and Friesland on his own wife, Margaret of Holland, in defiance of the hereditary claims of Margaret's sisters. On 11 July 1346, the electors assembled at Rhens agreed to depose Louis as emperor.

The Luxemburg claim to the imperial crown was thus revived, and had more support than the last time, but the other electors favoured skipping a generation in the election and elevating John's son Charles, formerly Wenceslaus, then Margrave of Moravia. Perhaps the electors knew of John's prowess as a chivalrous king heaped with honours, but understood how two-dimensional his image really was, and his obvious lack of real application when the more mundane business of government demanded his attentions. His blindness did him no favours either. Passed over again in the election, John still wished to establish the House of Luxemburg as emperors, and Charles IV, his succession number even mirroring the King of France he was renamed after, was elected King of the Romans.

As expected, a new civil war ensued and Louis and his supporters made every effort to frustrate Charles replacing him. Louis himself suffered a stroke during a bear-hunt in October 1347 and died. For a while his sons supported a rival candidate, but Charles was established and finally crowned Emperor in 1355.

Soon after his son's election as King of the Romans in 1346, John received news from France and his reaction was fateful. Edward III of England had again invaded and John decided that he was honour-bound to come to the aid of King Philip. Accompanied by his son Charles, he set out for Paris. John of Luxemburg's final campaign is quoted in the annals of chivalry. He produced 1000 *livres tournois* from his own funds, which he contributed to Philip's war chest. He soon departed on the campaign with the French army. Another king, Jaime, the titular king of Majorca, was also present. In June 1346, when the truce expired, Edward of England landed on the Cotentin peninsula and his army went plundering through an almost-undefended Normandy. They besieged Caen for three days. This might sound like unwarranted aggression, but once in the town they found written orders for a French invasion of England, and they were simply first to act. They had planned to march on Paris, which Philip expected and prepared for, but soon diverted their route and crossed the Somme near Abbeville into Picardy, thinking it a better plan to leave an adequate route for retreat to Flanders if needed.

On 23 July, an English advance force came to Pont-Remy, where they met an enemy defence commanded by John of Luxemburg and were sorely beaten back. John could not see the enemy but showed that he could still lead an effective defence.

Three days later, on 26 August 1346 in the late afternoon, the French and their allies had sight of the main English army near a small town called Crécy-en-Ponthieu. It was where Edward the Black Prince 'won his spurs', as runs the potted history. It was also the field where many on the French side met their end, John of Luxembourg included.

The 'flower of French chivalry' as it rode into the battle was truly impressive, as was the presence of such prestigious commanders as John. But poor overall leadership was the French side's undoing. The opening engagement of the battle went badly for the Genoese crossbowmen and men-at-arms. Without their pavises, or wooden defensive shields, they advanced close to the enemy lines despite the setting sun in their eyes. A sudden thunderstorm caught them off guard, and the ground grew muddy and their crossbow-strings damp. The English longbowmen did them serious damage, and their confusion made the charge of knights behind them all the more difficult. The rain of English arrows and Edward's guns were both unnerving for the horses.

The Count of Alençon, in command of the vanguard, led the knights on, though obviously exasperated at the confused Genoese. The charge was poorly executed as a result. Some of the French knights did reach the main English force, most falling en route. It was said that Alençon himself touched the royal standard before the English cut him down.

King John of Bohemia is then mentioned in despatches. He commanded a force on Alençon's left flank, and as soon as he was told that Alençon was in trouble he ordered these men to advance. According to Froissart, he asked the whereabouts of his son the King of the Romans and was told that Charles had left the field. The young man was in fact still there, and would be wounded later, but apparently did not share his father's penchant for heroism. 'One does not risk the crown of the Holy Roman Empire on the back-roads of France,' he was reported as saying. John was said to have ordered the attendants to bring him into the thick of the battle. 'Sirs,' he said, according to Froissart,

> 'Ye are my men, my companions and friends in this journey: I require you bring me so far forward, that I may strike one stroke with my sword.' They said they would do his commandment, and

to the intent that they should not lose him in the press, they tied all their reins of their bridles each to other and set the king before to accomplish his desire, and so they went on their enemies.

A Bohemian chronicle has him declare: 'Let it never be the case that a Bohemian king runs from a fight!' With the blind king and his attached attendants at their head the force rushed into the fray, shouting 'Prague' on their charge. It was a magnificent gesture, typical of those wars. It was also a magnificent suicide. Even if John was not completely blind, as some believe, his act of charging into a crowd of armed enemies he could hardly see defied any description of sensible behaviour. He had shown himself able in commanding troops with impaired vision, but he could not reasonably be expected to engage the enemy personally. John lashed with his sword in front of him but could only last so long before he fell. As his following were falling, two of his men fought their way back to the French lines; they felt bound to tell their king's story.

The French then charged fifteen times before they admitted defeat. The death-toll was large and included many important nobles: the Duke of Lorraine, eight counts including Alençon and Flanders; and the King of Bohemia. Philip returned to Paris with a resounding defeat behind him, and Edward proceeded to Calais, where he settled to his year-long siege before taking the town. The body of John of Bohemia was found the next day, his attendants lying around him. His funeral cortege passed through Paris and then to Luxembourg, where he was interred with his ancestors.

Legend has the Black Prince so impressed with John's act that he adopted the three feathers of his crest and his motto *Ich Dien* ('I Serve') and every English Prince of Wales since has continued to display both. In reality, John's crest was a pair of black wings and the feathers came from elsewhere. But if 'I Serve' was John of Bohemia's motto, who or what exactly did he serve? He was every inch the chivalrous knight; brave and terrible in battle, pleasant in courtly dalliance, the crusader, jouster and judge. He was a picture of chivalry as the book described. But what was John's personal agenda, besides promoting this image?

Much of his endeavours centred round his thwarted hopes of succeeding his father as Holy Roman Emperor. His activities in Italy, Poland and Lithuania are almost certainly linked with such ambitions. John could be pragmatic when ambition called for it, but he was essentially a great performer of chivalrous acts and spent much of his life engaged in fighting as became a knight. It appears, however, that he took it all too seriously, and ignored much else. He may have been thought of with affection in Bohemia itself, but his record as its king was poor, given that he was seldom seen within its borders for over half his reign and delegated his responsibilities to regents. His presence in Luxembourg itself was minimal too, and had he succeeded in gaining the crown of either Poland or Lombardy, it is unlikely that either land would have seen much of him afterwards.

'To fight like King John of Bohemia,' was once an idiom in France, which meant to charge into a fight blindly with no perception of the opposition. What possessed John to ride into certain death on that battle which was not even his own cause? Surely, honour would be satisfied if as commander he stood out of the actual fighting, especially when unable to see the enemy in front of him?

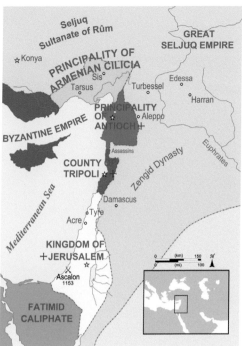

Above left: Croyland Abbey and Parish Church of Crowland. After his beheading the body of Waltheof, Earl of Northumbria was thrown into a ditch but was later retrieved and buried in the chapter house of the Abbey. (Creative Commons)

Above right: The Near East in 1165. At that time Reynald of Châtillon was incarcerated at Aleppo. (Creative Commons)

Statue of Saladin in Damascus. Reynald of Châtillon may have died at his hand.

In 1182 Reynald was trapped in the castle at Kerak by Saladin's besieging armies.

Saladin seizing the cross from King Guy at the Battle of Hattin.
(From Matthew Paris)

Jean Leclerc's *Doge Enrico Dandolo Recruiting for the Crusade* at the Palazzo Ducale, Venice (1621). Dandolo and the Crusader Captains are in the Basilica of St Mark swearing loyalty before leaving for the Fourth Crusade.

Delacroix's *Entry of the Crusaders into Constantinople* during the Fourth Crusade.

15-century miniature of the conquest of Constantinople.

The island of Sark was used as a base by Eustace the Monk for piracy.

Left: Progression of the Lithuanian state, showing areas annexed or temporarily controlled during Mindaugas's reign.

Above: Mindaugas.

Above right: Celestine V, depicted at the Castel Nuovo in Naples.

Below right: Statue of Jacob van Artevelde in Vrijdagmarkt Square, Ghent.

Below: The Royal Arms of England, from 1340. By quartering the lilies of France with the lions of England, Edward III claimed to be ruler of both countries.

William of Ockham depicted in a
stained-glass window of All Saints'
Church, Ockham, Surrey.

1370s sandstone bust of John, King of Bohemia in St. Vitus Cathedral, by Peter
Parler's workshop.

The Battle of Crécy, where John of Bohemia fell, as depicted in *Froissart's Chronicle*.

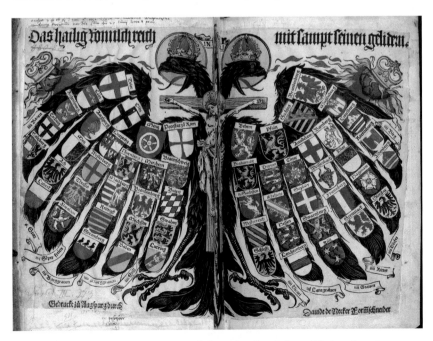

A later, magnificent representation of the prize that John of Bohemia never won: the *Quaternionenadler*, an eagle of the Holy Roman Empire showing the shields of the member states by rank.

Above: The defeat of the Jacquerie, 15th century. *Grandes Chroniques de France* (Bibliothèque nationale de France)

Left: A fanciful depiction of Guillaume Cale in an assault during the Jacquerie.

Right and below: Peter of Cyprus. Details from Andrea di Bonaiuto's *The Way of Salvation*; see the final page of the plate section.

The assassination of Peter of Cyprus. From *Froissart's Chronicle* (Bibliothèque nationale de France)

Right: Bust of Ibn Khaldun in the entrance of the Kasbah of Bejaia, Algeria.

Below: St Michael's Mount, near Penzance in Cornwall, occupied by John de Vere, Earl of Oxford, in 1473.

Above left: Christine de Pizan in her study at the beginning of the 'Cent ballades'. (British Library)

Above right: Justice enters the City of Ladies, depicted in the Collected Works of Christine de Pisan, France, 1410-1411. (British Library)

The burning of Lollard John Oldcastle for insurrection and heresy. (Wellcome Collection)

Jean Poton de Xaintrailles and La Hire, Joan of Arc's lieutenants.

The Penance of Eleanor, Duchess of Gloucester by Edwin Austin Abbey, 1900. (Carnegie Museum)

A statue of Henry the Navigator in Massachusetts.

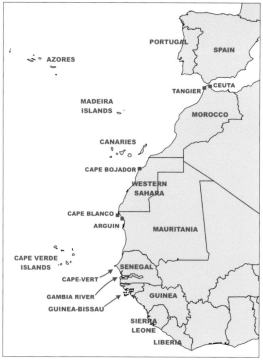

The slowly extended route along the African coast under Henry the Navigator.

Right: Vlad the Impaler, portrait made c.1560, reputedly copied from a portrait made in his lifetime.

Below: Vlad's Romania.

Above: Andrea di Bonaiuto's *The Way of Salvation* features both William of Ockham and Peter of Cyprus. The black-cloaked figures are Dominican priests (the Blackfriars, the Order of Preachers), and the black-and-white dogs are their symbol. Founded by St Dominic to preach against heresies, they were referred to as '*domini canes*', hounds of God. To the victims of the Inquisition they were hounds of Hell.

Left: This oil on panel portrait, *c.* 1535 by an unknown artist held at the National Portrait Gallery was always assumed to be Margaret, Countess of Salisbury, but there is now doubt as to the identification.

10

'Jacques Bonhomme'

The Rebellious Peasant

Unlike the others depicted here, this character never really existed as a man of flesh and blood, or was at best a title a man assumed. He was a role that many filled, mostly, but not all, peasants. 'Jacques Bonhomme' or 'Jack Goodman' as translated, was an idea, a kind of Everyman. From his first appearance in the popular revolt of 1358 in the Beauvaisais in France until fairly recently, his image has been reinterpreted many times; and he has been in different eras the peasant of the revolution and the rising proletariat. Jacques Bonhomme has been presented as 'Joe Ordinary', the simple Frenchman who laboured on the land from Roman times to the present day; although in this chapter we are looking at a narrower interpretation, as the peasant who takes arms against his lord.

This Jacques Bonhomme was essentially of the same stuff as such as Robin Hood and General Tom Thumb were made on, and a close relative of Jack Straw and Robin of Redesdale. From the fourteenth to the sixteenth centuries, peasant revolts were common throughout Europe, a challenge to the severely immutable world-picture that placed the peasants perpetually on the lowest rung on the ladder of society.

There certainly was a leader for some of the time in 1358 who used the title Jacques Bonhomme, who was named as Guillaume de Cale. This is beside the point: little is really known of this Guillaume and this chapter in reality concerns an abstract, the peasant in revolt. The name Jacques certainly came from the jack, or jerkin, a peasant traditionally wore. The stereotype showed an earthy worker in rough homespun, often wearing the jacket of leather in which he laboured;

the cloth cap would later serve the same purpose. A 'bonhomme' is what we could call a 'fellow', an ordinary man.

It would not be a complete picture of medieval society without the appearance of the peasant, the agricultural labourers who formed the majority of the population, yet there are problems researching individual peasants given the lack of documentary evidence. Records do exist, mostly of peasants taxed or censured for their behaviour, but given the limited spread of literacy we seldom hear their own voices or see much of their own lives; though when the rigid feudal system temporarily broke down some light can be shed.

The original intention for this chapter was to examine the Peasants' Revolt in England in 1381 with Wat Tyler as the focus, but in keeping with the criteria of the book it is clear that both have been too widely studied. Tyler was not a peasant as such, it appears. In examining the '*Jacquerie*' or peasants' revolt in France earlier the same century, the lot of the ordinary peasant comes into perspective, as does the previously unthinkable act of peasants rising against their masters. Such an event might either be interpreted as an explosion of anger, or an early manifestation of the Marxist concept of inevitable class warfare.

From the time that Neolithic humans turned from hunting and gathering for sustenance and towards herding and cultivation, people were driven by the demands of growing and harvesting crops, of raising and tending animals and a range of related activities. Such work required sustained and backbreaking effort and the failure of a crop one year could bring starvation. Yet such labours could produce a surplus, which would be traded for other goods or could be used to support others not directly engaged in this process. As a result, there appeared the craftsman, the trader, the priest, soldier, noble and king and thus the development of civilisation proceeded.

In Europe during the Carolingian period, the eighth and ninth centuries, it was recognised that some separation of roles was in order, the reasoning being that while a cadre of skilled warriors would protect the lands and people from invasion, the majority would labour to provide the group with material sustenance. The institution of the knight, and also the lord of the manor, came from this recognition and by the twelfth century there was a definite division within society, although it was essentially parentage that determined membership of the noble military class or else of the peasantry that laboured in their service. King Alfred is often quoted as saying there were three kinds of men: those who prayed, those who fought and those who laboured, and that the third supported the other two, which was already a platitude by his day. Whereas in England Anglo-Saxon society had afforded some social mobility and fewer constraints on peasants, the Normans imported a more rigid interpretation of the manorial system.

Medieval peasants were subject to a variety of agrarian economic systems. Depending on the custom they might pay rent in coin or in kind to the lord of the manor, or work on the lord's lands three days in every seven, on top of which they were liable to a number of charges. The peasants on the Bishop of Durham's estates rendered both rents and labour services. The legal status of a peasant varied throughout Europe, even in the same locality and sometimes within the same manor. Many were practically owned by the lord, almost as slaves, while others would simply pay rent and consider themselves free. But all depended on this manorial system for survival and most had few personal rights other than what were vaguely accepted as traditional limits to what the lords could expect.

A fourteenth-century peasant's lot was often harsh, thankless and offered little hope of respite. Many might long for the life of their lords or even of townsfolk, but for the unfree peasant, the serf or villein, life was circumscribed. In England a runaway villein could consider himself legally free if he lived a year and a day within town walls, but few ran away from their manors before 1350, for where could they go to find employment? The townsfolk jealously guarded their own financial opportunities, except when labour was much in demand.

The life of the peasant in France was as noted for its severity. Fields were ploughed, crops were sown, watered, tended to fruition and harvested. Beasts were guarded, brought to graze, sheltered, milked, mated, slaughtered. At the same time every year a French peasant was concerned with exactly the same activities. In March he would tend his vines and in November drive the pigs into the wood to fatten on acorns while he collected winter firewood. All this had to be done if he and his family were to see the next year. Although by such back-breaking work some surplus or gain was possible, the French peasant would render part of this at least to his lord. In addition, there were a number of dues payable to the king, including the *gabelle*, a tax on salt, and the *corvée*, the conscripting of peasant labour for building roads, fortifications and similar works. There were also periodic taxes exacted by the crown, especially in times of war.

The Black Death would change so much. Once the first outbreak had run its course in 1348-49 it left the population of Europe reduced by over a third. In England this did not in itself end villeinage but did reduce both the labour force and the market for grain, bringing economic and social change. One ramification was to give English peasants some bargaining power, which eventually eroded the hold their lords had over them. A peasant could more easily leave a manor for better conditions, for there was now much demand for labour, and the constraints of villeinage could not be enforced so easily. Villeins, now more often known as customary tenants, would blur with free tenants and it was difficult to distinguish between the two. This was not mirrored in France and many other places, where servitude continued for centuries longer.

The Hundred Years War, as it is misleadingly known, brought new hardships to the French countryside. Whether Edward III and his heirs had a legitimate claim to the throne of France was a thorny legal issue, but from the late 1330s there was fighting between the English and French in the roads and fields of France over this matter from year to year. While the kings and their feudal nobilities fought, it was often the common people who suffered severely.

An advancing army of either side would as a matter of course send out foraging parties who would grab any produce or livestock they came upon to feed the troops. It is not difficult to see how peasants often suffered the ravages of war and in fact even worse fates awaited those who were simply performing their designated labours. In 1360, a hundred villagers were massacred at Orly, and similar atrocities took place at Châtres, which was reduced to rubble. Rapes were common, of peasant women and young boys. One raid the English made at Cambrésis in 1339 left a path of destruction some fifty kilometres wide.

France suffered other serious ills in the spring of 1358. The French had in 1356 suffered an appalling military defeat at Poitiers that brought the nation to a new low in humiliation. King John II, known inexplicably as 'John the Good', had been captured in the battle and for the next few years resided in England while his ransom was raised. His eighteen-year-old son Charles, the first to hold the title of Dauphin, was struggling despite inexperience and poor health to hold the country together as regent. He faced decided opposition from the Estates, a form of parliamentary assembly who withheld their assent to taxes unless changes in governance and the dismissal of unpopular officials were enacted. The Parisian cloth merchant Etienne Marcel headed an opposition that sought to constrain the regency with governing committees. The Dauphin also contended with his uncle Charles King of Navarre, often known as Charles the Bad, who pursued an agenda of his own. In February 1358, Navarre, then representing the Estates, stormed Paris, started a riot where some of the ministers were murdered and made the Dauphin his prisoner, but the young prince escaped a month later and regained control. France was hardly a stable nation in the months before the Jacquerie appeared.

The Beauvaisais did not suffer many of the well-known ills of the time. In this region the peasants were free, more tenant-farmers than serfs, and the Black Death had not ravaged this area as much as in some places. Nor had it seen much of the English or French armies or any sign of the Free Companies' excesses. It is often remarked that many taking part in the Jacquerie were not particularly poor and few were really starving. While famine was usually not far away, such peasants could live on their labours and might hope for some surplus of produce each year. Perhaps the fact that they had something to lose caused their discontent.

Though the Beauvaisais peasants were in fact feeling the pinch of falling agricultural prices following depopulation. There was also concern over a possible English attack on Paris through the Oise valley and the rulers were seeking to close this route by strengthening the defences, and this meant extensive use of the *corvée* to build and maintain fortifications. The increase in knights and soldiers brought problems of supply, and ill-feelings rose among the peasants.

The first sign of the Jacquerie appeared at Saint-Laye-d'Esserant, a village in the Champagne region not far from Paris, in the spring of 1358. When a noble named Raoul de Clermont was attempting to install a garrison of soldiers at the abbey there in order to secure control of a bridge over the Oise, he made the mistake, as it turned out, of requisitioning property and provisions from the locals. Such a practice was not unusual and both sides would plunder the countryside for their sustenance. But there was a local custom that nothing could be thus requisitioned without payment, and this flouting of what the peasants considered their inalienable rights brought a swift reaction. The Dauphin had recently prohibited such appropriation, and the peasants of the Beauvaisais had come to believe they were legally in the right. Unfortunately, Charles had also practically encouraged his nobles in plundering for the war effort, giving different messages to separate audiences.

A mob of peasants set upon a party intended to join this garrison, killing four knights and five squires. This triggered a more general rising and once the revolt began it spread first through the Oise valley and then southwards, thousands of peasants joining. Throughout the Île-de-France, in nearby Champagne, Artois and even as far as Normandy, peasants took to storming the region's castles. The Beauvaisais countryside exploded into violence, where aristocrats and their families soon had good reason to fear for their lives.

There followed what was reported as a bloody nightmare by chroniclers of the time. Throughout the Beauvaisais masses of peasants rose and stormed the castles and great houses of the locality. They burnt down the buildings, killing and raping those aristocrats they could find. The Duchess of Orleans fled from the region with some other ladies, narrowly escaping the Jacks' assault on the castle at Beaumont-sur-Oise while the invaders slaughtered her retainers.

There are stories that the chronicler Froissart related featuring rape and cannibalism among other atrocities he found it difficult himself to report. While such second-hand reports can acquire exaggeration in their retelling, and perhaps some of the horrific details can be discounted, there was no doubt some of the stories were true. Marauding gangs in their characteristic leather jackets could then be seen about the countryside and the castles of the nobles lay in smoking ruins, the signs of carnage littered around them.

While cannibalism sounded like the ultimate atrocity, and one could question whether even rebellious peasants would go that far, this practice was not altogether unthinkable. During the First Crusade there were tales of the wild *Tafurs*, mostly Flemings, who had followed the crusading army to the Holy Land and who acted as irregulars and labourers. The *Chronique d'Antioche* claimed that they made use of Turkish enemies as a source of food. Again, this story may have little substance to it; Flemings were not degenerate, even by medieval standards. But even if cannibalism went on in the Jacquerie, it was only one of the terrible deeds that did.

Soon after the initial explosion of revolt there emerged one Guillaume de Cale (also Calle or Caillet), who assumed leadership of the Jacquerie at a meeting in his own village of Mello. From that point the revolt took a clearer direction, something more akin to modern revolutionary movements. Froissart tells of how the peasants elected one of their own as king, who took the name of Jacques Bonhomme. This abstract figure now had a human representative.

Guillaume was believed one of the better-off peasants, but the company he kept is surprising, and there were knights and others of higher social standing named among the rebels. German de Reveillon, Colm de Maunier and Jean Bernier were all aristocrats, and the first two had been in the knightly retinue of greater nobles. There is a reference to an unnamed Knight Hospitaller also of this group. Towards the end, one of the Jacquerie's leaders was Jean Vaillant, once an official of the royal mint. At its largest, some 5,000 marched in this rebel army, including several lesser aristocrats and quite a few bourgeois of the towns among the peasants.

Such data begs the question as to how men of high birth would defer to a son of the soil, as the upper classes always claimed leadership by virtue of parentage. Was this Guillaume someone other than the sources said he was? Were the knights bowing to the will of the masses who chose him, mindful of their own credentials in an egalitarian movement? Or were they content to see Guillaume as figurehead, who would draw attention away from them should the revolt fail?

Accounts of the time describe Guillaume as charismatic, as 'well-informed and well-spoken, pleasant of face and form', characteristics which do not fit with the stereotypical peasant. Perhaps he was only posing as a peasant. He showed some idea of military strategy, as an element of this appears in the Jacks' activities from then, and Guillaume could have been a knight or lesser noble with some experience fighting in the wars. No clear evidence has appeared to identify Guillaume's social status, but there is an air of something not being quite as believed.

The Jacks under Guillaume's leadership now took a more systematic approach. They overcame the castles lying in a ring around Senlis, a little to the south of the Oise region, including Chantilly, Cortreuil, Thiers, Fontaine-Chaalis and Brassure. There was support for the Jacquerie in Senlis – its mayor raised a hundred men to fight on its side – and this act hints at a strategy of limiting aristocratic strength in the region, possibly with the intention of consolidating territory. Having marched south to Senlis from the Oise, the Jacquerie attacked the castle at Montmorency in the Île-de-France, coming close to Paris itself. The revolt also spread to Picardy.

The political struggle continued as the Jacquerie came into full swing. Etienne Marcel and his faction at first showed a tacit support for the Jacquerie, for in a way they had a common enemy. Marcel thought that the destruction of fortifications around Paris that could be of use to his enemies would serve to his advantage. But the support of the Parisians was ambivalent: they feared the Jacks as much as the nobles did, for the peasants could hardly be trusted not to rampage through Paris as they had through the countryside. The Parisians closed the gates but set out tables of food in the suburbs. When Montmorency and other castles in the Île-de-France burned, the flames to be seen from Paris itself, the Paris bourgeoisie considered that the Jacquerie was not the best of allies.

It was not strictly true that the Jacquerie was nipped in the bud. If it had been allowed to continue beyond those few weeks there might have been a more lasting effect, even though there is reason to believe that it was already losing impetus. In conjunction with the current political struggle, the movement could by an association with Marcel's faction have at least consolidated its position. But less than two months after the rising began, it was savagely and decisively crushed.

Charles of Navarre saw his advantage and appointed himself the defender of the status quo against this murderous rabble. Putting himself at the head of an army raised in the king's name, Navarre set out to Mello itself in order to confront the Jacks in their territory. He recruited a company of English mercenaries under William Scot as one contingent, for while the truce was holding there were many redundant English soldiers to be found in France.

Guillaume de Cale was by this time seeing the initial drive fade from the revolt. Bands of insurgents were drifting away from the main body and pursuing their own agendas. Discipline was deteriorating; Guillaume had little more to offer with his leadership. On 10 June, Guillaume probably realised that the game was up, as now an army of knights and well-equipped soldiers had arrived. He set up archers in defensive positions and marshalled a body of cavalry to be held in reserve; again, a departure from the image of an undisciplined horde of peasants.

In the manner of a noble leader he went forth to parley with Navarre. He probably wished to offer terms to end the revolt, or else such an act was a formality, in the manner of a chivalrous exchange before battle as commanders of opposing armies were wont to make. If Guillaume was simply posing as a low-born peasant, he had now backed the wrong horse. For as soon as Guillaume entered the royal camp, Navarre had him seized. This Jacques Bonhomme was only a peasant, he declared and entitled to no chivalrous treatment. He sent Guillaume to Clermont where he was soon beheaded, although one account has Navarre's men heating an iron tripod stand in a furnace and crowning Guillaume with it while red-hot.

Navarre ordered the charge on the now leaderless Jacks and the expected bloodbath followed. Many were killed in the fighting and the rest dispersed. Navarre's army rounded up scores and had them beheaded or hanged from nearby trees. They locked some 300 in a monastery which he had set on fire. In many villages four inhabitants each were chosen as ringleaders and executed. In the Meaux district his army slaughtered every peasant they could find.

The contingent of Jacks led by Jean Vaillant attempted to plunder Meaux, where at the time the Duke of Orleans and the duchesses of Orleans and Normandy had fled, together with several other ladies. Froissart related how two nobles, one French and the other Anglo-Gascon, came quickly to their relief as chivalrous knights were honour-bound to do. Gaston Phebus, Count of Foix, and Jean de Grailly, the latter known by his Gascon title the Captal de Buch, had taken advantage of the truce and had gone crusading together in Prussia. Hearing as they returned to France of the Jacquerie, they rode with their following of about forty lances to the rescue.

It was an engagement of heroic proportions, Orleans, Foix and the Captal with their meagre forces holding the marketplace and defending the ladies against what Froissart believed were seven thousand Jacks and rebels of Meaux itself. Although disadvantaged in numbers, the well-armed professional soldiers fought off the crowds of peasants, finally driving them away. Froissart tells of the knights killing thousands, probably much exaggerated, and then somewhat unchivalrously setting Meaux on fire on their departure, for many in the town had supported the Jacks.

Soon after, the Seigneur de Coucy led an army that hunted down the scattered rebels. After the events at Meaux the revolt was over, apart from in Picardy where a few small bands of Jacks survived living by brigandage, knowing that they could only last so much longer.

Now the French monarchy regained prestige. The Dauphin had fewer problems with opponents and the Estates and showed his coming of age with an effective resistance to the English and tougher negotiations. In November 1361, the first instalment of the ransom was paid and King John went home. He voluntarily returned to captivity in England soon after when one of his hostages broke agreements and John died there in 1364. There was an attempt to end the war with the Treaty of Brétigny in 1361, where in return for large territories in France and other large concessions Edward would relinquish his claim to the French crown and his quartering. But this violation of the ransom terms prevented the final ratification of the treaty, and the Plantagenet claim to France persisted for centuries more.

Succeeding as King Charles V, the former Dauphin showed his worth in recovering his kingdom's prestige. Known as Charles the Wise, he never rode again into battle but used his intellectual skills, his flair for diplomacy and his noted cunning to their best advantage. He broke the power of Charles of Navarre, conscripted some of the Free Companies into royal service by sending them on expeditions, and in 1369 renewed the war with the English. Etienne Marcel met his end when a mob of Parisians turned on him. Charles eventually regained almost all the invaders had taken in the previous three decades, leaving England with the Pale of Calais and part of Aquitaine, and also the Ponthieu region, which France regained later. Charles's death in 1380 unfortunately left a boy as King Charles VI, whose reign first as a minor then as an adult madman saw the war turn again in the English direction.

There were many revolts of a similar nature in the following two centuries, usually in response to tax increases. The insurrection of the *remensas* in Catalonia in 1388 took the form of protest over taxes and the peasants were finally granted exemption from many harsh dues. There were popular revolts as far afield as Iceland, again usually over taxation and feudal dues. In France, smaller risings appeared from time to time. The *Tuchinerie,* a similar revolt, occurred in the southern provinces but also disappeared without lasting effect.

Later in the fourteenth century a new dimension was added to this unrest, where rebels challenged established religion as much as secular authority. The Catholic Church formed part of the ruling class; the abbeys and the bishoprics owned vast estates between them, and resentment of their demands on the peasant was tempered by the argument that as God's representatives they were entitled to such material benefits.

Once the challenge was first made, it was not so difficult to question what entitled both secular and clerical lords to such incomes and power. In England in 1381 the radical preacher John Ball emerged as one of the leaders of the Peasants' Revolt and threw down his gauntlet to the entire social order with the oft-repeated rhyme:

When Adam delved and Eve span,
Who was then the gentleman?

This couplet survived as a mantra down the centuries, repeated by the Levellers in the English Revolution and by late-twentieth-century anarchists. For John Ball it presented an alternative ideology to medieval feudalism; it used a simple Christian belief as its central point and denied the inequalities that characterised feudal society. Later in the century French revolts echoed this sentiment by questioning the right of church and nobility to exemption from honest labour, again citing the Book of Genesis.

There was an element of this in the Hussite rebellions in Bohemia early in the fifteenth century. In 1524, with the Lutheran Reformation under way in Germany, there were popular risings in Swabia, Thuringia and Franconia. These revolts were not closely related but often mixed calls for religious reform with those of economic easement of the peasants' lot. Luther himself came to condemn insurrection in no uncertain terms and called for brutal suppression as the only remedy, although at a later stage, probably when preachers more radical than himself became prominent.

The Jacquerie did not appear to follow any ideology to speak of, it could only have been an explosion of anger and frustration. Once this anger was spent, little more could be expected but to prepare for reprisals. The revolt of 1789 was channelled by those steeped in the ideals of the Enlightenment and in the Russia of 1917 the Bolsheviks translated the tenets of Marx into a solution to the ills the ordinary people suffered. For all that Marxism presents history as the story of class struggle, there are many examples of popular risings, but whereas the common people provided the muscle in each case, only a leadership seeking to put an ideology into practice could produce lasting results by revolt.

This chapter does not identify Jacques Bonhomme as Guillaume de Cale, although he took the leadership and the title for a time. Nor can Jacques Bonhomme be taken broadly as the French peasant throughout the ages, from those who laboured on the estates of the Romans to those who still raise crops by their own hands, jealously mindful of their subsidies from the European Union. We are talking of a peasant who was moved to action contrary to all that he understood as his position in the divine scheme.

Jacques Bonhomme, whatever his real name, knew a life of hard work and severe demands from his superiors. Although starvation was seldom far away, he might have won a little personal comfort through his labours. But the economy was changing as the demographic reversal caused by the Black Death and the demands of continual warfare took their toll on the margin of comfort his labours might bring. The combination of excessive financial demands, fear of war and political instability created an atmosphere of discontent. The incident at Saint-Laye was only the spark; where the lords went further than accepted, the peasants of a large part of northern France rose in a massive explosion of fury.

The Jacquerie's principal targets were aristocrats and castles. They were bent on lynching anyone of the noble or knightly social class they could find, which was understandable. They were also very meticulous in their attacks on the castles, and certainly by the time Guillaume de Cale had taken command these structures became prime objectives. When Robert de Lorris, who had amassed fortunes in royal service, was set upon in his castle at Ermonville by an attack led by Guillaume personally, he slyly declared his support for the Jacquerie, renouncing his knighthood. His life was spared – but he could not stop the rebel army tearing down his castle in front of him.

There was a logic to attacking the fortified homes of the high as much as their persons. The castle has a place in history and literature as the home of the knight and noble, and as a seat of chivalry. It immediately comes to mind when medieval society is discussed and images of battlements, towers and dungeons appeal to our sense of the romantic. But we mostly see the castle from the viewpoint of its residents. Perhaps to the peasant a castle was a forbidding place, where lived those who demanded their wealth and labour, and armed men who could enforce such demands. The Jacks often vented their anger on castles as instruments of oppression. In one case when they tried unsuccessfully to burn out the roof timbers, they conscripted local carpenters to complete the destruction.

A castle essentially functioned as a refuge for knights and soldiers who would ride out to do battle and then rest safely within its walls. Until the development of cannon they did not really command movements on a route, but advancing invaders ignored enemy castles at their peril while their garrisons could ride out to attack supply trains. Those who made war on aristocrats in 1358 believed that gutting such strongholds would weaken the hold the nobles had over them.

It is remarkable how successful the Jacks were in capturing over eighty castles. They proved far more successful than the English army on campaign. A castle was built to resist determined attacks by armies: its walls were high and strong and might be encircled with a moat. If under attack it should have an adequate defence, where there would be archers and soldiers prepared to push away scaling ladders and to repel attackers by dropping large rocks, lime powder and cauldrons of boiling oil. At least in theory, a garrison would be able to defend such fortification against seasoned, well-equipped soldiers. Yet in 1358 so many castles were overcome by what are believed bands of peasants, their weapons mostly no better than scythes and pitchforks, unless some were archers. There is cause to wonder how the Jacks succeeded for so long.

Perhaps the element of surprise allowed this at first. Whoever garrisoned the castles probably envisaged only defending them from the English, who were not immediately expected, and might have grown lax in their vigilance. The Jacks might stealthily scale the walls at night avoiding the alarm being raised until it was too late. One can only speculate in the absence of proper records, but once the Jacquerie was under way the chatelains of the region must have prepared for defence. Even then the rebels often overcame the defenders.

Some form of strategy would then be required. Even the early attacks would have needed some direction. Some of the leadership surely had military experience, and this has a bearing on Guillaume de Cale's real identity. It is reasonable to speculate that he was someone with some training and experience in the arts of war. Leaders of popular revolts have followed a similar pattern, and appeared not to be of peasant stock. In England, Jack Cade, the leader of the 1450 rebellion, is believed to have been either a sailor or a lesser gentleman and himself claimed membership of the royal family. Robin of Redesdale was almost certainly Sir John Conyers, who led a popular revolt in 1469 on behalf of his patron the Earl of Warwick as a prelude to Warwick's own rising against Edward IV. Wat Tyler of the 1381 Revolt was probably a craftsman, and it is far from certain who his confederate Jack Straw really was, if he existed at all. The other leading light of 1381, John Ball, was a priest. Such shadowy figures often appeared where there was a body of peasants in revolt.

Guillaume and others, some of whom were definitely knights, provided leadership for the revolt. They appeared after the initial explosion of anger and for a time channelled the peasants' aggression into some strategy. We do not know what Guillaume promised the rebels, although we have a vague reference to the 'commun'. If he was offering some kind of communism or utopianism, he would have had difficulty gaining acceptance for it, as such ideas certainly went against the grain. For Jacques Bonhomme, there was only a vague sense that to attack the rulers would solve his problems.

While the story of every individual involved in the Jacquerie is different, if that of Jacques Bonhomme were told it would be of a peasant who either snapped when the demands enforced on him suddenly became unbearable, or who stood to lose what little material gain he had made. Jacques and his female equivalent worked incessantly with little respite and could look forward to little advancement and scant material benefit. When even this small margin was threatened, Jacques might react, even against all his ingrained acceptance of lordship. Perhaps the aristocracy should have realised that the peasants' forbearance was not infinite, and in an age where we expect redress for grievances, it is difficult not to see Jacques' point of view.

It is certain that even when the leadership is accounted for, not all the Jacks were simply rural labourers. There is reference to townspeople, and to lesser aristocrats among the ranks of the Jacquerie. Where Guillaume found his cavalry is not explained. Although the peasants formed most of the strength of the rebel army, many other elements of French society were present, all with grievances against the nobility or else pursuing other agendas.

In our day we can easily understand why a peasant living in the fourteenth century would revolt. It was the tragedy of Jacques Bonhomme that no political alternative was available once he had revolted, and that there was little prospect of making any lasting difference to his lot.

11

Peter I of Cyprus

Too Late the Crusader?

The Moslem reconquest of the last Frankish state of the eastern Mediterranean in 1291 by no means marked the end of the Crusades. Even as the entire Holy Land was again lost to Islam, crusading went on in practice for over a century, and as a serious proposition for much longer. For a time, the Kingdom of Cyprus was a centre from which a form of crusading continued, particularly in the person of its King, Peter I of Lusignan.

Although the total area of the Frankish territories was reduced to a fraction after the Third Crusade of that before 1187, the three remaining states survived for another century. Partially as a result of the Moslems' failure after the death of Saladin to produce leadership or even any unity that could challenge the Franks, the Kingdom of Jerusalem, the Principality of Antioch and the County of Tripoli at least remained on the map, even if none of them stretched too far eastward from the coast. More crusades did appear in the thirteenth century but regained little and nothing that lasted. The German Emperor Frederick II did retake Jerusalem in 1228, even though the pope condemned this action because Frederick obtained it by negotiation and not by fighting, and the Saracens took it back in 1244.

Crusading had by 1291 come to mean much more than expeditions to the Holy Land. It involved fighting Slavonic peoples on the eastern borders of the German Empire and in the Baltic coastal region. It took place against the Albigensian heretics of southern France and even against the excommunicate Frederick II. All manner of ulterior motives interfered with the simple act of using martial skills to promote the Christian cause, and the crime the 1204 Crusade became was only the most spectacular of many committed in the name of fighting the good fight.

Still the ideal continued for centuries. In 1492, one of the reasons the King and Queen of Spain sponsored Columbus's voyage was the expectation that it would bring such wealth that it could finance their own crusade to liberate Jerusalem once more. The last officially sanctioned crusade against Moslems took place in 1396 against the Ottoman Turks at Nicopolis in Greece, and even after that the Portuguese in North Africa in the next century considered themselves crusaders. For many European nobles, knights and even kings a crusade was often intended for the next year, or for when the kingdom was quieter, or for some future date. Henry IV of England was determined to embark for Jerusalem soon after his accession, but continual rebellion and afterwards ill-health prevented him from ever doing so.

After 1260, Islam had new champions who treated the residual Frankish states as a threat. The Mamluks, a corps of freed Turkish slave soldiers in the service of the sultan in Egypt, rebelled against his successor in 1250, made one of their number sultan in his place and imposed their rule first on Egypt and then on Moslem Syria. The Mamluks, the term meaning 'one who is owned', maintained their membership with new former slaves and for over two centuries it could be said that almost every powerful amir and most of their sultans had begun their time in Egypt as another's personal property.

In 1260, against all expectations the Mamluks turned back the relentless westward conquest of the Mongols by defeating their advance force at Ain Jalut in Palestine. After this, the new Mamluk Sultan Baibars I embarked on a series of campaigns to reduce the Mongols' potential allies in the Syrian region. Perhaps not forgetting how the northern Franks had collaborated with the invaders in 1260, Baibars set out on a long-term project of driving all the Franks into the sea, capturing and destroying individual towns and fortresses in a series of annual campaigns. His successors continued this strategy and in 1291 Acre was the last Frankish city to fall.

Once the Third Crusade had regained part of the Kingdom of Jerusalem, the question of maintaining this territory meant awkward decisions for its leaders. It is not difficult to understand why many did not wish Guy of Lusignan to remain king, his poor performance on the Hattin campaign the most obvious indicator. Even Richard of England, of whom the Lusignans were vassals in Poitou, had to admit that Guy could hardly be relied upon to defend the kingdom once the crusade had returned to Europe. Henry of Champagne was the eventual choice.

On his way to the Holy Land Richard had captured Cyprus, then in the hands of a renegade Byzantine governor. As part of the settlement of 1192 Guy became King of Cyprus, and the Lusignans ruled the island until 1475. In 1197 Guy's brother Amalric succeeded him, married the Jerusalem heiress and thereafter the two kingdoms were linked, despite others claiming the crown of Jerusalem later. The Lusignans would dispute this succession with Frederick II and later with Charles of Anjou, but after 1291 all such claims were notional.

The front line of the Christian defence against Islam, or so it seemed, now took the form of three states. The Kingdom of Cilicia, an Armenian state on the borders of Syria and Anatolia, suffered ongoing and damaging Mamluk campaigns for over a century until its final destruction in 1375. The Knights Hospitallers had set up their naval base on Rhodes, their rival order the Templars suppressed by the Inquisition in 1314. It was Cyprus that provided the most serious threat to the Moslems as a base for seaborne raiding. The Mamluks, who prided themselves on light cavalry tactics, were never the most enthusiastic of sailors, and their attempts to take ship against their enemies were usually half-hearted and ineffective.

Peter of Lusignan was born on 9 October 1328, second son of King Hugh IV of Cyprus. He was first created Count of Tripoli, a title which, like all lordships of the mainland by this time, was only a title. At an early age he married Eschiva, heiress to Humphrey de Montford, Constable of Cyprus and titular lord of Toron. This marriage was childless and ended early with her death some time before 1350. In 1353 Peter married Eleanor, daughter of Don Pedro of Aragon, a pretender to the Aragonese throne. This was a typical dynastic marriage, linking Peter politically with Aragon and producing children. Peter would later object to her alleged unfaithfulness, although he himself kept Joanna l'Aleman as his mistress for many years.

Peter's eldest brother Hugh had predeceased him and his father in 1343. Hugh had a son, also called Hugh, but the Cypriot succession custom made the next son of the *last* king the heir and Hugh tried very hard throughout Peter's reign to contest the succession. Peter was crowned in 1358 in his father's lifetime, as a means of avoiding any succession dispute.

Peter's story, or rather a version of it, was immortalised by Guillaume de Machaut, who would write *The Capture of Alexandria* within a generation of the events. This is literature rather than history and presents Peter as a chivalric hero. He tells the story of how as a boy Peter visited the relic of the Cross of Dismas, the Good Thief of the Calvary story and heard voices exhorting him to crusade against those who occupied the Holy City. The relic was in fact kept at the Cypriot monastery of Stavrovouni, but it is unlikely that Peter needed any divine prompting to follow his life's ambition. He was no doubt conscious of how close the Moslems were, and one of his professed roles as King of Cyprus was king-in-exile of Jerusalem, or so he was brought up to believe. Only Machaut tells the story of the cross.

Another story, also not verified, tells of young Peter and a friend running away to Europe to either raise or join a crusade. His father eventually had him brought back and imprisoned.

Many times the Cypriots attacked the Anatolian coastal cities. In 1333 they raided the important Turkish port of Izmir (or Smyrna) and occupied it again in 1344. Hugh had also extracted tribute from Satalia. As heir to the throne Peter continued this policy, sailing to the Moslem-held towns on the shores to the north of Cyprus, doing damage and collecting plunder. His father eventually considered this impolitic and tried to curb his expeditions.

But in 1359 Peter became king on his father's abdication and put new energy and resources into this raiding. In 1361 he led an attack on Adalia once again. There was little to be achieved with these raids, apart from booty and some damage to trade. Before he had been long on the throne Peter revealed larger ambitions: in 1362 he outlined plans for a crusade.

This was a better time than most. After the Treaty of Brétigny was signed (but not ratified) in 1360, the Anglo-French wars had ceased for a while. In October 1362 Peter went to Pope Urban V's court at Avignon and received the papal endorsement for the crusade proclaimed at Easter 1363. John II 'the Good' of France expressed his interest, and he and some French nobles pledged to come within two years. Yet it must have surprised Peter, living as close as he was to the Islamic world, that enthusiasm in the west for crusading seemed so muted. A mountain of excuses and prior commitments confronted him, and he soon realised that France would not provide a large crusading army.

As John himself was a prisoner when taken at the Battle of Poitiers in 1356 he was technically in the custody of Edward III. At this point he was back in France, his son standing hostage for him, and still seeking to satisfy the terms of his ransom. He thus had a good reason for not embarking for Cyprus and was probably over-optimistic with his promise, given his financial obligations. When John died in 1364 with his ransom unfulfilled Peter realised how unlikely it was that the French would rally to the crusade in large numbers. Peter had travelled as far as England, Kracow and Vienna trying to drum up support for his project. He was fêted wherever he went, but there were few concrete commitments to a crusade, mostly good wishes and vague promises with the words 'when the time is suited' spoken or implied.

Peter had made agreements with the Venetians to transport a crusading army when the time came, but when he returned to Venice the agreed time limit had expired. The French crusaders waiting there had come to the conclusion that the crusade would not happen and had gone home. But Peter had received some financial aid from the pope, which made it possible to raise some troops and he also gained the support of the Hospitallers when he called in at Rhodes on the way back in August 1365. The recruiting mission had not been entirely a failure.

He had many Cypriots ready to sail. There was also his friend and principal supporter Philippe de Mézières, a minor French noble who had previously fought in the service of the Duke of Milan and then the King of Hungary. He had taken part in a small Neapolitan crusade in Asia Minor and in 1347 met Peter in Cyprus. The two men appeared to think alike and Peter made him his chancellor on his accession. De Mézières went with Peter on his European tour and was one of his main supporters at the Cypriot court. There were many others, probably those nobles and knights who enthusiastically followed him in his raids on Anatolia.

The terms of the papal bull authorising the crusade were quite vague and allowed for attacks anywhere on the eastern Mediterranean coastline. Landings in Palestine itself were inadvisable as there were no more footholds on the coast. There was a possibility of using Cilicia as a base to invade the Levant, but the governing faction there opposed co-operation with Latin Christians.

The crusades of the thirteenth century had nearly all involved an attack on the Nile Delta. As their main source of wealth and supply, to occupy this region would do the Moslems such harm as to force them to concessions at the very least. The Fourth Crusade, as already shown, was originally intended to have gone this route. The question of going a step further and conquering Egypt by attacking Cairo from the Delta was brought up in the Fifth and Seventh crusades and Damietta at the eastern branch was seized both times.

The crusading army Peter had raised in 1365 was hardly big enough for the major campaign needed to subdue Egypt, but it was larger than the forces used on the raids on Anatolia. For an attack on Alexandria, Peter might have just enough troops, if not for a march on Cairo.

Alexandria was Egypt's second city and remains so. Founded by Alexander the Great and his final resting place, it had ever since been a prime commercial centre of the eastern Mediterranean. On the coast at what is now the dried-up mouth of the Nile Delta it was a major port for the lucrative trade from the east. The sultans had understood the demand in Europe for spices, as they had of silks and precious metals, and decreed that merchants from India and the Orient could only sell their wares in Cairo, and some of this merchandise was then taken to Alexandria as the only port open to westerners. This trade brought the sultans gigantic revenues, and the overall cost of spices increased at every stage on the way from India to northern Europe. For most of the time the Venetians held a near-monopoly of the spice traffic to Europe and Venice grew rich, provoking widespread resentment.

The mid-fourteenth century had seen the Mamluk sultanate sink into economic and political decline. Baibars and his eventual successor Qalawun had built a powerful, unified empire in which Cairo, Damascus, Aleppo, Jerusalem and many other illustrious cities of Islam had flourished once again, now that the Mamluks had appointed themselves protectors of Islam from the Mongols and their allies. Once the Mongols had destroyed Baghdad and laid Iraq and Persia waste, Egypt and Syria were the last refuges of the learning, arts and sciences that Islam had promoted. Even the Abbasid line of Caliphs still resided in Cairo, as powerless puppets in the Mamluk sultans' hands. The long and celebrated reign – three reigns in fact –of an-Nasir Muhammad, Qalawun's youngest son, had at his death in 1341 bequeathed the sultanate sound government and economic prosperity, where there were few threats from outside.

An-Nasir had re-established the principle of an hereditary sultanate in defiance of a tendency of the Mamluk amirs to usurp, but the poor performance of his heirs spoiled his achievement. His sons were mostly impetuous and self-indulgent youths who offended too many powerful elements, or else were manipulated by intriguing amirs and harem politics. Several were powerless child-sultans and few lasted more than three years, often deposed and sometimes murdered at the most powerful amir's convenience. Of the thirteen sultans that followed an-Nasir, few showed any capacity for ruling, and fewer still were allowed to reign for any length of time. Adding to this poor leadership the ravages of plague, together with other natural disasters such as the failure of the Nile to rise in some years, the Mamluk sultanate, dependent on an agrarian feudal economy, was suffering.

In 1365 Shaban, yet another boy-sultan, served as figurehead for a government led by Yalbugha al-Umari al-Khassiki. This amir had already deposed two other sultans and was constantly watching for intrigues against him. Even his own mamluks, traditionally the most trustworthy followers of all, were inclining towards rebellion. Needless to say, Egypt was far from prepared for an invasion by the Christians.

Peter could not have chosen a better time to attack. Not only was this political uncertainty at its height, but the Mamluk governor of Alexandria was then on pilgrimage and the annual flooding of the Nile had virtually cut the city off from Cairo. Perhaps Peter had excellent intelligence. In the first week of October the crusading army embarked, and on the ninth of the month the ships reached the harbour of Alexandria.

With the crusaders came Peter Thomas as papal legate. A Carmelite Friar, Peter had served at Avignon and since become Archbishop of Crete and Latin Patriarch of Constantinople. He had accompanied an expedition to Smyrna in 1359 and appeared even more belligerent than the king. Philippe de Mézières, a man of many talents, later wrote Peter Thomas's hagiography following his canonisation. Peter Thomas urged immediate attack on the Moslems, and the chancellor had to talk him out of it.

The following day the Franks landed, swiftly gaining control of the peninsula where the Pharos or lighthouse had stood in ancient times, and they soon breached a weak point in the city walls. It was not difficult to predict the result: carnage, slaughter, mass enslavement, looting and pillaging. Over seventy shiploads of loot went back to Nicosia. It was similar to Peter's previous raids, only on a much larger scale.

But what to do next was debated. Having succeeded in capturing and plundering Alexandria there was soon disagreement among the senior crusaders over which way to go now. King Peter was all for a swift descent on Cairo, and both de Mézières and Peter Thomas supported him. Given the unreadiness of the Mamluk leadership there was at least an outside chance of this succeeding. But it would have been a gamble; news of the invasion would have reached Cairo by this time and the Mamluks might still rally to its defence. Above all, the original problem, that so few had come on this crusade, made such a campaign foolhardy. Many European knights refused to follow him to Cairo and some were already talking of returning to Europe.

Peter then advocated that they hold Alexandria against the Mamluks, but William Roger, Viscount of Turenne, pointed out that this would be impossible to sustain. At this time of year it might have been viable as the inundation continued, but Yalbugha and an army would have come sooner or later, and few of the crusaders shared Peter's resolve to defend this city against him. To what purpose, the European knights asked? If a larger crusading army followed up this victory it would be an ideal landing point. But Peter was lucky to have mustered as much support as he had in the first place and could not reasonably rely on any further arrivals. Peter Thomas believed that reinforcements would come as soon as word of the victory reached Europe and exhorted the host to stand firm. But the majority of the crusaders did not wish to stay and be killed, and some were already drifting away, taking ship back to Cyprus. The legate was himself wounded by arrows and died in Famagusta some months later. On 16 October the king reluctantly ordered the evacuation, and the crusaders had all left before the Mamluk army finally arrived.

Peter and the other crusaders had collected mountains of loot and had dealt a severe blow to the prestige of the Mamluk sultanate, but apart from gaining the permanent animosity of the Mamluks towards Cyprus they had achieved nothing else. It is hard to see what Peter could have otherwise done; it was probably a mistake proceeding at all once he had failed to raise an army large enough. Perhaps he had to give the crusaders something better than yet another raid on Anatolia, or else they would not have followed him. But as soon as many European knights had taken the city and collected their booty, they quickly thought of going home. The sensible campaigners among them knew that little else could be achieved given such resources and conditions and saw withdrawal as the only course.

The Moslems' anger could only be expected. Christians in the Mamluk Sultanate suffered persecution and seizure of their property. Despite the Mamluks' aversion to seafaring, Yalbugha immediately ordered the building of enough ships to transport an army to Cyprus. Baibars had once tried a seaborne invasion of the island to no avail, but revenge for the 1365 outrage was now driving the Moslems.

Events in Cairo saved the Cypriots. The following year Yalbugha attempted to depose Shaban but met with opposition, and soon his own mamluks rose against him and killed their patron; the expedition never sailed. Shaban remained sultan for a total of fourteen years, maintaining an understanding with the Yalbughawis, but this broke down in 1377 when they revolted again and killed him. There followed the expected power struggle over the heads of two more puppet-sultans, and eventually in 1382 the Amir Barquq, formerly of Yalbugha's following, declared himself sultan. Succession by usurpation again became the norm. Although the Mamluks would not invade Cyprus for some time, they did not forget Peter's raid.

After his expedition Peter was far from ready to give up his dream and called for a new crusade, but he had even less response. He still had a number of Europeans whose obligation to the crusade for a fixed period had not expired and in 1366 he made use of these when he raided Tripoli on the Lebanese coast. Again, this furnished the Franks with plunder, but they withdrew before the Mamluks could retaliate.

The Pope urged Peter to make peace with the Sultan. There had been reprisals against Christian merchants in Egypt and Syria, and there was after all little to gain at this time. But Peter was hard to dissuade, and he toured Europe again in 1368 seeking to raise a new army. When his efforts produced pitiful responses Urban prevailed upon Peter to join him and the Venetians in a treaty with Shaban.

While this was going on Peter received a deputation from Cilicia. The nobles there had elected him king and called for his leadership to defend them from Mamluk depredations. The Sultan's troops had reduced the little kingdom bit by bit for over a century and were close to destroying it altogether. The Armenians knew that the end of Cilicia was close, and this decision, together with entering into communion with Rome, were acts of desperation, ineffective in the event. Peter accepted the crown and made promises of aid which he never provided.

It appears that for all his crusading fervour, Peter had little skill managing his Cypriot vassals. He was unpopular among the nobles of the island, even those who had grown rich under his activities. There is a story that Queen Eleanor had been unfaithful while he was in Europe, and on his return he conducted vendettas against various nobles, even his own brother, for their alleged affairs with her. Having heard that John of Morphou had lain with the queen Peter demanded that he answer in public for this. John offered to prove himself innocent by trial of combat but was eventually imprisoned for life and died soon after.

There are worse tales. Guillaume de Machaut relates how in 1369 Peter's son the Count of Tripoli coveted two hounds belonging to a son of Henry de Giblet, then Sheriff of Nicosia. The affair escalated, and Peter had Henry imprisoned and stripped of his position and wealth, and his daughter (who was planning to take the veil) dragged from sanctuary and tortured. This account presents Peter as a tyrant, despoiler and violator of women and the factual basis for this story is debatable. The action sounds somewhat hackneyed, and few kings would have attempted such a course without knowing how serious it would have been to risk alienating their nobles. If it happened that way, it was probably the event that sealed his fate eight days later. Yet Peter made many enemies in his last year, and his assassination could have come from one of several quarters.

On 17 January 1369 as Peter lay in bed with his mistress, three knights burst into his chamber in the Palace of La Cava in Nicosia. Machaut names Henry de Giblet as the ringleader. They stabbed Peter to death before he could reach his sword. He was buried in the church of St Dominic's of Nicosia with his predecessors and succeeded by his son Peter II 'the Fat'.

Cyprus remained a centre for Frankish raids on the mainland long after Peter I had gone. No more serious crusades took place from the island, but attacks on the Syrian coast continued from time to time, much to the Sultan's annoyance. For a few years from 1403 Charles d'Albret, the Marshal of France, later killed at Agincourt, led seaborne raids on Alexandria, then on Tripoli, Beirut and Sidon.

This raiding of the coast of Egypt and Syria might have been a way of assuaging guilt, as for the chivalrous knight of Europe to liberate Jerusalem for Christianity was the real quest. They knew it could not be done when such small numbers turned up to crusade, but it seemed while such raiding went on that at least something was happening, if in all honesty it made hardly any difference.

In the 1420s, as depredations from Catalan corsairs using Cyprus as a base became a serious problem, the Mamluk Sultan Barsbai finally acted. Cypriot and Catalan raiders became very bold and even took merchant ships from the harbour of Alexandria, and there was a rumour about a new crusade. After Barsbai's ambassador was captured while travelling to Constantinople, the sultan was moved to action. Three seaborne expeditions from 1424 brought vengeful

Mamluk armies to the island itself, and in July 1426 the Mamluks defeated the Cypriots at Choirokiotia.

Peter's descendant King Janus, captured in the battle, was brought to Cairo to swear fealty to the Sultan, where he was first paraded in humiliation through the streets, his banners dragged in the dust. Cyprus continued as a Mamluk vassal kingdom until 1475, when a succession dispute between the Lusignans resulted through a complicated series of inheritances in a Venetian annexation. The Ottoman Turks took the island later.

Peter I was considered a harsh and impulsive ruler. He was also believed a promoter of the ideals of chivalry and crusading. In 1347 while still Count of Tripoli he founded (or re-founded) the Order of the Sword with the motto 'To Maintain Loyalty', whose knights committed themselves to recovering Jerusalem. Such a vow was typical throughout Catholic Europe, and almost every country had at least one such order. In chivalric fashion Peter always carried an unsheathed sword with him as a symbol of his intent.

It is possible that Peter was simply using warfare as an aid to damaging commerce in the Levant, and perhaps frustrating Mamluk plans to dominate the eastern Mediterranean. There were genuine fears of Turkish expansion into the Aegean and threats to the trade routes to Constantinople. If Peter was simply out to disrupt Moslem trade his aims during the raid of Alexandria show something of a break from this, from a pragmatic commercial policy into the realms of old-style idealistic crusading. Did he genuinely believe in the mission he professed? He did not attempt to invade the Palestinian coast before 1367. Then again, he would just fight the nomadic tribes that the Mamluks had settled there, and only until the Mamluks sent an army from Cairo. None thought it a good idea to approach Jerusalem this way by this time.

'Winning Jerusalem on the Nile', that is, to capture the Moslems' source of supply, was already an old idea in Peter's day. It was a strategy that would have done much harm to the Mamluks and the best way to bring the sultan to terms, had it succeeded. Attacking Cairo from Alexandria was always debated. Despite the flooding, Peter might have attempted this if he had had a much larger crusading army under his command, but without a constant supply of knights and soldiers from the west it could only be a matter of time before any advance would be reversed. While holding Alexandria was a somewhat more realistic plan, he could have maintained it at a high human cost for a few months at best, and to little advantage in the end.

The problem throughout stemmed from the shortage of serious commitment among those would sign up for a crusade when the call went out but had too many practical considerations to overcome to actually set forth; even those who came mostly thought of going home as soon as the real fighting began. Peter Thomas blamed the failure of the 1365 crusade on the wickedness and cowardice of the Europeans, but perhaps their greed was more to blame, for they gained their rewards early and their fervour lessened as the prospect of a long campaign against the Mamluks loomed.

Crusading is not an easy ideal to live up to. Peter's failure to lead a fully attended and successful crusade was not due to the fact that he lived too late, for in the thirteenth and even the twelfth centuries there were always problems raising enough support for the desired crusades. It was his tragedy that he was all too willing to charge into battle for what was considered the divine cause while so few shared his enthusiasm enough to follow him. Crusading was still a serious proposition into the sixteenth century, but again the practicalities cooled the enthusiasm.

Peter of Lusignan was not the man who could have won back Jerusalem. His eccentricity was to have taken the ideal of crusading seriously, and unlike so many after 1291 to turn his ideals into action. The flaw in his plans was that not enough others had the same commitment as he did. Perhaps he should have put more energy into the management of his own kingdom.

Chaucer's Monk says of Peter:

O worthy Petro, king of Cipre also
That Alisandre wan by heigh maistrie
Ful many an hethen wroghtestow ful wo,
Of which thyne owene liges hadde envie
And for no thyng but for thy chivalrie
They in thy bed han slayne the by the morwe
Thus can Fortune hir wheel governe and gye,
And out of joye brynge men to sorwe.

(*Canterbury Tales* ll. 2581-88)

O worthy Peter, king of Cyprus, also
Who won Alexandria by great strength
To many a heathen you wrought great woe
About which your own lieges were envious

And for no thing but your chivalry
They have slain you in the morning in your bed.
Thus can fortune govern and guide her wheel
And out of joy bring men to sorrow.

The Wheel of Fortune was a common device in medieval literature, and Chaucer used it several times. Like the Monk's other examples, Peter fell from the heights of his achievement to utter disaster and his own death – but it was more of his own making than by any twist of fate.

12

Ibn Khaldun

Scholar and Double-dealing Politician

The presentation of medieval history in this country has often been criticised for being overly Eurocentric. We are of course usually more interested in what happened in our part of the world, and some regions have fewer written records than others. Despite this, the civilisation of Islam flourished alongside that of European Christendom, producing highly developed societies and many philosophical, scientific and literary achievements which are still relevant today. In the period from 600 to 1100 the Islamic lands, North Africa and the Near and Middle East, claim a better case for study than Europe at the same time in such a context.

Catholic Christians saw the Moslems as a permanent enemy and from 1095 were encouraged to go forth and annihilate them. Interaction between the Christian and Moslem worlds was minimal, but there still were points of contact between the two communities. The Franks in the states of Syria created by the crusades eventually developed a relationship with the Moslems living there, if not always amicable at least not fighting most of the time. Spain and for a time southern Italy, where Moslems ruled over Christians, Jews and Moslems alike, saw many cultural exchanges.

A large segment of the world's population looks back at the events in Mecca in the Arabian Peninsula, when in about AD 610 the merchant Muhammad ibn Abdullah spoke of the One God and His revelations as he gathered followers. When the powerful pagans of Mecca voiced their opposition he was forced to flee to Medina in 622, an act known as the *hejira*, which begins the Moslem calendar. After continual war between the two cities the Moslems gained control of

Mecca in 630, two years before the Prophet died. He was succeeded by his Companions Abu Bakr and then Umar, the first two to hold the title of Caliph, or successor.

Umar encouraged the emergence of the Arab armies from the peninsula and by the time of his assassination in 644 the Arabs had conquered Syria, Palestine, Egypt, Mesopotamia and most of Persia. They spoke of their activities as 'opening' such lands for Islam. Contrary to popular assumption, there was no enforced conversion of the peoples, as Christians, Jews and Zoroastrians worshipped without interference under the new regime. The previous masters had been mostly unpopular, their taxes high and religious intolerance the norm. All conversion to Islam was voluntary, its status as the religion of the rulers not harming its attraction.

By the end of the seventh century the Arabs had conquered the whole of the North African coastal region, lands they called the *Maghreb,* the 'west', which they still call the modern state of Morocco. In 711 an army crossed to the Iberian Peninsula and the centuries of Islamic rule in Spain began. This relentless spread of Islam by military conquest was finally halted in 732 when a small invasion force crossed the Pyrenees and suffered a decisive defeat at Poitiers by a Frankish army headed by Charles Martel. From the ninth century onwards, the Christians retook the Spanish lands piece by piece, a process only completed in 1492.

From the ninth century the gigantic Caliphate of the Arabs fragmented, and in these western lands there was a succession of short-lived empires. From 1042 to 1276 the Almoravid and then the Almohad amirs ruled over this region and Moslem Spain. Both began as religious reform movements, and both would fall into decay within a few generations. Afterwards North Africa was partitioned between the Hafsid, Zayyanid and Marinid amirates, of which the last was emerging as the most powerful by the mid-fourteenth century. It was in the wake of this fragmentation that Ibn Khaldun rose to prominence.

Abū Zayd 'Abd-al-Rahman ibn Muhammad ibn Khaldun Al-Hadrami was born on 27 May 1332 in Tunis, where his family settled after the Christian reconquest of Sevilla had driven them from Spain. Abd-al-Rahman was his personàl name; Ibn Khaldun had become a family name.

Ibn Khaldun wrote an autobiography, although it says little about his personal life. There is every reason to believe that it was a truthful account, although he probably embellished a few details. The Banu-Khaldun claimed distant ancestors who came from Hadramaut in Arabia and eventually settled in Moslem Spain, where they were known as warriors and scholars. In 1330, as the Christians fought southward, they fled to the Maghreb. Some biographers believe that the family were originally Berbers who invented an Arab genealogy, a practice not unusual in the world of Islam. His family gave him both an extensive education and opportunity for government service.

As a boy and then a young man Abd-al-Rahman had the best teachers that could be had at that time. The Banu-Khaldun were now highly placed in government circles and also attracted many scholars to their home. The young man had a broad education, not only on the Koran and the theology of Islam but in philosophy, logic, medicine and mathematics. The acclaimed philosopher al-Abili, who lived for a time in the household, introduced him to the writings of Averroes, Avicinna and other rationalist thinkers, while training him thoroughly in logic. Ibn Khaldun resolved that he would eventually join his tutor when al-Abili returned to Fez. Not all his studies were purely academic in their nature, and he did learn much of administration. In particular he received a diploma in jurisprudence, which involved interpretation of Islamic law.

Apart from research that has commercial value, it is often the lament of academics these days that funding for the furtherance of knowledge is not forthcoming. In the Islamic lands the scholar was something of a hero. Respect for knowledge of any kind was the norm and in the early days of the Arab conquests the Moslems absorbed whatever learning they could from the Greeks of Egypt and Syria. The works of Aristotle, Euclid and Pythagoras were only a few of the classical authors studied, and they disseminated the same learning as they could. The Moslem University of Toledo taught a higher standard of medicine than any to be found in Christian Europe; as only one example, the Arab doctors understood the process of blood circulation centuries before it was known in Europe. The stars mostly have Arabic names and a mass of words in use today, including *zenith, nadir, alcohol, alkali, admiral, magazine* and the root of the word *chemistry* are of Arabic origin. Spanish, Portuguese, Farsi and Urdu have a large Arabic content in their vocabularies. A scholar was also prized for his usefulness as a civil servant. A grounding in Islamic learning, science, law and philosophy was a suitable background for an administrator and diplomat, and it is not difficult to see why Ibn Khaldun was so much in demand by one prince or another throughout his life,

The North Africa of his formative years saw serious upheaval, for in 1348 the Marinid ascendancy was shattered. When its sultan Abul Hasan introduced reforms that reduced the powers of the Arab tribes to levy taxes, they understandably voiced their opposition. Attempts to placate them with compensation failed to stop their revolt, and Abul Hasan suffered a severe defeat when his army deserted him. There were risings all over his empire, particularly in Tunis where his officials found themselves under attack.

It touched the Banu Khaldun, although they did not suffer personally for their support of the regime. They sheltered some of the fugitive Marinid officials in their house. Eventually a Hafsid prince returned to rule in Tunis once more, although his *wazir* (or minister) Ibn Tafrajin was effectively in control. The matter was far from over, for the Marinids laboured for years to regain their North African empire.

At the age of sixteen the life that Ibn Khaldun followed as a scholar with an intense love of learning was turned upside down, he suffered personal tragedy and was forced to provide for himself.

Just as the commotion over the expulsion of the Marinids was over in Tunis, plague arrived via the trade routes from the east. The bubonic plague had already devastated Egypt and Syria with an astronomical death-toll and was then also creeping relentlessly through Europe and across north Africa. The young man escaped it himself, but both his parents died. Before the epidemic ran its course in Tunis many of his friends and teachers were also taken.

In 1352 young Ibn Khaldun decided on going to Fez, as nothing remained for him in Tunis. His elder brother Yahya persuaded him to delay his departure and urged him to find employment in the new government. Ibn Tafrajin himself took an interest in him as he had all the makings of a useful official. Ibn Khaldun took on his first administrative role when appointed Master of the Signature in Ibn Tafrajin's administration. This was a fairly junior post but required some skill. The officeholder would employ a precise calligraphy, writing out the name and genealogy of the Hafsid ruler on diplomas and proclamations. It was a much-desired position, if only as one rung on a ladder of advancement, but young Ibn Khaldun was far from pleased with holding it while his passion was reserved for the pursuit of knowledge and as events later show, he was too much the intriguer to be an obedient civil servant.

In less than a year he decided to vacate his position, although this was not so easy without incurring the wazir's wrath. During the commotion of a war with a rebellious Hafsid ruler in Constantine, he slipped away. He waited at Biskra until the fighting ended in defeat for the army of Tunis and then set out west, eventually for Fez. Ibn Tafrajin confiscated some of his family's wealth in reprisal.

While on the road to Tlemcen he met a military force that the new Marinid Sultan had sent against a rebellion in Bougie, which he had gained not long before. Its commander, a childhood friend of this Sultan, befriended the young scholar and Ibn Khaldun went with the troops, lending his services to the surrender of Bougie. He then went to Tlemcen with the mission from Bougie to offer homage.

On reaching the court of the Sultan Abu Inan, who was labouring to regain the Marinid empire in the east, Ibn Khaldun was given a sumptuous welcome. It is likely that some of the scholars in the Marinid court knew him from Tunis as a promising pupil. The support the Banu Khaldun had shown for the Marinids at Tunis in 1348 was not forgotten either. He also showed himself useful for his knowledge of Hafsid affairs. Ibn Khaldun related how he received gifts of rich clothing, horses, tents and money.

Thus Ibn Khaldun flourished under the patronage of Abu Inan. As Moslem rulers gained prestige by encouraging scholars, he lived well for a time, often appearing at the many gatherings of the learned the sultan sponsored. At this time he married the daughter of an important Hafsid official, although he said little of this in his own account. He set out for Fez in 1354, again as a much-feted scholar. It was now the Marinid capital. For three years more he lived the life of a celebrity and as secretary to the Sultan. He was not keen on writing out proclamations and diplomas but knew he had much to gain from Abu Inan's continued generosity. He was prominent in the philosophical and literary circles that the regime promoted.

It was in this capacity that he made his first big mistake and lost much. The former Hafsid ruler of Bougie, Abu Abdullah, had abdicated and was living sumptuously at Fez. It was useful for a ruler like Abu Inan to keep such potential pretenders and former enemies at his court, often as his guests and his prisoners at the same time, for they could be useful to him at some point. Ibn Khaldun became a close friend of Abu Abdullah, probably as they shared interests. As one in such favour with the ruler the scholar attracted envy, and tongues wagged about this association.

In 1357 the situation became explosive. Ibn Khaldun was accused of plotting the escape of Abu Abdullah and arrested at the sultan's command. It is not known how true the allegations were; Ibn Khaldun was always the intriguer, but it is uncertain what he could have gained by this act, risking so much. He was thrown into prison where he remained for two years.

When Abu Inan was dying after an unsuccessful expedition to Tunis, there was a struggle in the palace between factions and rival claimants to the succession. Ibn Khaldun was released by one faction who thought it politic, and for the present he stood by and observed the infighting, but it was clear that he had powerful supporters and diplomatic skills that many found useful. One pretender, Abū Salem Ibrahim III, offered Ibn Khaldun a large amount of money and an important post in government for his support, which he accepted. This faction, gaining much of its support from his efforts, eventually entered Fez in triumph, with Ibn Khaldun himself at the new sultan's side.

This revolution was not so easily won. The new incumbent began by arresting all his brothers, cousins and members of collateral branches and disposing of them in the guise of sending them in a ship to exile and drowning them all. There was fighting in the streets. The townsmen attacked the Christian and Jewish merchants and were separated by the Marinid troops. For a time Ibn Khaldun was secretary of state and head of the chancellery, together with an office as a judge. At twenty-seven he had certainly done well.

Abu Salem Ibrahim was murdered a year later, and the Grand Wazir who had initiated the infighting returned to power, to rule for six years in the name of four puppet sultans, three of whom he had murdered. The fourth, Ibn Amar, removed the wazir before suffering the same fate. Throughout this period Ibn Khaldun continued to perform important roles, his skills as an intriguer pushed to the utmost; it was difficult to stay alive in such a court.

But Ibn Amar was not as well disposed toward Ibn Khaldun and gave him no official position, and in 1362 the scholar requested permission to leave the realm. Given the general atmosphere, it was probably the safest course. The sultan granted his wish, specifying that he was not to go either to Tunis or Tlemcen, for he certainly did not wish him to join with Marinid pretenders exiled in either.

Ibn Khaldun accordingly crossed the Straits of Gibraltar and went to Granada, where once again his welcome was pronounced and generous. He wrote how Muhammad V, sultan of the Nasrid dynasty who ruled in this state in southern Spain, had a wing of the palace set up for him. Muhammad fancied himself a philosopher king, for he loved learning and valued Ibn Khaldun as a counselor and promoter of scholarship. Not long before, he was himself an exile in Fez and had enjoyed Ibn Khaldun's support, which had aided Muhammad's return to power in Granada.

It is very easy to read ulterior motives into Ibn Khaldun's affairs. Perhaps he thought it politic to cultivate Muhammad while in Fez as he might need to flee to Granada one day. Perhaps he simply valued his friendship as a fellow lover of learning. He must have planned far ahead for such a day if such a move was his intention.

Soon he was in demand for his skills. In 1354 he was sent to the Castilian court to negotiate a peace treaty on behalf of the remaining Moslem states in the peninsula. King Pedro the Cruel is known for his dealings with the Black Prince during a lull in the Hundred Years War, and has a generally poor press. The many achievements of Pedro of Castile are not as much publicized; he was, for example, opposed to the growing religious intolerance in that time and he is known in Spain as Pedro the Lawful. Perhaps his intriguing and his harsh disposal of relatives – he had five illegitimate half-brothers plotting against him as a beginning – can be weighed against the many attempts to depose and murder him. The talks were successful, and the Moslem states of Spain had some peace for a period, although the Castilians were preoccupied for some time with civil war.

During his stay Pedro suggested to Ibn Khaldun that he take a permanent position at his own court. It was not in fact unusual for Christian rulers in Spain to employ Moslems and vice versa. In the Iberian kingdoms Christians, Jews and Moslems lived together with some mutual tolerance, the cultures cross-fertilizing each other. Scholars came from Europe to study medicine, mathematics and other sciences under Moslem and Jewish teachers. Pedro wanted him to act as his liaison with his Moslem subjects, and even offered to restore the lands the Banu Khaldun had held in Andalusia before the Christian conquest. Ibn Khaldun mentioned in his autobiography how like an Islamic palace Pedro's residence was, and the ways of the court made him feel much at home.

Ibn Khaldun ultimately made the right decision by respectfully declining this offer. A decade later Pedro fought a war with his rivals, particularly his bastard half-brother Henry of Trastamara, and the English and French intervened on opposing sides in the persons of Edward the Black Prince and Bertrand du Guesclin. Henry's supporters played on the popular anti-Semitism that Pedro denied, and many nobles opposed him knowing that Henry would be a weaker king and easier to manipulate. Pedro was murdered in 1369, and this enabled the Trastamara dynasty to accede.

Ibn Khaldun had escaped these events but was far from secure in Granada. He was rewarded with lands and enjoyed a close association with Muhammad. He wrote poetry, and a commentary on the writings of Averroes at his patron's request. Deciding to settle in Granada, Ibn Khaldun brought his wife and children from North Africa, preparing for a new life there. However, his close relationship with its sultan, it was said, disturbed the wazir Ibn al-Khatib. Perhaps this was envy, or else the minister felt the scholar was encouraging Muhammad to ignore important practicalities, while Ibn Khaldun believed he was guiding him to become a wise ruler. Perhaps this was simply the clash of politicians, each believing their own approach the right way. In 1355, the wazir eventually prevailed on Muhammad to expel Ibn Khaldun from his court. In 1357, Ibn al-Khatib was accused of philosophical heresies and of blasphemous writings. He was imprisoned and murdered on Muhammad's orders, despite an attempt by Ibn Khaldun to intercede for him.

Ibn Khaldun eventually decided to return to Bougie, but only in 1365 after his old friend Abu Abdullah had succeeded in retaking his city and after promises of an appointment as grand wazir. The scholar was now growing cautious. Ibn Khaldun had given his support to Abu Abdullah raising troops for this venture, and now took the position as part of his reward. He was particularly useful in dealing with the Berber tribes. But his time in this position was short-lived. Abu Abdullah was a harsh ruler and made many enemies, some of which by 1366 revolted and killed him. Ibn Khaldun was asked to act as regent for his son but saw the dangers as the situation worsened and surrendered Bougie to the pretender.

Soon after, as worse instability was imminent, Ibn Khaldun took refuge with the Dawawida, an Arab tribe. Having sent his brother Yahya to be chief wazir to the Sultan of Tlemcen, he worked as advisor to this tribe, urging them to support this sultan. For four years Ibn Khaldun acted as intermediary between Tlemcen and the Dawawida. During this time he often led the Arab tribesmen on campaign, his role often resembling that of a bandit chieftain more than a politician.

When the Marinid ruler of Fez won a crushing victory against Tlemcen in1370, Ibn Khaldun was forced to flee, but while heading to the sea in search of a ship to Spain he was captured. He characteristically escaped execution by convincing the Marinid sultan that he was only acting in self-preservation and also made himself useful for his local knowledge and influence with the tribes. For a time, he entered a dervish monastery, but soon the Marinids had work for him, bringing the tribes' support to their cause. Again, he was successful, although on a different side.

In 1472 the situation in the Maghreb became chaotic once more, when a new Marinid sultan was ousted by Muhammad of Granada and the second of two Marinid pretenders. After some further machinations Ibn Khaldun returned to Granada. But now Muhammad had abandoned the role of an enlightened Moslem prince and acted as an unashamed tyrant. Having no further use for his former mentor he had Ibn Khaldun taken to the coast of Tlemcen and left there in the certainty of him being caught by his enemies. He miraculously survived this, for an influential friend entreated for him, and he was allowed to retire again into a monastery. Soon he was again called to act on behalf of this sultan and raise tribesmen on his behalf.

Around that time Ibn Khaldun confessed to wearying of politics. The price of high office was too high and he really wished to study and advance knowledge. He was forced to intrigue as much as everyone else in the courts did if he were to survive, and it was remarkable that he was still alive after so long serving so many masters. The life of a Moslem holy man or mystic, to which many politicians and amirs resorted after leaving public life, was not strictly for him, and his energies were taken up in study and scholarship.

Of course, Ibn Khaldun appears throughout as the great intriguer who turned his coat again and again. But such machinations came with the territory. In order to conduct his studies he had to make himself useful, and if he was not to fall victim to intrigue he had to be more devious than the others. His main achievement in those years was to have survived while a ghastly death often awaited a failed politician in the Moslem world of that time.

All though his adult life Ibn Khaldun busied himself with one piece of scholasticism or another. He wrote his first book at nineteen, a commentary on the theology of al-Razi under the supervision of al-Abili. He produced much more work, although comparatively little survived him. In the days before specialism in fields of knowledge, a scholar in the Islamic worlds was often a polymath and Ibn Khaldun was forever working on treatises on philosophy, astronomy, mathematics or law. History was then a subject that commanded respect, although subject to standard forms, mostly narratives on rulers and political events. At first, when Ibn Khaldun had retired from public life, he envisaged a history of the Berbers. This became more ambitious, and resulted with *The Book of Example and the Commenced Diwan, from the Days of the Arabs, Persians and Berbers and their Powerful Contemporaries,* a history of the world in seven volumes.

Most of the actual body of the text is not very original work, apart from the two books on the Berbers, which are an invaluable source to historians in the present day. It was the *Muqaddimah,* or the *Prolegomena* as often translated, that made all the difference. This introductory volume is often treated as a book in its own right. It lays down a methodology by which history can be understood.

The *Muqaddimah* is perhaps the first attempt by any historian to account for changes in society and government. In doing this Ibn Khaldun broke with traditional methods and developed a terminology of his own. He showed the effect of the environment on peoples.

One major theorem concerns the conflict of the 'town and the 'desert'. Tribal societies conquer and becoming ensnared by the 'civilising' influence of the towns, soon lose martial qualities and become vulnerable to a new onslaught from the desert. In North Africa, Ibn Khaldun was all too aware of such incursions, for the Fatimids, Almoravids, Almohads and so many other dynasties began that way. Even the Bedouin Arabs that conquered the region for Islam in the seventh century fit into such an understanding. Many have since taken Ibn Khaldun to advocate the cyclical view of dynastic change. To an extent this is so, but it would be simplistic to see his work purely in such terms.

Ibn Khaldun's main concept he called *asabiyyah,* which has been translated many ways, but could be accepted to mean 'group solidarity' or 'social cohesion'. A tribal society could be strong through such unity, by which it can gain an empire. But as this original unit is replaced by another group such as a dynasty or empire, the original loyalties fall into disuse. Ibn Khaldun spent much time exploring the nature of the *asabiyyah.*

There had been much discussion on his views ever since, and many interpretations of what exactly this *asabiyyah* really was. How accurate his findings were cannot be discussed here, but it is true that Ibn Khaldun at least sought a perspective and offered explanation as to how and why politics and society behaved as such, which was revolutionary for the time. To an extent the study of history has been occupied with this over the past two centuries.

What Ibn Khaldun offered was a view of the behaviour of society rather than the actions of individuals, and he is considered a forerunner in the discipline of sociology. His work also shows an understanding of economics, and some important theories can be traced back to him. Many modern thinkers – economists, sociologists and philosophers as much as historians – including Toynbee, Flint and Gellner acknowledged their debt to him.

But in keeping with his religious views, he did not fail to stress the hand of God in all of the affairs of man. His views might otherwise have been judged heretical.

He wrote the main part of the *Muqaddimah* in 1377 and went on adding to it for the rest of his life. For years he lived in the citadel of Taourzout working on his magnum opus. In 1382 he obtained permission to travel to Egypt for research. It was the best centre of learning he could select. Once he left the Maghreb he never returned. Egypt was the land where scholars could hope for the best patronage.

Ibn Khaldun might have considered the example of an older contemporary, a scholar from Tangier. Muhammad ibn Abdullah ibn Battuta had come the same way while on pilgrimage in 1325. In Cairo a conversation with a qadi roused his interest in travelling all over the Moslem world, and once he had visited Mecca Ibn Battuta continued journeying for the next twenty-five years: to Persia, India, Anatolia, West Africa, wherever Islam had taken root. Although there is cause to doubt the truth of his visit to China, the account Ibn Battuta wrote in his old age is a valued historical source.

Cairo in the late fourteenth century was truly a haven for scholars. The learning of the previous centuries of Islam was preserved there now that the Mongols had destroyed Baghdad and the eastern Islamic lands. The university-mosque of al-Azhar was and still is a major centre of learning which all Islam respected. Many of the Mamluk sultans and amirs had funded the building of *madrasas*, or college-mosques throughout the medieval city. The thirteenth-century sultan Qalawun had built the Maristan, a complex in the main street that comprised a mosque, a hospital, a library, an elementary school and his own mausoleum. It was still in use in the nineteenth century.

Although scholars and learned men abounded, and every subject was being taught somewhere in the city, the time for enthusiastic advances in knowledge was mostly over and much was simply repetition of that which had gone before. There had been few new discoveries in a long time, and perhaps Ibn Khaldun was a rarity in introducing his method of historical analysis.

He taught at al-Azhar for a time and was quickly a celebrity, distinctive for the Moroccan burnous he insisted on wearing for all his life. The atmosphere in Cairo lent itself to freethinking, but still the religious establishment was watchful: an associate who expressed similar views to Ibn Khaldun's was lynched as a heretic. Nevertheless, many flocked to hear him. One of his students was the Syrian Taqi-ad-Din Ahmad, known as al-Maqrizi, who, much influenced by Ibn Khaldun's method, later wrote a history of the Mamluk dynasty. He in turn would be tutor to one Ibn Taghri Birdi, son of a senior Mamluk amir, who was the principal source of the history of Egypt in the fifteenth century. Most of our understanding of Mamluk Egypt stems from these two narratives.

About the time Ibn Khaldun had arrived in Cairo, the Mamluk regime had ended four decades of instability under the sons and grandsons of an-Nasir Muhammad. When Ibn Khaldun wrote in his *Muqaddimah* that 'prestige lasts at best four generations in one lineage' and how the descendants of the vigorous founders of dynasties often undo their achievements by their ineptness, he might have had the events in Egypt in mind. Poor leadership, manipulated by intriguing amirs and exacerbated by such disasters as plague and Peter of Cyprus's invasion of 1365, had brought the Mamluk sultanate's best days to an end. In 1382 the Amir Barquq seized the throne, declaring with credibly that a strong, able man should be sultan, rather than those by virtue of their lineage.

Barquq was a Circassian, rather than a Turk as were most of the earlier Mamluks. The supplanting of more warlike Turks with Circassians was not as much a factor leading to Mamluk decline as has been thought, although Barquq and his successors did prefer their own race as slaves and advanced them with less regard to their individual merits than their racial affinity. As in the early days of the Mamluks, the sultans were once again nearly all senior amirs who seized control in the minority of each other's heirs and then usurped them as sultan.

Barquq took an interest in this new arrival and soon gave him a prestigious appointment. There are different schools of interpretation in Islamic law, and different regimes would favour one or another. From its early days Mamluk Egypt had not one, but four chief *qadis* or judges of the Shafite, Malikite, Hanafite and Hanbalite persuasions. This may have been designed to weaken the religious establishment as a potential challenge to the Mamluks' authority. In 1384 Ibn Khaldun was appointed Malikite Chief Qadi, where he acted as one of the supreme judges along with the others. In this capacity he soon sought reform, which provoked opposition, and a year later he was forced to resign. But he must have been highly regarded, for he was soon recalled to the position. In all, Ibn Khaldun was a Chief Qadi six times, but never for very long in each appointment.

Also in 1384, he knew personal tragedy. Having sent for his wife and children, the ship they travelled in sank off Alexandria. After a period in mourning Ibn Khaldun then set off to complete the pilgrimage to Mecca. He returned to Egypt in 1388, where he taught at various college-mosques for a time and eventually resumed his role as Chief Qadi.

In 1389 Barquq was overthrown when two of his provincial governors revolted. During this phase Ibn Khaldun was one of the religious leaders who issued a *fatwa* against Barquq, probably under duress and against his better judgment. But Barquq returned after nine months and executed the leading insurgents. Ibn Khaldun was removed from his office as a result, but reinstated a while after. Thus the pattern was repeated.

Barquq died in 1399 and his son Faraj succeeded, but plans to found a new dynasty came to naught due to the heir's disposition. Growing up alcoholic, paranoid and probably deranged, Faraj often turned against important amirs, meting out torture and executions almost on a whim. He suspected almost everyone else of plotting against him and was probably not far wrong in many cases. Ibn Khaldun spent his last seven years in Faraj's Egypt, and it is surprising for one with his record not to incur the new sultan's wrath. His last important role followed the Timurid invasion of Syria in 1400 and the defensive campaign, when with the other senior qadis he went with Faraj's army.

The Mamluks had first halted Mongol westward expansion in 1260 and for fifty years held it at the Euphrates. The Mongol khanate had long since fragmented, but a new leader and following emerged late in the fourteenth century. Timur the Lame, usually known in the west as Tamerlane, had built his own empire in a manner emulating Genghis Khan. In Barquq's reign he threatened the Mamluk lands but had never invaded in strength. Now he returned to conquer.

Tamerlane took Aleppo in September 1400 and approached Faraj's army at Damascus at the end of December. The Mamluks succeeded in holding the line, and the Timurid army might have withdrawn if contained long enough. But Faraj heard rumours of a plot against him and ran straight for Cairo with his retinue. His abandoned troops were soon hard pressed and without leadership most drifted away.

Ibn Khaldun was involved in the ensuing negotiations. He was let down from the walls of Damascus in a basket and requested admission to the presence of Tamerlane himself. The Mongol leader was impressed with this scholar whose fame might have reached him. During the meeting a peaceful surrender of the city was discussed, but during this exchange Ibn Khaldun offered to return to Tamerlane's capital of Samarkand with him.

Why he did so is not easily explained. It might have simply been a courtesy to so offer and be refused. He could very easily have been planning a new career move; Tunis, Granada, Tlemcen, then Cairo, then finally Samarkand, each time in the service of a greater Moslem prince. Faraj was hardly the most reassuring sultan, and the scholar might have reason during his reign to fear for his life. Perhaps Ibn Khaldun was seeking to escape the expected massacre in Damascus by the Mongols. If so, he was not exactly acting in an honourable manner.

After various meetings of Tamerlane with the learned men within Damascus, Ibn Khaldun among them, it was finally agreed that the city would open its gates without fear of reprisal. What then caused Tamerlane to order the massacre after all is unclear. Apparently, he was shown the graves of two of the Prophet's wives and finding them untended he vented his anger on the Damascenes. It is more likely that he was annoyed at the city's resistance and had acted in a conciliatory manner only to gain entry. His men ran through the streets in an orgy of murder, rape, pillage and destruction. The great Umayyad Mosque was burnt down, as was most of the city, and Damascus, then considered a magnificent jewel among Islamic cities, never rose again to its former glory.

Tamerlane spared Egypt from his wrath, but not out of charity. He turned east to deal with a vassal in Baghdad who had thrown off his submission. Afterwards he returned to Samarkand and set about other projects, leaving the Mamluk Sultanate for another day. He died in 1405 on the way to conquer China. No record on how Ibn Khaldun survived the carnage remains; he might have had the good sense to set off for Cairo immediately after the surrender. Tamerlane had questioned him in detail on the Maghreb, with the obvious intention of going there as a conqueror one day. Ibn Khaldun had even written a report on it at the Mongol leader's request. Now he wrote a detailed account on the Mongols, which included a character study of Tamerlane, copies of which he sent to the rulers of North Africa.

We know from Ibn Khaldun's autobiography that he lived out his remaining years in Cairo, where he completed his main scholarly projects. He founded a men's organisation, the *Rijal hawa rijal,* whose purpose was uncertain, and which brought him once again to the attention of the authorities. He died on 19 March 1406, surprisingly once more in his qadi's office, his sixth and fairly recent appointment.

Tamerlane's invasion was only one of the ills that now visited the Mamluk Sultanate. Syria had suffered this new Mongol invasion, but afterwards contended with brigandage, marauding Bedouins and the weakening of the sultan's control. Men feared to till the soil and the Levant sunk into ruin and impoverishment.

Faraj's paranoid intriguing finally had him removed, as Barquq's amirs deposed him in 1412 and had him murdered in prison. The succession pattern that followed was chronically unstable. Most sultans of the fifteenth century were succeeded by their sons, but few of these had real power over the amirs, who would struggle among themselves until one amir emerged powerful enough to usurp the sultanate; this repeating itself several times. Five of Barquq's amirs were sultans, and the last of these, Qait Bey, was succeeded in turn by five of his own. The story thenceforth was that of decay, as the Mamluks had difficulty even looking like an effective force of government. In 1517, after a short war of conquest the Ottoman Turks added both Egypt and Syria to their empire, and hanged the last Mamluk sultan like a common criminal.

Ibn Khaldun's work would have made a significant contribution to the early development of history as a discipline, but until comparatively recently was not known to the west. A French translation of his *Muqaddimah* was first published in 1806, but as the debate on the methodology of historical research only began a little later in the nineteenth century, there was still little attention paid to him before fairly recent times. His methods may have needed some revision, but his approach might have advanced historical analysis much earlier, had he been better known to western scholars. A statue of Ibn Khaldun now stands in Tunis, where he is belatedly honoured.

It would be misleading to see Ibn Khaldun as a Machiavellian intriguer in his earlier years. He served many masters, changing alignment swiftly and decisively. But none of these moves advanced him personally, and his main objectives throughout were his own survival and patronage for his scholarship. Once he left Tunis he owed no allegiance to anyone. It must be remembered that the politics of both the Maghreb and Granada were treacherous, a wrong move could have an official beheaded, or worse. Towards the end of this period the whole region was destabilizing, and perhaps the most astute move Ibn Khaldun ever made was to leave it. He showed a talent for knowing when to abscond.

In the lands of Islam, a man of letters was often drawn into the service of a ruler, and often prized for his expertise. It was often the way to put food on the table while he conducted his studies. Ibn Khaldun must have somewhat enjoyed his life of intrigue, or else he would have retired much earlier. But such a lifestyle had its price, and he was forced into a furtive and double-dealing stance, if only to stay alive.

13

Richard Scrope,
Archbishop of York

A Typical Prelate, but not a Typical Rebel

In England the events of 1399 and 1400 changed both the monarchy and the political climate. Richard II, last of the senior line of Plantagenet kings, had finally offended too many important elements and his cousin Henry Bolingbroke of the House of Lancaster led a revolt that swept him from the throne. The monarchy under Henry IV was widely resented, both for the usurpation and for the stiff taxes and saw two major rebellions. Why Archbishop Richard Scrope of York took part in the second of these is a tantalising mystery.

Richard Scrope was born about 1346, third son of Henry, Lord Scrope of Masham. His father was a distinguished soldier and of fairly comfortable means, but typically had the problem of providing for his younger sons. As the eldest son inherited the estates and titles and the daughters could be married off, there was always a need to find patrons or heiresses, or some other means for the sustenance of the other sons. It was a common remedy to point at least one, often the youngest, towards the Church. If the boy had some capacity for book-learning, and if the right patronage could be found among senior churchmen, this was at least a career that could lead to financial independence and could make him a bishop.

Young Richard was given the rectorship of the church at Ainderley Steeple, near Northallerton in Yorkshire, in 1368, and later of a private chapel at Tickhill, both before he was ordained. The second appointment hints at the patronage of John of Gaunt, as it was on the estates of the Duchy of Lancaster. He was eventually taken into the *familia* or close following of Bishop Arundel of Ely, later his opposite number as archbishop. In this service he was ordained priest by 1378. He also went to Oxford to study. He excelled both there and at Cambridge, and was for a time chancellor of the latter university. He later went to Rome and for a few years served in the Papal Curia as an auditor. On his return to England he was created Dean of Chichester in 1383, and three years later attained episcopal office, of Coventry and Lichfield. At the same time, he was appointed papal legate.

As bishop his successful but unremarkable career progressed to its logical climax. A medieval bishop was a powerful landowner in his own right and could easily be influential in affairs of state. Scrope, however, showed no interest in politics, nor did he distinguish himself as a theologian and hardly for piety either. He was a capable administrator, a skill valued in both church and state, and quietly served his time. Prelates were often chosen as chancellors, treasurers and for other administrative positions of government, but Scrope was never called to any post of that nature.

Perhaps his standing with the Papal Curia gave him his further advancement. In 1398 he was enthroned as Archbishop of York. This could be thought the highest achievement of all but a few English churchmen, and in his early fifties he was one of the two most senior prelates in England. Only if translated to Canterbury, a rare move in those times, or if the Curia gave him a cardinal's hat, could he aspire further. Given his lacklustre performance, it was surprising that he went so far.

There is no evidence that Archbishop Scrope was either a committed supporter or an opponent of the deposition of Richard II in 1399, when Henry Bolingbroke, heir of John of Gaunt Duke of Lancaster, finally defied Richard's order of banishment, returned and overthrew him. Richard's unreasonable and incongruous manner had left him with few supporters. Scrope was credited as a leading member of the committee called to depose Richard that year, and it was he who read out Richard's statement of abdication.

Scrope in 1399 was a grey man in the politics of the day. When the prevailing desire was for the removal of Richard II and to place Bolingbroke on the throne as Henry IV, it would take a churchman of conviction to speak against it, and Scrope was no such man. His position gave him seniority and for this reason only, he was one of those who read the judgment to Richard, then imprisoned in the Tower, and then to Parliament. If Richard Scrope had any misgivings over this business, he was not known to voice them.

The usurpation certainly harmed the standing of the monarchy, undermining the belief in the king's supreme authority and his divine election. In the fifteenth century the removal of a king was a far easier business to conduct than before, and four more kings were forcibly deposed that century, including Edward IV, who would also regain his kingdom by force of arms. After an attempt on his own life in 1400, Henry is believed to have ordered the murder of Richard, then imprisoned in Pontefract Castle. Some of his measures in these early years, including his taxes and levies, were unpopular.

The only noted event before 1405 concerning Scrope as archbishop featured the canonisation of St John of Bridlington. This local saint, an Austin canon, had from his death in 1379 been noted as the subject of posthumous miracles, and on his canonisation in 1401 his remains were 'translated' to a more appropriate tomb. Scrope was prominent in providing for this, but it was a local event rather than an ecclesiastical affair of any importance and by its nature apolitical.

There were also tales of friars in the Yorkshire area making seditious speeches in those years, when some claimed that Richard II still lived and urged his restoration. No evidence points to the archbishop concurring with them; secular clergy had little influence with the Orders.

In July 1403, the Lancastrian monarchy confronted its first crisis. Owain Glyndwr, styling himself prince of an independent Wales, was joined in revolt by Edmund Mortimer, whose nephew the Earl of March had at least as strong a claim to the throne as Henry. They soon gained the support of Sir Henry Percy, known as Hotspur, heir to the Earl of Northumberland. This coalition planned to divide the kingdom between them and had plenty of powerful elements on their side. But on 21 July the king defeated their army at the Battle of Shrewsbury, where Hotspur was killed, and the other leaders retreated into Wales. The Earl of Northumberland was accused of complicity in the affair but forgiven.

The regime was still unpopular, however. Aside from the questions of legitimacy, Henry's attempts to raise money were widely resented. Taxes on the clergy, although Archbishop Arundel agreed to them, were disliked among the rank and file. Two years later a new rebellion appeared in the north of England, and its leadership included the Archbishop of York. Joining with the Earl Marshal, the Earl of Northumberland and Lord Bardolf, Scrope issued their manifesto in April 1405, as Scrope's hagiographer later related:

The first reason was that he [Archbishop Scrope] urged the King to repent and make amends for the perjury that he committed when he swore an oath in the town of Chester by the sacrament of the Lord's body that he would neither rebel against nor consent to the deposition of King Richard. In fact, he did the opposite of what he had sworn when he forced King Richard to give up his crown by proxy in Parliament on the day after St. Michael's Day, the year of our Lord 1399, while in the meantime King Richard himself was locked up in the Tower of London. And yet previously he swore an oath of fidelity to King Richard in the presence of Lord Thomas Arundel, Archbishop of Canterbury, and many nobles.

2. Also, Archbishop Richard Scrope desired that the crown of the kingdom should be restored to the rightful line of descent, and he wanted the English Church to have its liberties, privileges, and customary rents and dues according to the just laws of the Kingdom of England which have been in effect since ancient times.

3. Also, he wanted the lords and magnates of the kingdom to be judged by their peers with the due deliberation of other lords who were their equals.

4. Also, he wanted the clergy and commons not to be oppressed by levies and taxes of tenths, fifteenths, and subsidies to the Crown, nor by any other unjust exactions, as is now the case. In the year after his coronation the King received a tenth, and sometimes he received two tenths in a single year, despite the fact that the King swore from the very beginning that in his lifetime he would do everything he could to prevent the English Church from ever paying a tenth and the people from paying a tax. That is what he swore in Knaresborough Castle, not far from York.

5. Also, after the crown had been restored to the rightful line of descent, he wanted some sensible counsellors to be appointed, men who were experienced in public office and who were knowledgeable; and he wanted other men to be removed from office, those greedy, avaricious, and self-serving men who are willing to say and do things which please the King but not God in order to fill their own pockets.

6. Also, he wanted the sheriffs in every county to be elected freely without any coercion on the part of the King or the barons.
7. Also, he wanted the barons, nobles, and the commons to have the right to act freely in Parliament in matters pertaining to them.

These grievances all have a familiar ring to them, and the manifesto was skilfully written in order to make the most political capital. Some, such as the issues of election of sheriffs, the right of magnates to judgement by their peers and free speech by the lords and commons, were traditionally guarded rights which many felt were encroached upon. There is much said concerning the privileges and tax exemption of the clergy.

But this does not so readily shed light on why Scrope forsook a lifetime's loyal (or rather uncommitted) behaviour and participated in this rebellion. He had shown no opposition to the usurpation of six years earlier, but here were clear references as to whether Henry should be king. There was also talk of the king's unpopular counsellors, a typical grievance in medieval rebellions. And there was the issue of overtaxing, a common cause for discontent. The Lancastrian regime had offended many, and Scrope – if it was he who wrote the manifesto – was cleverly playing on the prevailing grievances. The only demand Scrope was known to have personally supported was that against taxing the clergy.

His confederates were more typical rebels. Northumberland as survivor of the first revolt would have risen as easily as in 1403. In 1402, the archbishop's brother John had married Elizabeth, widow of Sir Thomas Percy, brother of the Earl of Northumberland. This shows at least a basis for association but does not in itself say why Scrope would join with the Percy cause.

There is no connection between Scrope and Thomas Mowbray, Earl of Buckingham and Earl Marshal. Mowbray's father and namesake the Duke of Buckingham had in 1398 famously challenged Bolingbroke to a duel after the latter had exposed his plot to Richard. The king had halted the tournament before fighting began and banished both. But while Bolingbroke later rose against and replaced Richard, Buckingham had died in exile, his dukedom annulled on his death. Now his son, usually known as the Earl Marshal, rose in rebellion.

How Scrope ever came to conspire with these two is surely a mystery, as much as why he abandoned a lifetime of political neutrality. It is far from clear who was the prime mover of the revolt, whether Percy or Mowbray, and what motivated either to act, but it seems unlikely that Scrope was the principal rebel. He was still a valued recruit to the cause, lending ecclesiastical gravitas and a semblance of legitimacy.

Many medieval churchmen had few qualms about riding into battle and killing enemies, as had been the norm as early as the Battle of Hastings. We have already seen from the twelfth century the orders of warrior monks whose principal role was to fight the heathens and other enemies of Christianity as the Knights Templar and Hospitaller, and the Teutonic Knights, to name the three main orders. There was a vague canonical tradition that a man of the cloth should not shed blood, and therefore fighting bishops often carried the mace into battle to break heads instead. It is unlikely that even this constraint was much observed.

Would Archbishop Scrope have even fought in battle, had one ever taken place? It would not have been sensible for a man of nearly sixty without any military experience to have charged into the thick of fighting. Perhaps his role as an eminent and respected figure was the best contribution he could make, and the other rebel leaders would have been content for him to add his ecclesiastical authority to the rising and grant benedictions from the sidelines.

On 29 May 1405, the rebel host was gathered on Shipton Moor, an open ground to the north of York. There were many of the common people, and also a number of knights and lesser peers. The archbishop said Mass and read out the manifesto. It is not certain what the rebels would have done next. Perhaps they were waiting for Northumberland to arrive with his contingent.

At this point a small force from the Crown appeared and its commanders requested a parley. Prince John of Lancaster would later excel as military commander in the French Wars as Duke of Bedford, and as third son of the king he was then Warden of the East March towards Scotland and the most senior royal representative in the north. Lord Fitzhugh rode with him. The two swiftly brought the revolt to an end using trickery as a better weapon than force.

Scrope was probably thought the best intermediary, and Lancaster appeared all too willing to parley with him. The archbishop proved too trusting and lacking in political astuteness when he agreed to go to Lancaster's camp, for there he was promptly seized and placed under guard. The royal contingent announced that an agreement had been made, and the rebel assembly almost immediately began to drift away.

Many were probably in conflict over their loyalties to the king and the archbishop, and glad to leave without being further implicated.

Only a small contingent under the Earl Marshal and William Plumpton remained and Lancaster ordered his forces to attack. The rebellion ended hardly a step away from its assembly point, and all who stayed to fight were soon dead or surrendering. The leaders were imprisoned, and all that remained for judgement to be made upon them.

The king came north soon afterwards and stayed at Bishopsthorpe, a residence of the archbishop. Henry ordered that all the men of York should prostrate themselves naked before him, in imitation of the Day of Judgement. He was certainly in a mood for draconian reprisals, but aware of the problem that Scrope posed. No senior prelate had ever been executed in England for treason before, and the archbishop had a strong popular following. But to pardon him, Henry thought, would weaken his own position. He took into account that this was the second of two serious revolts and there could easily be more to come. Henry IV himself had come to the throne at the head of a rebellion, and by his usurpation he had made insurrection against a reigning king that much more acceptable. To enact harsh reprisals against those who rose against him was the only way he could deter others.

At this point not even Archbishop Scrope believed he would be executed. It would be a very serious matter, as no king would lightly make an enemy of the Church. Henry II had in 1173 done penance for his alleged part in the murder of Thomas Becket by submitting to a public flogging; the alternative would have been the Church's support for his enemies. But in 1405 the Papacy in Rome was much weaker than at any previous time, in serious competition for recognition with the rival pope in Avignon, and any protest from the Curia would be muted. Archbishop Arundel supported the policy of coercion but other prelates would have had misgivings. Arundel had himself been convicted of treason under Richard II, but had kept his head. To execute Scrope would provide a precedent that many of the Church did not wish for and would have been inconceivable were the Church not as seriously afflicted by schism.

On 3 June, the king came with his retinue to Pontefract where Scrope was then held. The Archbishop confronted him in a defiant manner, in his robes of office and bearing his crozier before him as if it entitled him to immunity. It seemed at this meeting he seriously believed that Henry had no jurisdiction over him. Sir Thomas Beaufort, the king's half-brother, immediately wrested the crozier from Scrope's hands and took it to the king. Whatever the prelate expected, and opinion was much divided over this issue, Henry's advisors felt that it would be a mistake to let Scrope live.

Henry spoke to William Gascoigne, a northerner and royal justice, insisting that the death penalty was required. Gascoigne angered him by refusing, as he believed that no bishop could in law be sentenced to death. The king was clearly on dangerous legal ground in this matter, but eventually appointed William Fulthorp to try the case and pass the sentence he wanted.

Partially out of an old friendship, Arundel rode at speed to York and pleaded for clemency for his fellow archbishop. Henry made reassuring promises but had the death sentence read while Arundel slept, exhausted from his journey. Archbishop Richard Scrope was beheaded.

Within two years Henry fell ill, plagued with many serious maladies, and for the rest of his reign struggled both with illness and with attempts by his son Prince Henry to take over government of the kingdom, even when some tried to persuade him to abdicate. But Henry IV lasted until 1413, despite what some believed was divine retribution. This unprecedented act in York had not brought him down, and there were no more serious revolts in his reign. The Lancastrian monarchy survived two more generations, ending in 1461 during a new series of civil wars.

Henry probably wished at times that he had sent Scrope into exile instead. Soon after the execution the king had to send to the Dean of York and the city's mayor, requesting that they discourage the growing cult surrounding the dead archbishop. Crowds came to pray at his tomb and a number testified to miracles seen there. Scrope was now a martyr and there was already a campaign for his canonisation. This movement did not, as the king feared, become a focus for his opponents, and did not gain much support outside of York. Even in the late twentieth century the campaign for Scrope's canonisation was resumed and is still under way, but it has so far made little more progress in Rome.

Questions as to why Richard Scrope took this incredibly foolhardy course of action remain unanswered. Was Henry's attempt to sting the clergy for money enough to bring the archbishop over to the rebels? It is unlikely for such a political neutral to be so spurred into action; and not only against the king, but against his opposite number Arundel. It requires a major leap of the imagination to see how this came about.

Had he been moved by personal ambition, there was little to gain. He had practically reached the limit already of all he was likely to achieve. If he wished for advancement in the Papal Curia no revolt would have accomplished this when he had received all he would from Rome. He was hardly tempted with political office, given his behaviour to date.

It is more likely that Scrope was duped by the other two and believed that his grievances over clerical taxes would be redressed. They thought he would add respectability to the revolt, and he did at least attract half-hearted support. Scrope also believed that he would not suffer too much, as he was archbishop: perhaps at worst he may be exiled. Given the controversy over his execution, he certainly had good reason to believe so.

To think of Richard Scrope as a gullible old man who cast aside a lifetime of cautious time-serving on a wild impulse might be simplistic, but what other possible explanation can be found? He might have otherwise passed into history appearing on lists of prelates without much further reference. His bold and ultimately fatal act so late in his career remains a mystery.

14

Christine de Pisan

A Woman Forced to Make Her Way in the World

It is a general impression that the lot of women throughout much of history was bleak. At the very least denied opportunity to develop their professional and political identities, they were often treated as the personal property of their fathers and husbands. In the Middle Ages women knew little respite from such treatment and often contended with extreme Christian doctrines that defined them all from the first woman onwards as objects of temptation and accomplices of Satan. Of course, much has altered in the last two centuries, but many would argue not enough, and it is still difficult for a male writer to talk of this without sounding patronising. There was one woman whose achievement shines out in those barren later medieval times for the entire female gender: Christine de Pisan.

The principal role of the majority of women in the medieval centuries, as for most of recorded history, was that of wife to a man and mother of his children, although there was scope for a working woman in some trades. Mostly for ladies of aristocratic birth, the cloister was one viable alternative, but other than in such roles whatever women achieved would have been in spite of what was designated for them.

Girls might be educated in nunneries as it stood to reason that as some such houses might take girls as boarders, they might extend classroom facilities to the daughters of the more substantial men of the locality. There are also references in Froissart to boys and girls being taught together, although this was probably at a young age. In whatever schools there were, only boys received an education in the arts, sciences and other fields of knowledge, and few girls learned Latin. Perhaps an aristocratic girl might have a governess, but it was clear that a serious education was not considered appropriate, as no career for a learned woman was ever envisaged. It was often the practice to teach a young lady to read, but not to write.

One of the most accomplished of medieval women was Hildegard of Bingen, whose position as an abbess in the Rhineland of the twelfth century enabled her to become both a figure of standing among the ecclesiastics of the time and a writer of many mystical, moralistic and scientific treatises. She also created an alternative alphabet and was a celebrated visionary and candidate for canonisation. There has been more recent interest in Hildegard as a composer, and her liturgical works and sung moral drama *Ordo Virtutum* have been produced and recorded.

There were other women writers, but precious few. Also in the twelfth century, *The Lais of Marie de France* appeared; twelve short narrative poems in Anglo-Norman on courtly love themes. Almost nothing is known of Marie herself, or whether she was a real person. One more was the fourteenth-century anchoress Julian of Norwich who wrote of her intense mystical experiences. Her contemporary in Lynn, Margery Kempe, produced similar works.

Apart from this handful, Christine de Pisan was almost one of a kind. Driven by personal disasters she made a way in the world that no woman had yet trodden. Christine de Pisan was the first ever professional woman writer. Very few women had the opportunities of the learning that Christine received; she was fortunate that her father encouraged her education, and she was accepted in the milieu of the learned at the French court at the turn of the fifteenth century. It was a major achievement to establish herself and hold her own as Christine did.

Pisan (or Pizzano) was a small village in Italy north of Bologna, and birthplace of her father, the scholar Tommaso di Benvenuto da Pizzano. The Church no longer had such a hold on higher learning as in previous times, and as Tommaso had a family he had not set himself on a path to Holy Orders. He was trained in medicine and at times practised as a physician, but his forte was astrology, in which from 1348 he lectured at the University of Bologna. In 1357, Tommaso first re-located to Venice and then in 1368 became Court Astrologer to King Charles V of France.

Few academics take astrology seriously today, but astrology is an exact art which involves calculating the picture of the heavens at the moment of an individual birth. Those who even now protest its validity often quote Sir Isaac Newton's defence of the discipline in the face of Sir Edmund Halley's derision: 'Sir, I have studied it; you have not.' It was never disproved, they also point out; belief in astrology simply went out of fashion among the generation of intelligentsia that followed Newton. In the Middle Ages there was no doubt about the truth of astrology. It was used in medical analysis, and popes and emperors alike had resident astrologers. Some such as Tommaso must have gained a reputation for predictions with some accuracy, or else would not have attracted such patronage.

Christine de Pisan, who took a French version of her father's name, was born in 1365 when her father practised at Venice. She had two brothers. Soon after gaining his position at the French court, her father sent for his family and Christine spent the rest of her life in France. Unusually for women of her time she grew up literate, well-read, knowledgeable and proficient in several languages. It is certain that her father sought to give her an education, although a woman could never enter university at this time, nor aspire to any scholarly profession, and until Christine changed it all she would not see their writings taken seriously.

By the references she used in her work it is certain that Christine read widely in Classical literature. She knew of Homer, Plato, Virgil, Ovid and others, and also mentioned several pieces of contemporary literature in her writings. Although she always wrote in French, she must have understood enough Latin to do the research for all her work. Although her education was far from formal, Christine was as well-versed in the literature to hand as most men of letters alive at the time. Some have speculated that Christine's father was advisor to the Royal Librarian on scientific books and Charles's library was renowned for the size of its collection, which might have allowed Christine access to the best books then available in many subjects.

As she approached an age to marry, Christine's father insisted that she continue learning, which did her much good in the long term. In 1380, the fifteen-year-old Christine married Étienne du Castel, a royal secretary a few years older than her. It seems very much a love-match: her poems hint at the joys of a young wife in her conjugal bliss. She was devoted to her husband, and for nine years her marriage flourished as she bore him two sons and a daughter.

Charles V died the same year and Tommaso did not remain as influential under his successor: Charles VI was a minor and his regents did not honour the late king's commitment to his servants, and Tommaso died impoverished in 1387. Christine's husband did remain as much in demand for his service, but in 1389 far worse befell Christine and her family. Étienne accompanied the king to Beauvais on some royal business, where he contracted the plague and died.

Christine was devastated. Fourteen years later she still talked of the sorrow of losing the captain of her ship. Much worse for her there were practical issues; she was left to support her three children, a niece and her widowed mother. Her brothers had returned to Italy after their father died. Her husband's estate was contested in more than one lawsuit. Needing support, she fought the suits and spent much of these fourteen years in court seeking the means to maintain her family, finally gaining a settlement that allowed her to make ends meet.

Christine was widowed at only twenty-five, without financial support and with five dependents. Most women in her position would have been forced to remarry, usually beneath themselves, but Christine remained devoted to her husband's memory. She was a one-man woman, it is certain. A widow might also enter a convent, but this would not have solved the problem of maintaining Christine's family. While the litigation dragged on, she went to work, but in a different manner from most women of the time. She supported her family as a professional writer.

Many a poet or writer might seek a patron. Perhaps a noble or even a monarch would make a gift or a payment on being pleased with a literary offering. Christine had a talent with the pen, and this is the route she followed. She found her patronage in the French court, and survived.

For a medieval writer there was no need for originality in material. There was a limited number of themes an author would treat. One might at the most give a new slant on an old story, but innovation was frowned upon. There was Christian theology and mythology; there was whatever material that survived from classical literature, that of the Trojan Wars in particular. Every country had its pseudo-history of heroes, including King Arthur, Charlemagne and the Cid, usually reincarnated as chivalrous knights. To read the works of Chaucer, Dante or Malory shows how important such themes were in the literature of the fourteenth and fifteenth centuries.

One of the most enduring of such preoccupations was that of courtly love. Rather than a simple sexual issue this approached the relationship of man and woman in elevated terms. It puts the lady on a pedestal and makes the man her servant and idolater. It deals in such themes as worship from afar, unobtainable, forbidden, and unrequited love. It involves a cast including the confidant, the tempter, the slanderer, and the walled garden. Chaucer shows the Trojan hero Troilus struck down by Cupid's arrow and illustrates at length the efforts of his friend Pandarus to obtain the attentions of Criseyde for him. Malory in his retelling of the story of King Arthur and his Knights related Sir Lancelot's forbidden love for Guinevere his queen and how the traitor Mordred exploited it to destroy the Round Table. Such themes were instantly recognisable in late medieval literature. They have never departed from the consciousness of the western world.

For generations the *Roman de la Rose* was one of the most read books in Medieval Europe. The first part was written around 1230 by Guillaume de Lorris. The poem describes at length an allegorical wooing and is a deeply symbolic treatment of the entire question of love. At least for this first 4 000 lines, for fifty years later Jean de Meun added a further 17,000 or so showing a more sensuous aspect to the affair. Chaucer produced a partial translation. It was this work to which Christine turned her hand as a first major project. Christine wrote several treatises on courtly love themes: *Letter of the God of Love, The Debate of Two Lovers, The Judgement of the Three Loves* and *The Tale of Poissy*, written between 1399 and 1402. Soon after she produced her own addition to the *Roman de la Rose* discourse, as *Le Dit de la Rose*.

Although from the twelfth century the poetic tradition idolised women, there was a more cynical vein growing in the fourteenth, which now stressed the worst aspects of the female gender. Jean de Meun had somewhat satirised the idealisation of woman in his continuation of the *Roman*, and this being the latest word, Christine tackled his presentation as the first female voice in what would become a vigorous debate on the concepts presented in the poem. In 1399 she presented *The Letter of the God of Love*, also called *Cupid's Letter*, which began a series of writings. Her *Treasure of the City of Ladies* is the culmination of her writings on this theme.

Christine is often described as a feminist writer, even though the concept of feminism did not exist at the time. Where feminism calls for women gaining parity in the world with men, Christine's work does not even consider this alien concept. Modern western society knows the benefit of nearly two centuries of the struggle of women to gain equality in law, careers and public life, a struggle that continues. As in the fourteenth century, organised religion is still male-dominated. While the Anglican Church only recently created female bishops, having only allowed women into the priesthood about thirty years earlier, the Catholic Church is still as vehemently opposed to the ordination of women as they were in Christine's day.

Christine writes about the woman as a person in her own right, not as a rival to man, but one who needs to have her thoughts and feelings known. This in itself was revolutionary for her times, where the thread of misogyny stretched from the Papal Curia to expressions of popular culture. Men wrote almost everything, and few gave space to women in their writings. Christine had to contend with a general view of woman as seductress or as victim to predatory males.

While she did not claim perfection for women in the manner of courtly love, she basically stated that women were not the source of all evil, but people with feelings and aspirations, and with minds of their own. This, revolutionary for its time, was the first piece of common sense written on the subject in ages. It would initiate a new direction on what would be called 'La Querelle de la Rose'. Around 1440 Martin LeFranc took Christine's part in *Le Champion des Dames*, which spoke of many virtuous women. At least the balance was partially redressed.

The same theme inspired Christine's most accomplished work, *The Treasure of the City of Ladies*, a sequel to *The City of Ladies,* which she completed about 1405. While serious literary criticism is beyond the scope of this study, it can be said that this treatise is a milestone in women's literature. Christine first wrote her *City of Ladies* through 1404 and part of 1405. She introduced three allegorical figures who she said visited her in a dream: Lady Reason, Lady Rectitude and Lady Justice. The first of these talks of the construction of her allegorical city and its fine Gothic buildings. The treatise then populates this city with ladies of virtue, beginning with the Virgin, Mary Magdalene and various female saints, and then the reigning queen Isabeau of Bavaria and other contemporary ladies, including the duchesses of Berry, Orleans, Bourbon and Burgundy. But high birth was not in itself indicative of good disposition, and the citizens came to include women of all social backgrounds.

The influences on this work include Augustine's *City of God* and also *On Famous Women*, the first book in western literature to talk about virtuous women, which Boccaccio had produced some fifty years before, although he had confined himself to discussing the women of Antiquity. *The City of Ladies* is often criticised as paraphrasing Boccaccio, but of course one must remember that much of medieval literature was repetitive, and Christine was not inconsistent with the conventions of the day. Yet her own original contribution was to write from the viewpoint of women, supplying a missing dimension.

The City of Ladies is a formidable work in its own right, but it was when Christine finished it that the most significant development took place. Christine often spoke in her work of her personal journey to produce each piece, and now she talked of how the ladies Reason, Rectitude and Justice visited her again, and exhorted her to write more. 'One day as I was sitting alone in my study surrounded by books on all kinds of subjects, devoting myself to literary studies' she relates, the three archetypal ladies returned and exhorted her to pick up her pen once more.

'Hear our lectures, and you will accomplish good work. We do not want to overwork you, but we have considered our virtuous labours, discussed them and made a decision with the counsel of virtues and the command of God... Similarly may that preceding work of ours, *The City of Ladies*, which is good and useful, be blessed and exalted throughout the entire world so that this same work may be further disseminated.'

What emerged was Christine's masterpiece, initially as a sequel to *The City of Ladies* but on its own an eminent moral treatise. As the City was for virtuous women, the *Treasure of the City of Ladies*, also called the *Book of Three Virtues*, makes a detailed study of attitude, and how a woman can best address her life according to Christian values and as a person in her own right. She completed it before the end of 1405.

The *Treasure* is an encyclopaedic illustration of the lives of medieval women. Most of the two first sections concern the behaviour of the lady, and how she ought to comport herself. In the guise of Lady Prudence Christine stresses Christian values as the principal criteria. She shows an understanding of how easy it is to persuade oneself against better judgment. She knew how the inner person could invent excuses and make compromises with what one knows is the correct approach to an issue.

It would be a mistake to see this simply as a lecture on morality, as it appears in places more as a survival kit and a manual for what appears a precarious social milieu. Christine was not one for platitudes there; she knew much of it at first hand. She talks at length of how the culture of flirting that went on at court could compromise the virtuous woman, were she drawn into it. In particular she was mindful of the shabby treatment a widow could suffer, as it was her own experience. Those who had behaved with deference and respect while her husband lived might turn dismissive, and all manner of scoundrels and opportunists would seek her out. It would be in a widow's interest to remarry at an early stage, if only as a means of self-preservation.

Christine's advice covers practical issues, too. She shows how to manage revenues, where a prudent lady would divide her income in such a way as to meet her essential needs first and only then answer her desire for jewels and raiments. The Treasure gives advice to women of all walks of life, as well as those of high birth. There are sections on the best behaviour for the wives of merchants, and it even gives uncompromising advice to prostitutes: ie that they forsake that lifestyle.

By the standards of today Christine might appear limited in her outlook. Above all she states that a woman should devote herself to her husband, and that her calling was as a wife and mother, and to do good works in the community. This might fall short of feminist ideals but for her day Christine was revolutionary. Female emancipation (as for that matter parliamentary government) was still centuries away, and nobody seriously advocated any change to the roles women automatically took. It was Christine who presented women as people, and if she appears to lecture her own gender on virtuous behaviour and thought, she allows no questioning of the fact that women were capable of being virtuous, in an age where women on the whole had such a bad press. Few women were as highly literate and articulate as she was, and fewer still had the opportunity to express themselves so widely.

The years from 1398 to 1407 saw some easing of her personal affairs. Her lawsuits at least yielded her some income and she was often in demand while her writings brought her modest fame and patronage. Christine was the first official biographer of Charles V when Philip the Bold, Duke of Burgundy, commissioned her to write it. She also produced *The Book of Feats of Arms of Chivalry*, a paraphrase of the fifth-century writer Vegetius on military activity. She recognised that as a woman talking of such matters she was appearing presumptuous, but her work was much read. Decades later, on Henry VII's command Caxton produced an English printed edition of the same book and other works of the time refer to it. She was obviously writing for the market in both books but showed her skills as a researcher and classical scholar.

Her children were finally provided for. In 1397, the Earl of Salisbury agreed to take her elder son Jean de Castel as a page in his household. This was a promising opportunity which could lead to great things but ended two years later when Salisbury was executed for plotting against Henry IV. This king tried to persuade Christine to come to England, but she declined and had serious trouble having her son returned to France. He later entered the household of the Duke of Burgundy. Her younger son is believed to have died before 1399 and at any rate disappears from the records. By 1398, her daughter had entered the convent at Poissy. She declined overtures from both Henry of England and the Duke of Milan to attend their courts, for she loved France and never left it.

She stated in her book that a lady should seek to bring peace when lords quarrelled. Perhaps this was already on her mind in 1405, and this issue would demand her attention in the years to come when Christine's close association with the royal court exposed her to the politics of the realm.

In the years following the completion of her masterpiece, the same politics deteriorated and turned into civil war. As Charles VI was clearly of unsound mind, the factions headed by his uncles the Dukes of Orleans and Burgundy fought each other for the governance of France. In 1407, matters became dire when John the Fearless, Duke of Burgundy, had Orleans murdered. The act was condemned and Burgundy banished, but he later gained control of the government. The rival faction, now led by the Count of Armagnac, struggled to unseat him and control of the realm changed hands several times.

While this feud went on Henry V of England renewed the war for his claim to the French throne and the civil war left France vulnerable. The Armagnac following refused to countenance a military command for Burgundy, and his faction mostly did not appear on the 1415 campaign. The defeat at Agincourt hit the Armagnacs hard, many of their higher nobles killed or captured on the day itself. It might have been sensible for the Armagnacs, now enjoying the support of the Dauphin Charles, to make peace with Burgundy, but instead they used their overtures to lure John the Fearless to parley on the bridge at Montereau in 1419, where they had him murdered. His heir Philip the Good then pledged his support to Henry and by 1420 Paris and most of northern France was firmly held by the English and their Burgundian allies.

Christine took it all to heart. As early as 1405 she was imploring Queen Isabeau to call the dissenting dukes to make peace. She later wrote her *Lamentation on the Ills of France* in 1410 and *The Book of Peace* in 1413, both calling for an end to this struggle and for cooperation in the fight against the English. She cared deeply that this quarrel was harming her beloved France. She never commented when Isabeau joined with Burgundy and in 1420 made a peace that repudiated the Dauphin's paternity and recognised Henry V of England as heir to the French crown.

Why Christine ended her remarkable life in a nunnery could be put down once again to practical considerations. All her dependents had either died or were provided for, and she was advancing in age. Many of her old friends were either dead or prisoners in England after the Agincourt campaign. Her concerns over her own safety in the worsening political situation might have prompted the final move and she probably gained admission to the convent of Poissy, where her daughter was already a nun.

There is also an element of her wearying of the evils of the world in her later writings. In *The Book of Peace*, written about 1413, and then her *Letter on the Prison of Human Life*, written shortly before she took the veil, she shows an increased interest in spiritual issues. In her last work of 1429, she stated that she had been in seclusion for twelve years. If so, she probably opted for a life of quiet devotion almost on entry to the convent.

There is a hint in this final piece that she ran for the abbey while in danger of her life. In 1418 the Burgundians conducted a horrific massacre of Armagnacs in Paris, the Dauphin Charles himself barely escaping after running to the Bastille in his nightshirt. The Count of Armagnac himself was killed then. Christine was not known to favour either faction, although many of her associates were Armagnac supporters. She later blamed the way Charles ran from Paris for her ending up in the cloister. While in the nunnery she probably heard of the death of her remaining son Jean in 1426.

Yet Christine put her pen dramatically into action just once more after forsaking the world when she sang the praises of Joan of Arc.

The deeds of the Maid of Lorraine reached even Christine's ears in her seclusion, as Joan drove the English back from Orleans and regained territory on behalf of the disinherited Dauphin. Christine waxes lyrical on the 'Little Maid' whose efforts placed the crown on the head of Charles VII at Rheims in 1429 in her offering in verse, 'In Praise of Joan of Arc', which she dated the last day of July that year, only days after the coronation.

The cult of Joan of Arc could very easily have been kick-started by Christine. It treats the Maid in the contexts of both divine intervention and of French patriotism. Much controversy still surrounds the seventeen-year-old girl who presented herself to the Dauphin's court at Bourges in 1429 and declared that God had sent her to save France and the Valois monarchy, but when the Dauphin agreed to her riding to relieve Orleans at the head of an army, he never looked back. Joan in Christine's account was exactly as God ordained, and she praised God for sending the deliverer of France. She placed her alongside Moses who led the Israelites from bondage, and with other Biblical liberators. The Pucelle, she said, was the subject of prophecy, which was in part true, although Christine quoted Merlin, Bede and the Sybill as her sources, none of which can be verified. She refers to the 'dreary cage' of the abbey she confined herself to and says that this news has changed her lament into song.

It was certainly the best news that she could have had since her flight in 1418. Following the French counter-attack with Joan at its head, the Dauphin had regained hold of valuable territory that the English and their allies of the Burgundian faction had taken, and once the Dauphin was crowned as King Charles VII in Rheims, he could better present himself as a legitimate ruler who had reached a milestone in the recovery of France from the English.

Although Christine's elation was premature in the event, she saw great things to come. Joan would restore union and harmony in France; she would ride east and destroy the Saracens, and would escort King Charles to the Holy City restored to the Christian faith. Christine railed at those Parisians who then collaborated with the English, but had faith that Joan would restore to the king his capital.

O thou, Jehanne was born at such good time
Praise be to Him who made you
Maiden of God ordained
In which the Holy Spirit endowed

His immense Grace, in which by
Great generosity and gift
Let all wish to see you
Who would render praise enough...
(ll.169-76)

It is a departure for Christine to laud a woman who had made herself
a resounding success in a man's occupation, as her writings mostly did
not advocate this direction. It is not certain how much fighting Joan
in fact did, and her contribution was essentially to lead and encourage
the army. But it must have appealed to Christine that Joan had the
opportunity to show her mettle and scored points for womanhood.
Whatever had been said of her since, there was no doubt that Joan was
personally very brave and committed to her mission. The coronation
of Charles VII was then seen by many as the turning point in France's
fortunes.

History tells the story that follows differently. While on the
campaign to regain Paris the following year Joan was dragged from
her horse at Compiègne by a Burgundian archer, delivered to the
Duke of Burgundy and eventually sold to the English. Her trial and
subsequent burning at Rouen in 1431 are a matter of record. The
English enjoyed a brief revival of their progress, but after 1435 when
the Duke of Burgundy switched his support to Charles, the French
eventually regained nearly all their territory. Joan definitely had a role
in this, but she did not live to see the English driven out.

After this trumpet blast on Joan's behalf, no more was heard of
Christine. The date of her death is not known, but as she was about
sixty-five when this last work was released it was probably not very
long after. It would have been a sore blow to Christine to have heard
what became of her heroine. Some speculate that she did not live to
hear of Joan's capture, trial and burning, for she would have been the
first to lament it. If Christine did know, she wrote nothing of it and her
powerful voice was now silent forever.

Christine's work was widely read for some time after her death.
Those who were known to have owned and read copies of her books
include Margaret of Austria and Mary of Hungary, both of whom
acted as governors of the Netherlands on behalf of the Emperor
Charles V almost a century later. Louise of Savoy, regent of France
during the minority of Francis I, and Anne of Brittany, queen to
two kings of France, were also admirers of Christine. But strangely,

although Christine was still popular to 1500, she was virtually forgotten within the next fifty years. Voltaire knew of her, although he gave her the wrong first name. It was only during the French Revolution that she was rediscovered, partially through the efforts of Louise de Keralio who published an edition of the writings of women. Since then and increasingly so, Christine's work is subject to much scrutiny and publication. As late as 1924 a French critic dismissed her as a mediocre bluestocking, which showed a poor understanding of her achievement. It is only in the last half-century that Christine has regained her place in literature. The first English translation of her *Treasure of the City of Ladies* appeared in 1986.

For more detailed analysis of the literary achievement of Christine de Pisan there are works of greater expertise than the present writer can muster; it is the person that is discussed here. While there is no doubt that her intellectual and literary abilities put her on a par at least with many of the well-educated men of her time, her predicament practically forced her into a life of letters. She was a woman in a hostile world, deprived of the love of her life and needing to provide for her family. She survived by making use of her sharp mind, her wide learning and her highly expressive pen. She accomplished most of what she wished and became respected among the intelligentsia for her works. She never attempted to compete as if she were a man and she developed a genre of literature from the woman's viewpoint. She certainly had strong convictions on the virtuous life, and seriously tried to live up to them.

15

Sir John Oldcastle

Valiant Knight, Stout Heretic and Reluctant Rebel

When William Shakespeare created the character we know as Falstaff, he was doing a gross injustice to a hero of English Protestantism. The flamboyant, roguish, heavy-drinking and somewhat endearing aged knight, who would encourage Prince Hal in his licentious behaviour in three of the plays and die offstage in a fourth, was originally presented on stage as Sir John Oldcastle.

In the original text of *Henry IV Part One* the Prince's objectionable companion was named as Oldcastle, and a reference to this survives the rewrite when Hal referred to him once as 'my old lad of the Castle'. When the play was first presented its writer met a furore. He had presented a much-revered Protestant martyr as a drunkard, a thief and an encourager of the Prince's dissipation. This reaction was understandable in an Elizabethan England in a continual state of paranoia over the recurring Catholic threat. Shakespeare was obliged to change his character's name, grabbing a corruption of that of Sir John Fastolf, a knight he had heard lived somewhere around that time, and who had gained an undeserved reputation for cowardice. For the second part of *Henry IV* he even wrote an epilogue, which stated categorically that Falstaff was not Oldcastle, in order to deflect further criticism.

The real Sir John Oldcastle, alias Lord Cobham, alias Lord Oldcastle, was a charismatic and accomplished magnate of the early days of the Lancastrian monarchy. He certainly was a personal friend of Prince Hal, the future Henry V, but not the feeder of his riots; the

Prince was not in fact as unruly as Shakespeare portrayed him. There is no evidence that Oldcastle was crooked or cowardly, nor that he was old: he was probably in his thirties when Hal was Prince of Wales. Over a century later Oldcastle would be venerated as one who suffered and died in the Protestant cause. He appears in *Foxe's Boke of Martyrs*, first published in 1563, and in a hagiography written by John Bale among other works, all with the most favourable comments on his character.

Oldcastle might otherwise have been a counsellor and servant of King Henry V, and certainly an able and loyal soldier on the campaigns in France. He would have been counted among the respected and accomplished nobles of this colourful reign. Instead, he spent this time as a prisoner and then a fugitive, a rebel against his former royal friend with a price on his head, finally to die in a horrific public execution, burned as a heretic. Sir John Oldcastle was a Lollard.

Heresy, the holding of religious beliefs incompatible with the doctrines of the Catholic Church, was condemned as an abomination, an agency of Satan. Over the centuries many movements appeared in support of one alternative religious understanding or another, usually answered with harsh and destructive reprisals from the established Church and its supporters. Such heresies included in the early Christian centuries Arianism, Monophysitism and Docetism, in the twelfth Catharism and Waldensianism, and in the late fourteenth and fifteenth centuries the related movements of Lollardy and Hussitism. Controversies over the nature of Christ, the nature of the Trinity, whether the Church should give its wealth to the poor, on reincarnation and so on, each had their time. Those who proclaimed such deviant doctrines were usually persecuted savagely at the Church's urging and it was only from the Reformation of the sixteenth century that any alternative interpretations of Christian doctrine and practice established themselves in western Europe. Martin Luther, it could be argued, was just another heretic, but one who succeeded in establishing his teaching because it was politically expedient for his prince, although at one point the Catholic Church came very close indeed to burning him.

In England there was little appearance of heresy before the fourteenth century and the ecclesiastical and civil authorities were scarcely equipped to resist it. Although the penalty in canon law for unrepentant heretics was excommunication and then delivery to the secular authorities for execution, this was hardly practicable, as the Common Law of England did not provide for it. But late in that century the Oxford academic John Wycliffe had caused much serious debate on his theological pronouncements, many of which explicitly contradicted Catholic dogma. He questioned the validity of the Eucharist, and both the temporal wealth and role in the administering of divine grace of the ordained clergy. He called for a Bible in English, which all should interpret according to their conscience. Many of his views were later echoed by Luther, Calvin and other leaders of the Protestant Reformation and Wycliffe is considered a precursor of Anglicanism. For a time, powerful protectors made it possible for Wycliffe to continue, but the more extreme tenets of his teachings caused even John of Gaunt to withdraw his support. Wycliffe was eventually forced out of the university and ended his life in 1384 as a parish priest.

His followers, dubbed Lollards, or 'mumblers', came from every rank in society. Many known Lollards were craftsmen or lesser tradesmen, although priests and academics appear too. This mirrored the early Reformation a century later. But Lollards were also knights and gentry, including Oldcastle. There were many women, often of the towns, the prospect of their preaching anathema to the established Church. The Lollards had no formal organisation to speak of, but a loose association was in evidence with a traffic in written material on issues of religious thought.

Throughout Europe the Catholic Church was weakened, divided and its influence impaired. From 1378 there were popes in Rome and Avignon, and nations would recognise the authority of one or the other as suited them. In the early years of the fifteenth century, Jan Hus, Rector of Prague University, was preaching doctrines that almost paralleled those of Wycliffe. It is not clear whether Wycliffe influenced the rise of the Hussite heresy in Bohemia at the end of the fourteenth century when Bohemian scholars heard him preach at Oxford, or whether Hus drew on influences closer to home. Either way, the Hussites held views that the Lollards mostly agreed with.

Lollards were persecuted in the reign of Richard II, but the English Common Law could do little to curb the heresy and Wycliffe's doctrines gained support from every stratum of English society. There was even a small group of Lollard knights at Richard's court, who were more or less tolerated because they did not voice their beliefs too strongly. Some of these were at court in the early years of the next reign, still discreet about their views.

It was the coup of Henry Bolingbroke in 1399 that brought a dramatic change of attitude, when he seized the throne from Richard and styled himself Henry IV. Such usurpation on very suspect legal grounds could only benefit from the endorsement of the Church, and the new king had the support of Archbishop Arundel, who had previously joined him in exile. Arundel who called for draconian action against what he saw as the threat of heresy, and he expected recompense for endorsing the Lancastrian coup.

Henry agreed to this in the Parliament of 1402 by granting the statute *De Heretico Comburendo,* which made burning alive the expected final penalty for heresy in England. Rather than bringing the Inquisition to England, the bishops retained the right to confine suspected heretics and to give them the opportunity to abandon their erroneous beliefs, and so the established religious courts still tried cases of heresy. For obstinate or lapsed heretics, it was now envisaged, the penalty would now be death by the flame. Although only one Lollard, William Sawtry, was burned soon after for declaring that the bread of the Eucharist remained bread, and no other until 1410, such a fate was now established as a deterrent. Even Wycliffe's remains were exhumed and burnt in 1427.

To be a Lollard thenceforth had more serious political significance. Now Lollards were accused of seeking to overthrow the monarchy. Such heretics did indeed have an interest in who ruled over them, and the need for secrecy to survive in a hostile state was vital. Not all were politically motivated, but each now had cause to fear for their lives. Many people, Lollards included, believed that the murdered King Richard still lived, somewhere far away, and such rumours spread, to the chagrin of the Lancastrian regime.

The birth of Sir John Oldcastle is not recorded and is given varying dates between 1370 and 1380, some say even as early as 1360. He was born into a substantial gentry family of Herefordshire, a county bordering Wales, at his own family seat at Almeley close to the border. The Oldcastles had been loyal servants of the Crown in that county for generations, at times sheriffs and members of Parliament. After 1400, fighting on the Welsh Marches intensified as Owein Glyndwr led his successful revolt against English domination. The young Sir John Oldcastle was serving as a knight in the retinue of Lord Grey of Codnor by 1400 and soon gained positions of responsibility. In 1401 he was given the keeping of Builth Castle and not long after, that at Kidwelly. In 1409 he also did service on the Scottish border and for a time was appointed Joint Keeper of the West March.

Oldcastle married three times, although only the third, long-lasting marriage was significant. First, probably as a youth, he married Catherine, the daughter of Richard ap Jevan, evidently one of many cross-border matches of the time and his eldest son John was born of that union. The date and manner of her death are not known and Oldcastle married a second time, but no details survive of this marriage apart from its issue: another son and three daughters. In 1408 he made his third match to Joan de la Pole. Daughter of a gentleman of Essex, she had already been married three times, including once to Lord Cobham, and had inherited his extensive lands in Kent, which included the new castle at Cooling. The title and estates then passed to Oldcastle, but it is uncertain whether he was styled Lord Cobham, for although summoned to the 1409 Parliament as a baron he was often addressed as Lord Oldcastle.

Oldcastle probably became a friend of the future Henry V when the Prince campaigned in the Welsh marches early in his father's reign, and by 1410 the knight was a well-established royal servant. He had already been a justice of the peace in 1406 and sheriff in 1409 and had sat in Parliament, first in the Commons before his summons to the Lords.

Oldcastle served on the English expedition to France in 1411. This campaign, to aid the Burgundian faction against the Armagnac, was ordered by the Prince during his father's illness. It accomplished little in the event, although Oldcastle's association with the commanders the Earl of Arundel and Sir Gilbert Umfraville gained him some further prestige. Oldcastle's military record on the Scottish border and in France had brought him some regard. In 1411 he participated in a celebrated tournament at Lille, where three English knights fought against three Frenchmen. The result is not known, but none were badly hurt as they all dined together that night. Sir John Oldcastle was therefore a much-acclaimed knight, and of high regard among the great. He could easily have advanced in rank and service in the oncoming reign.

Where he was first attracted to Lollardy is not known for sure. Lollard preachers such as William Swinderby and William Brute were active in Herefordshire by 1390. Oldcastle was well-educated and cultivated, was known to have read at least some religious tracts of this kind and was probably a heretic from his youth. He must at first have been discreet about his views, for he would not otherwise have gained such favour in the reign of Henry IV.

Did the Prince know that his friend was a Lollard? There is no way of knowing, but if so, he made no issue of it at the time. The House of Lancaster relied heavily on the support of the Church, but perhaps not as much the Prince of Wales personally. He publicly resolved with others in 1406, following a petition to Parliament, to take steps against the spread of heresy, but did little in reality. Perhaps he thought that as long as Oldcastle kept it secret there would be no cause for concern. But when Henry became king he was forced to defer to the prelates, and when his friend was exposed he could not easily protect him. We do not know what Henry's personal religious views really were, or whether he would be prepared to tolerate heresy in a good friend. Or perhaps Oldcastle succeeded in keeping his secret even from his friend and patron.

On his accession in 1413 Henry V presented himself as paragon of religious orthodoxy. His hair cropped in a fashion that made him look like a priest, he gave his full support to the war against heresy that his archbishop was waging. Many Lollards disliked the new king, dubbing him the 'Bishop's Prince'. Henry had on his accession chosen the Carmelite Friar Dr Stephen Partington as one of his confessors, who had once fought Wycliffe tooth and nail at Oxford. How much of this sprang from the need to maintain the support of the ecclesiastics is uncertain, for it is not easy to separate genuine religious fervour from pragmatism. Henry was not pleased about some of the excesses of the bishops in their attack on heresy, as events later show, but made little attempt to curb them.

While Henry IV was suffering his last illness a new climate of religious intolerance was growing and Archbishop Arundel embarked on a renewed persecution of Lollards. He had been active in recent years purging Oxford University of Lollardy, and the Oxford academic Master Peter Payne, who fled the country to live in Bohemia, was one victim. In 1410, Arundel had arranged the burning of one John Badby, the first so sentenced since Sawtry. The Prince, present at the burning, at one point had the fire put out in order to offer a final chance to recant. Badby chose martyrdom instead, and the fire was rekindled.

There was an attempt at the parliament of 1412, which Oldcastle attended, to repeal the Comburendo statute, but without success. Arundel decided that the coming new reign should begin with a clean sweep, and shortly before the old king died in March 1413, the

Archbishop summoned a convocation for the purpose of organising a new onslaught against heresy. Oldcastle's was the first name under discussion on the opening day.

The archbishop's interest in Oldcastle probably began with an incident in April 1410. Arundel had written to the Dean of Rochester stating that a certain John, a chaplain in Oldcastle's household, had been preaching Lollard doctrines in Cooling and nearby villages, and instructed the Dean to place these areas under an interdict, where Mass and most other sacraments were prohibited. This prohibition was not too effective; it was relaxed for the marriage of Oldcastle's stepdaughter to a knight of proven orthodoxy and not strictly enforced afterwards.

Oldcastle was known at the time to correspond with the Hussite heretics in Bohemia. It is unlikely that he actually led the English Lollards, but he was among the most senior in social status and often considered a leader, whether he took an active part in the movement or not.

Arundel summoned a chaplain named John Ley to the convocation, who may have been Oldcastle's priest. Soon after, he gained some more useful evidence. An illuminator of Paternoster Row in London had recently been found with a collection of short Lollard tracts in his possession, all explosive in their content. The man claimed that they belonged to Oldcastle, and this was taken as evidence enough.

A few weeks later, as the death and funeral of Henry IV soon followed and delayed the proceedings, Arundel read one captured book out to the new king, then lodged at Kennington. Oldcastle was present at this reading and claimed that he had only read two pages of the book. But Arundel now had enough to accuse him of heretical beliefs, sedition and the harbouring and protecting of unlicensed priests, none of which could be simply disregarded.

Henry V reminded the Archbishop of the loyal support and friendship of Oldcastle, and tried to resolve the matter by persuading the baron to recant, at least by outward show. But being exposed, Oldcastle now affirmed his convictions, refusing to retreat from them. Henry saw him in his privy chamber, trying to diffuse what was becoming a dangerous confrontation. As king and still in need of the endorsement of the Church to remain so, he was now constrained by Arundel's demands and found it difficult to protect his friend.

But still Oldcastle refused even to pretend to repudiate his heresies. He may have believed that he should stand on his convictions, or perhaps he did not think he was in danger. But Arundel resolved to proceed with his charges. Oldcastle sped away to his castle at Cooling and shut himself inside, refusing to receive anyone. The archbishop's summoner could not gain entry to perform his office. Arundel would not be denied; he had letters nailed to the door of Rochester Cathedral summoning Oldcastle to answer charges at Leeds Castle on 11 September. When the baron did not appear on that day, he was excommunicated.

It is not known how Oldcastle was apprehended and imprisoned in the Tower of London, but likely that he called on the new king at Windsor with a confession of his faith. Henry refused to listen but referred this document and its author to the prelates, who quickly decided to have Oldcastle arrested. Henry was now unable to prevent the proceedings, and he was forced to break with his friend.

There was something of the stance of Martin Luther a century later at Oldcastle's trial. At the Diet of Worms in 1517 Luther was similarly required to recant his beliefs on possible pain of death and was apparently obliged by his conscience to answer, 'Here I stand... I can do no other.' Even if the quotation is inaccurate, the sentiment is true and Luther refused to recant. For Oldcastle, it was a similar choice that confronted him; martyrdom is not a fate that one invites lightly. Not long before, Oldcastle had written to a contact in Prague that one should never lose hold of truth, even unto death, and by the look of it he was seriously practising what he preached, dire as the consequences could be. He did not begin with this stance when he was questioned on 13 September on four tenets of faith, but at first set out on a course of sophistry.

At first, Sir John eloquently presented his case to the tribunal that he was a good Christian whose views were not incompatible with those of the Church. He affirmed that the Sacrament was the Body of Christ and that true contrition was the only route to forgiveness of sins. These at face value echoed Catholic doctrine. On addressing further allegations he then tackled two more sensitive issues that Lollards had often spoken of. The worship of images was condemned in Scripture, he pointed out. As to whether pilgrimages did any good, as Lollards disapproved of them, Oldcastle stated that 'every man dwelling on the Earth was a Pilgrim' (according to John Bale).

This well-considered defence might have him acquitted in a more sympathetic court, and many present at the gathering showed a favourable disposition. But Arundel was determined to see this heretic brought down despite any eloquence on his part. He now quizzed the knight on the finer points of his convictions. When the bread turned into the Body of Christ, did any of the bread remain? And was forgiveness for one's sins only effective when confessed to an ordained priest? And was the Eucharist not a sacrament, *delivered by a priest*? There now followed a lengthy wrangle. The knight walked a tightrope, between refusal to lie about his beliefs and avoiding condemning himself. His opponents sought to catch him out.

Eventually, the defendant's composure was worn down. He became more aggressive as he argued from Scripture against what he saw to be erroneous Catholic doctrine. He compared the prelates to the Pharisees. At one point he turned to the public there assembled and burst out: 'These men who are bent on damning me mislead themselves, and will drag you down to Hell. Therefore beware of them.' The verdict was exactly as expected. The Archbishop, in consultation with Dr Walden the Prior of the Carmelites, finally pronounced Oldcastle to have declared himself a heretic.

All he had said were standard Lollard tenets, enough to condemn him to the flames. Some of the bishops favoured caution however, and the king's reluctance to see his former friend burn also stayed his execution at this time. Oldcastle was returned to the Tower and given forty days to reconsider.

Before this time elapsed, he had escaped. He had some assistance and went into hiding in the house of William Fisher, a parchment maker on Turnwell Lane Clerkenwell, which was then part of the Cobham estates. How Oldcastle 'broke' the Tower on 19 October as Bale described, is a mystery. The very nature of this stronghold made it the most secure prison in which the kings would confine their enemies. A double set of walls around the Norman keep, themselves surrounded by a moat and guarded at every point, made escape seem impossible. In its long history only a handful of people ever made good an escape from the Tower, and usually through subterfuge, which involved leaving through the main door in disguise or with the connivance of the guards. There is no surviving account of Oldcastle's flight, except that Robert Wrothe and William Fisher aided his escape. It has been suggested that he was allowed to get away, that by some means the vigilance of the guards evaporated at the appropriate time, and the keeper of the Tower was accused at one point. If so, it would need a powerful friend of the knight to order it.

Some even think the king himself allowed his friend to escape. If he had, it would have soon proved an ill-advised action. Perhaps Oldcastle had well-wishers who did not want to see him burn, whatever his religious views. None appear to know how exactly Oldcastle got away, and only some suggestion of the connivance of the mighty is present, but not enough to present a case for it. Oldcastle was a popular figure with the Londoners, described as 'a stout knight of Christ'. Many would at least do little to prevent his escape.

The Lollards, allegedly under Oldcastle's leadership, planned a coup for Twelfth Night 1414. As the king and his brothers were set to keep Christmas at Eltham a band disguised as mummers were to gain entry and overpower the court, a strategy that reprised an attempt on the life of Henry IV in 1400. Meanwhile there would be a gathering of Lollards at Fickett's Field, an open space near Temple Bar. Such were the secret plans, soon related by traitors in the Lollards' midst to the king's officials.

What the insurgents really wished to do is not at all certain. The stories that reached the king told of Oldcastle's intent to kill him and his three brothers, that the mob would occupy London, slaughter the senior clergy, seize relics and church valuables, and so on. Some have suggested that Oldcastle wanted to capture the king and impose an agreement of toleration, but no evidence supports this. It is not even established that Oldcastle was directly involved in this rising. The fact remains that the Lollards knew that under this regime they would be hunted for their beliefs and burned for them. Large crowds journeyed to London in the days before from Leicestershire, Daventry, Hertfordshire and throughout the Midlands. On meeting on the road, many would ask other travellers their destination, and if told 'to Cobham,' they would be greeted as fellow Lollards. Sir John might not have led this movement, but he was certainly its figurehead.

The king was already aware of all this. Over the holiday period all strangers seen in the vicinity of Eltham were arrested. Fisher's house was being watched. On 8 January, Henry and his court suddenly decamped to Westminster, and on the next night he and his men went out to confront the gathering at Fickett's Field. Latecomers on the way to London were already being arrested.

Henry ordered that the gates of London be locked, preventing those inside from joining the rebels. By the morning an army had arrived, and the assembly was dispersed with many captured. The king soon ordered the erection of 'Loller's Gallows', communal gibbets at nearby

St Giles' Fields, and set about hanging many of those caught at the gathering. Accounts vary, but one says sixty-nine met their end there. There are on record five knights, five esquires and six priests hanged. Sir Roger Acton, a Lollard knight formerly of Richard II's court, was hanged at St Giles, his body left hanging for a month before it was interred under the gallows. Soon afterwards the king pardoned some rebels, contented that most of the prominent ones had been dealt with.

Of Oldcastle, however, there was no sign. No account shows him even at the assembly. The king's men broke into Fisher's house where they found heretical tracts but the heretic himself had gone. The knight had disappeared and a four-year search began to bring him to justice. Within days the king issued a proclamation: a thousand marks for anyone who brought about his capture, and any village who informed on him freed from tallages, subsidies and other taxes for ever.

Oldcastle's possessions were then declared confiscated, and he was ordered to appear to answer charges at Brentford on 7 June. On not appearing he was outlawed. His wife was arrested and thrown into the Tower, but released soon afterwards. The hunt for him went on, but as he was nowhere to be found Henry turned his attentions toward France.

In 1415 the king made his celebrated expedition to France, and his spectacular victories at Harfleur and Agincourt are covered in many an account. From 1417 Henry continued to campaign, winning territory in northern France and bringing the Plantagenet claim to its crown closer to reality than ever. Had Oldcastle not clashed with the archbishop and as a result his king, he would have been a trusted and no doubt successful captain in these wars. He lived as a fugitive during this time, none knew where or how.

The Schism that had harmed the Church for so long was in the process of repair in these years. A new widespread belief that such issues could be solved by councils of the senior clergy of Christendom turned into action at Constance in 1414. Eventually, after three years of council there was only one pope in Rome, and Hus, lured to the Council under a false safe-conduct, was burned for his heresy. Also in 1414, Archbishop Arundel died, but the Lollards had little reason to breathe more easily for this. His successor, Henry Chichele, was as determined to eradicate heresy and would burn a number of Lollards over his three decades in office.

It was the continuing link between the Lollard heresy and political sedition that kept the repression alive. War with Scotland accompanied the fighting in France for a time, and there were by 1417 new rumours of Richard II still living and at the Scottish court. The Duke of Albany in fact had an imposter living in his household, hoping to use him against the Lancastrian regime. The Lollards, who saw Richard as their benefactor, were inclined to believe this. In reality he did nothing, but this was preferable to promoting persecution as Henry and his father had done.

There was a tale that Albany and Oldcastle met in secret at Pontefract. Although this is not verified, there is evidence of some understanding between the Lollards and the Scots. Albany was in fact weary of maintaining this pseudo-Richard and wanted him to act. Soon there were Lollards in the shires proclaiming Richard's imminent return. It was alleged that Oldcastle was hiding out in a peasant's cottage near St Albans. Soon after the king's men raided a house at Barnet and found Lollard writings and conventional religious books with the names of saints and the Virgin rubbed out. These were exhibited with a sense of outrage.

The Duke of Bedford, Henry's brother then acting as regent, renewed the reward for Oldcastle's capture. This finally produced the desired result, and Oldcastle was taken near Welshpool in 1417. It is said he was discovered at the village of Broniarth by two gentlemen and two yeomen who were tenants of Edward Charlton, Lord of Powys. Oldcastle fought valiantly, making good use of his martial skills. According to the legend a woman banged his shin with a footstool during the scuffle and the four only then overpowered him. Gravely injured, he was taken to London on a horse litter.

Oldcastle was brought before a new tribunal where Arundel's successor Archbishop Chichele read the original indictment. There was little effort on either side to bring about a recantation. Oldcastle threw himself on the court's mercy, but the Lord Chief Justice urged the regent to proceed with the penalty. Oldcastle then stated that he only recognised the justice of King Richard, who was in Scotland, the final defiance of a doomed man. Henry V, then in France on campaign, was at least spared the sight of his old friend burned to death. Sir John Oldcastle was taken to St Giles Fields on 14 December 1417. He was suspended on a gallows by a chain passed around his body and a fire built beneath him. It was a terrible death, but his accusers would hardly settle for less.

This was by no means the end of Lollardy. Long after Oldcastle's execution there were Lollards meeting in secret, circulating writings and keeping their doctrines alive. A few were burned at Smithfield in later decades, and in fact there were still Lollards at the time of the English Reformation the following century. But the loss of Oldcastle saw the end of aristocratic leadership of the movement.

There remains one mystery. While there was no doubt that Oldcastle was a heretic, and his views unacceptable to the established religion of the time, his alleged actions as a rebel do not appear fully consistent. From his escape to his final capture Oldcastle was demonised by the authorities. He was reputedly the leader of a conspiracy to kill the king and all his family and would have destroyed the Holy Church and all its true priests, take away Communion plate and scatter the relics of saints; such was his portrayal. Arundel wrote to Pope Martin telling of his vile intentions, and why all good Catholics had cause to live in fear. But first it must be remembered that while Sir John was accused of all manner of heterodox religious beliefs, there was no allegation at his trial in 1413 that he advocated any attack on *secular* authority. He was in his time a loyal servant of the king and the Prince of Wales, and while in favour he showed no such tendency. Although he was credited with calling the assembly at Fickett's Field, he was almost certainly not even there. Did he escape as the royal troops attacked, or was he absent from the gathering? The king's men hoped to find him at Fisher's house before he appeared, but he had obviously fled by then. This does not seem the action of a leader of an uprising.

Sedition and Lollardy had been linked before. Even the Peasants' Revolt of 1381 is believed to have had some Lollard influence. Arundel's persecution propaganda included sedition as one of its accusations of Lollardy. Only after Oldcastle had escaped would this strange gathering of 1414 happen, and this of a pitifully small number.

Of course one cannot assume that the average Lollard entertained serious intentions of overthrowing the Lancastrian monarchy, but survival was uppermost in their priorities. To worship as they thought fitting, to read prohibited books or even to appear unenthusiastic over the Mass, confession or pilgrimages, would mean living in fear of discovery. The prospect of being burned alive was sobering to even the most resolute of Lollards. Arundel and the other bishops did not seem to let even a lukewarm response to Catholic observance go uninvestigated. So it would have been an attractive proposition to replace the regime with one with greater religious tolerance.

This meant treason against the king – but the legitimacy of the House of Lancaster could be questioned. Henry IV had been threatened by attempts to overthrow him and Henry V's military activities in France were in part designed to bring his house prestige and keep his nobles occupied with thoughts other than rebellion. The belief that Richard II had been amenable to Lollardy, together with the rumours of Richard still living, attracted many Lollards to opposition to the Lancastrian monarchy. At least politically, the Lollards were not united in their views, but politics and religion overlapped on the issue of the Lancastrian kings' support for repression of Lollardy.

If Oldcastle was the leader of this Lollard-inspired revolt, he might have been forced into it. Some suggest he wanted to defeat the regime and gain a pledge of tolerance as the price for peace. If so, it would have been a naïve course of action, as hindsight shows. It is true that Oldcastle still regarded Henry favourably but, like the king, he might have been forced to consider serious measures even against old friends.

It would be far-fetched to see him hiding in Clerkenwell oblivious to this planned gathering, when it was certainly the worst-kept secret of the time. The assembled rebels saw him as their leader, which hints that he did not repudiate such a course of action. Although his part in the 1414 rising is in doubt, Sir John was known to intrigue with the regime's enemies. He certainly showed support for the false Richard II. In the weeks before his capture he was in Wales in conference with Mareddudd, son of Owain Glyndwr. Glyndwr had twice supported revolts against Henry IV. Was Oldcastle seeking to build a new coalition against the Lancastrian monarchy?

The manner in which the Tudor writers revered Sir John Oldcastle was little short of how Catholics saw their saints. He suffered and died for his beliefs, it is true, but not exactly because he refused to repudiate them. His strategy at his trial was chiefly to affirm his Christian views without committing himself to doctrines clearly heretical. This only failed to save him because Arundel was determined to burn him whatever he said. Furthermore, he had every reason to believe at this time the new king would protect him if it went badly, but then he had not reckoned with Henry's new-found zeal for orthodoxy, or else his sense of pragmatism. Sir John can still be commended for not speaking against his convictions, but then he almost certainly realised during the tribunal that Arundel was already stoking the fire for him, set on making an example. Rather than repudiate Lollardy without saving himself, he first prevaricated and then affirmed his creed.

Oldcastle's tragedy was to live too early, when the Catholic Church demanded no compromise as to thought and belief, at a time of repression of heterodoxy, and when the only way to replace a vindictive regime was rebellion. He is thought to have been forced by necessity to become a rebel against his nature. Was this a justifiable act? The majority of Lollards simply worshipped in secret, fearing discovery. Oldcastle by the look of it eventually decided on armed revolt, seeing this to be the only course of action, in order to survive. But one alternative remains; he could have followed Payne to Prague, where those of similar views flourished.

Those were harsh times for believers. It is not difficult to see how Sir John Oldcastle was drawn into extreme reaction. His intentions are still cause for debate.

16

Etienne de Vignolles, Called La Hire

The Freelance Plunderer and the Holy Maid

It has always been the case wherever wars are fought that the civilian populations suffers where the armies come. The Hundred Years War was no different, despite the insistence of the commanders on the tenets of chivalry, it was the common people of France who suffered mass murder, rape, plundering and all manner of atrocities, from French knights and soldiers as much as the English invaders. The French also fought a civil war in the later stages, and the Lancastrian phase of the wars, the last part from 1412 to 1453, showed a serious disregard of fundamental human values.

One feature throughout the wars was the result of poor management of the armies, intermittent as the fighting often was. How easily soldiers fighting in France could turn into marauding brigands, detaching themselves from the armies and setting themselves up as plunderers and protection racketeers. All too often the English commanders called a campaign to an end somewhere in the depths of France, leaving many soldiers and their aristocratic captains with no means of getting home, and it stood to reason that many turned to brigandage. French troops, not as far from their homes, might also take that route, and bands of *routiers* might include former soldiers of the English, French and Burgundian armies in common cause.

One routier captain was Segun de Badefol, whose band in the 1360s formed part of a larger army called the *Tard-Venus* ('the Late-Comers'). Another was the English adventurer Sir John Hawkwood, who eventually led his company to Florence, where he flourished as a mercenary. A third, John Fotheringay, based his company's activities on the road between Paris and Compiègne where he was known to have made over 100,000 marks on letters of safe-conduct alone. These were genuinely 'free-lances' often nominally in the service of their king, but in practice they made their way as they pleased. At times it would not be easy to tell the difference between a regular army and these routier bands, except when campaigns were not under way. Some such bands were known as *écorcheurs,* or flayers, as they would often divest their victims of even their clothes, if they did not actually flay them alive. They struck terror into the local populations wherever they were, whatever side they supported.

One such *routier,* Etienne de Vignolles, called La Hire, lived this lifestyle and at the same time served the Valois monarchy. He is revered as a national hero, even though he was at least as bad an oppressor of the French people as the English enemy.

The campaign that Henry V of England took to Agincourt in 1415 began an important and dramatic phase of the Hundred Years War. Although the Agincourt expedition did not gain in territory as much as it did in prestige, it was reprised in later years by more effective campaigning, which brought Normandy under English occupation and made possible the Treaty of Troyes in 1420, which sealed Henry's marriage to Katherine de Valois and his own succession to the crown of France.

Domestic affairs in France made that time the best for the English cause. Charles VI being insane, and the Armagnac and Burgundian factions, each headed by senior members of the ruling Valois family, fighting a civil war. After John the Fearless, Duke of Burgundy was murdered by the Armagnacs, his successor and faction took to supporting the English claim to the throne, at least in name, which made the Treaty of Troyes possible. The Armagnacs, now supporting the claim of the Dauphin Charles against the English, carried on the war, although it was most of France south of the Loire that they could claim as their territory, while the Burgundian faction dominated most of northern France, and gave the English access to Paris.

When in August 1422 Henry V died of dysentery only weeks before Charles VI's demise, there was no radical change to this situation and despite the reign of the infant King Henry VI, the English war machine trundled on. John Duke of Bedford, brother of the dead king, acted as regent in the lands the English held in France and in his time this territory expanded to the fullest in the entire period of the wars. He did not find it easy, given a shortage of funding from the home country and the attitude of Philip the Good, the new Duke of Burgundy, who was really conducting a civil war independently with the Armagnacs and did not make a reliable ally. Still, the conquest of France by the House of Lancaster proceeded, if less rapidly or dramatically.

Etienne de Vignolles was born in 1390 or thereabouts, son of a knight of the town of Vignolles in the Bigorre region, his birthplace given as Préchacq-les-Bains, In a county that had been signed over to Edward III thirty years before, Etienne was raised to hate the English bitterly. We know little of his life before he entered royal service. Where he gained the name La Hire is not certain; it is believed that it simply meant 'Anger', and that the Burgundians saw him as anger personified. The name might also contain reference to a hedgehog, for his prickly nature. Etienne de Vignolles was soon known for a violent nature and a foul temper. He was also known for his brightly coloured clothes and the bells on his scarlet tunic.

From an early stage it was said that La Hire was a routier. Records on this time in his life are practically non-existent, but soon he took on the role of steadfast soldier in the service of the Dauphin.

While Henry V embarked on his conquest of Normandy in 1417, the Burgundian and Armagnac factions continued to fight each other. It was in 1418 that La Hire turned from brigandage to royal service. In that year John the Fearless gained control of Paris and executed the Count of Armagnac. The Dauphin Charles, heir to the throne, was forced out of the city and the Burgundian faction could claim to be the government. After John was assassinated the following year by those Armagnacs who now sided with the Dauphin, the Burgundians now recognised the claim of Henry V to France. The English derided the Dauphin for an army composed of knights-errant as it seemed.

La Hire's offer to bring his following to aid the Dauphinist (or Armagnac) cause was much welcomed. The Dauphinists made much use of irregular soldiers, and La Hire was simply one of those taken into royal service. La Hire was soon created Bailly of Vermandois, and installed himself at Laon. Another like him was Jean Poton de Xaintrailles, who also offered his services. Poton and La Hire were virtually two of a kind, routiers from south-west France, landless warriors who sought material gain by force of arms, and often fought the English together; their bromance was legendary.

In 1421 the two captains were fighting in Picardy, and heard that Coucy Castle, of which Poton's brother Pierre Poton de Xantrailles was chatelain, had been taken over by Burgundians. Two of the brother's servants had released a number of pro-Burgundian prisoners. Poton and La Hire stormed the castle, but the former captives countered by throwing large rocks. The two fought on but were forced to admit defeat. La Hire captured sixty Burgundians and took them to Guise at swordpoint.

La Hire took part in the Battle of Baugé, the first French victory since Agincourt. On 22 March 1421, Thomas of Lancaster, Duke of Clarence, brother to Henry V, was returning from a raid across the Loire and decided on impulse to attack a French force reinforced by Scottish troops that outnumbered his own forces. The result was not only defeat, but Clarence himself and three commanders were killed and Clarence's stepsons John Earl of Somerset and Sir Thomas Beaufort captured. King Henry and his two surviving brothers were much aggrieved at Clarence's death, but there was no sign of the English conquest reversing.

In fact, both at Cravant in 1423 and Verneuil the next year, the English soundly defeated the Dauphinists. After Henry V died in August 1422, his next surviving brother John Duke of Bedford acted as Regent in France on behalf of the infant King Henry VI and showed himself no less able a commander. He had at least the nominal support of the Burgundian faction, as much as the Duke of Brittany. The English either held most of northern France or the pro-Burgundian nobles did, and the powerful elements of Paris gave the English access.

But after Verneuil the impetus of the English advance was slower. Even though they expected to win in the end, there were fewer spectacular victories, and it was now more of a relentless grind. Bedford was constantly uneasy over the attitude of the Duke of Burgundy. Philip the Good might not act so much in tandem with the English forces but would often withdraw his forces when they could have aided the conquest, and at times he made truces with the Dauphinists independently of Bedford. He was fighting his war with the other faction, and obviously using the English for his own purposes. Bedford was constantly worried, as the Burgundian alliance was the keystone of English attempts to gain recognition for their king. Bedford even married Anne of Burgundy, Philip's sister. His brother Humphrey's designs on the Low Countries where Philip was empire-building did the alliance no good, but Burgundy decided to continue it for the present.

In the last years of that decade the English had consolidated their hold over the right bank of the Loire. Thomas Montague, Earl of Salisbury, had laid siege to Orleans but found it a longer-term project to force its surrender. Salisbury was killed at the siege by a cannon ball and his replacement the Earl of Suffolk carried on the siege in a pedestrian manner, withdrawing the soldiers to winter quarters for a time. The English saw it only as a matter of time before their final victory and had become complacent. When the Dauphin's armies attempted to lift the siege and made little impression, they had every reason not to expect serious opposition.

La Hire had campaigned incessantly through the 1420s, a hybrid of guerrilla tactics and unashamed brigandage. During this time he was injured when part of a chimney collapsed as he slept, and he walked with a limp ever afterwards. By early 1429 he was at Orleans, and fighting as valiantly as ever, even though the English had the advantage. The Battle of the Herrings was one engagement. On 12 February a Dauphinist-Scottish force intercepted an English supply train of some 300 carts, bearing arrows and other armaments, and also barrels of herrings that were much needed to feed the English during Lent. Sir John Fastolf beat them off, many barely escaping with their lives. La Hire commanded the rearguard and at least enabled the main force to escape after what was a sore defeat.

It is well known how Joan of Arc, the peasant girl from Lorraine professing to be the choice of God himself to save France from the English, led the Dauphin's army to regain important territories and had the Dauphin crowned as Charles VII, and how she was captured, tried as a witch and burned alive. Closer scrutiny begs questions. We have mostly heard the story as based on the hagiography that the Catholic Church endorsed, our perception probably then coloured with theatrical versions by George Bernard Shaw and Jean Anouilh. There are other interpretations; some on the French side as well as the English saw her as a satanic witch. Shakespeare agreed with this and had her attended by demons to which she fed her blood. Some have wondered if she was simply psychotic, or if a deficiency of sugar in her diet convinced her that saints and angels attended her as she guarded the family's goats on long days in the field.

When she came to the court of the Dauphin in 1429 Joan found a highly attentive audience in its head. Dauphin Charles had heard little other than discouraging news for some time, and was then at his wit's end. The English had laid siege to the city of Orleans, that dominated an important crossing of the Loire and had beaten off any attempts by the Dauphinist army to drive them back. Many simply saw it as a matter of time before Orleans fell, and the English armies poured into central France. Allowing for how persuasive Joan was once she made her mind up, Charles agreed to sending her to Orleans as an act of desperation. He might also have thought that if she really was a divine choice, he should not say her nay.

It is not as well-known how sceptical so many of the French commanders were at the prospect of this Holy Maid as saviour. It was in fact La Hire who first endorsed Joan as she arrived at Orleans on 3 May. Why he did is unclear and perhaps he was not as cynical as one might think. Perhaps he pragmatically saw her as a morale booster, but it is certain that he thought highly of her, and their association continued while Joan was active.

When Joan reached Orleans in May, Jacques Dunois, Bastard of Orleans and a commander of the Dauphinist forces, was faced with his expedition across the Loire being held up when the winds blew the wrong way, and his latest attempt to outflank the besieging army was frustrated. When Joan arrived the wind suddenly changed, making the crossing possible. Very soon La Hire and others led the troops to engage the English, forcing the Earl of Suffolk to lift the siege and retreat to the upper Loire valley. From that point the Armagnac (or Dauphinist) persuasion applied its augmented morale and the English advance of previous years was rolled back. The Pucelle was definitely a divine appointee, the commanders decided, and she was proof that God was ready to save France from the English.

Now rather than simply La Hire, the Duke of Alençon, Dunois, and Gilles de Rais the hereditary Marshal (and almost certainly a mass murderer), all showed their faith in Joan. The Dauphin himself appears to have been ambivalent but did not complain about how the tide had turned. One might wonder how much input Joan gave to the fighting itself; she had little real idea of military strategy and was probably not strong enough to take on adult soldiers or knights herself. It was in fact the Duc d'Alençon in overall command, despite all the legends. But her presence at the head of the army giving the impression of both righteousness and invincibility was the best weapon the Dauphinists had. She was 'lucky' when she was there. La Hire was her close associate when the French laboured to take Jargeau, Beaugency, Patay and other towns and castles to the north of Orleans.

At Patay it was La Hire that struck the most serious blow against the English. While Joan exhorted the men, La Hire led an onslaught without waiting for the next wave of the attack. Even though Joan was kept in the third wave, her lack of experience in cavalry tactics would be risky in the front line at that point, she exhorted them with 'You have spurs, so use them.' La Hire's men now felt they had all to play for. Sir John Fastolf barely escaped the slaughter and on reporting defeat to Bedford he was temporarily relieved of the Garter.

It is not easy living with a saint, though. Joan declared that the soldiers must refrain from playing cards and foul language, which might not have gone down well, unless the army was gripped by the sense of a religious mission. La Hire himself, long noted for his profanities, moderated his language: he then would only swear 'on my baton'. Double entendres apart, this may have shown a remarkable influence the Maid had on him. He was even known to pray too, although his prayers were somewhat idiosyncratic. One was 'May God do for La Hire what God would have La Hire do for Him if God were La Hire and La Hire were God.' This sounds vaguely blasphemous and was certainly not a conventional orison. La Hire was said to speak of himself in the third person.

At one time Joan rode out on impulse with a small force to engage the enemy, eventually becoming embroiled in an unplanned action where she attacked an English fortification and was trapped between it and other English troops. With Gilles de Rais, La Hire raised what troops he could and they fought their way in to rescue her. This may mean that they cared about her mission, although it may also signify how much they valued such a valuable mascot.

By the end of the year Joan had initiated a dramatic new scheme. Together with the Dauphin and many of the French commanders she led an army that fought its way over a hundred miles into Anglo-Burgundian territory and arrived at Rheims, where on 17 June according to French tradition the Dauphin was crowned as King Charles VII. She was soon after disappointed when her king showed a desire to relax military activities and she railed at him to press on and regain Paris. During one attack on the city she was wounded by a crossbow bolt and was left lying on the field all night. Her following believed (and some probably hoped) she was dead. This was the end of the belief that she was invincible, and many must have cause to wonder if God really gave her his support.

Soon after, worse followed. On 23 May 1430, while she took part in a raid at Compiègne Joan was famously pulled from her horse by a Burgundian archer and given up to the Count of Luxembourg. She was eventually sold to the English at Rouen, who were determined to try her as a witch and heretic and burn her, to destroy the icon as well as the person. It is not as well-known that Charles VII immediately dissociated himself from the Holy Maid, abandoning her to her fate. Ungrateful as he seemed, it was far from practicable to seek her rescue at Rouen, still a long way into English-held territory. His counsellors must have advised against it; it would have meant serious military resources invested for one person, and the spell she had over them all had since evaporated. Strangely though, it was La Hire who apparently made a serious attempt at rescuing her. He apparently still believed in her.

At the time he was occupying Louviers, a town on the edge of Normandy, having acted independently of Joan's campaign to regain Paris; such is the nature of the freelance warrior. At that time he took Chateau Gaillard, forcing the English Captain Kingston to surrender. He did make two attempts to fight his way to Rouen and save her, but soon contended with an attack by an English force on Louviers. It took six months to besiege the town, but La Hire was finally forced to surrender and was held prisoner at Dordan until a ransom was paid. During this period Joan was burned.

There are allegations that Joan was a bastard daughter of the Duke of Orleans and the tale of the Domrémy shepherdess may have been fabricated. The truth cannot be determined here, but Joan is presented as many desire her to be. Decades later she was cleared by both English and French of accusations of witchcraft and heresy and in 1921 was canonised, to become joint patron saint of France. In the past hundred years or so she has been presented as Joan the Patriot, Joan the Suffragette, during the German occupation simultaneously Joan the Collaborator and Joan the Resistance Fighter, and subsequently Joan the Feminist. Her latest incarnation as Joan the Fascist is the least endearing, now that in almost every public event held by the *Rassemblement national* (the former *Front National*) in France a young girl in armour rides a horse.

Joan did not command armies; the Duc d'Alençon was in overall command during the Orleans campaign, even though she had a knack for getting her way when she urged dangerous ventures, but her main contribution was her role as a divine representative, which made all the difference to a previously demoralised army. Charles VII had endorsed her as an act of desperation but once the crown was on his head and some of his sources of income recovered he was lukewarm about her further drive at reconquest. When Joan was captured, her king abandoned her, and most of those she had stood with disowned her.

La Hire was different in that he apparently made a serious attempt at rescuing her. It would have been very difficult for anyone while she was held far into English-held territory, and even Charles would have needed to organise a large campaign to Rouen, and Joan could not be safe while it was going on. Her spell was broken too; it was unthinkable that a messenger from God could be so captured. La Hire did try, but he was unfortunate. Did he still believe in her, had Joan won over such a battle-hardened cynic? Was La Hire's occupation of Louviers part of his rescue strategy? Some say he and the other captains concurred with Charles's assessment that she was not what they thought she was. Demons are cunning, they were told, and the Pucelle was simply leading them to damnation. In any event Joan was of no further use to the Valois cause.

La Hire continued his activities. In September 1432 he fought Bedford at his siege of Lagny, and the following year he ravaged the Duke of Burgundy's lands around Cambrai. In December 1433 he took Ham and Breteuil from the Burgundians and defeated the Earl of Arundel at Gerberoy in 1435. But after the death of Joan of Arc, Charles VII was hearing of the English recovering their losses. In 1435 a new game-changer appeared.

The French met with the English and Burgundians at Arras in August that year to discuss peace. Philip the Good contrived this meeting, even though the English were not too keen; they were winning and wanted to consolidate their hold on Paris. Philip had decided that his English alliance, vague as it actually was, no longer gave him what he needed, and he instructed his negotiators to make peace with the French king even if the English would not. After making demands the French could not agree to, Cardinal Beaufort led the English walk-out, leaving the way clear for the Burgundians to make their own agreement. With Philip and his faction on the side of Charles VII, the English lost more and more ground from this point. In 1436 not only were they dislodged from Paris, but Philip threatened Calais, and in later years, after a number of truces, all English possessions were retaken. In 1453 Calais and its march was the only territory they had left.

At first La Hire disregarded the new accord by attacking Burgundian territory, waging guerrilla warfare in Artois around Caux, where he was taken prisoner at Beauvais in 1437. He later took part in the sieges of Harfleur and Pontoise, and in the Battle of Tartas. He continued in his combination of predatory activities in whatever area he was in and to grind down the borders with the lands the English still held. As long as his activities helped Charles regain French territory, there was no objection from above. La Hire was designated Captain General of Normandy in 1438, although there was not much land there where Charles's writ ran.

The career of Richard Venables, the English routier, merits some consideration. This chapter was originally planned as a larger comparison between him and La Hire, but there is not really enough information on Venables' side. Venables probably came from Cheshire; it was a common gentry name there. A Hugh Venables of Kimlaton was deputy constable of Chester Castle at this time and there is a Richard Venables mentioned in Chancery records, but as these coincide with events in France it is unlikely he was the same man. There are also Venables in Gloucestershire. Richard Venables was almost certainly an esquire, a gentleman who was a younger son of a knight who sought advancement and wealth in the French wars. No estates were recorded to his name.

Venables was first known to have appeared in France in 1428, at the head of three men-at-arms and a dozen archers. These were probably all he could afford to raise when he came, but his activities soon brought men to his service. He was said to have between 1000 and 1200 men following him, probably an exaggeration. These came from English, Dauphinist and Burgundian armies, either deserters or stranded from previous campaigns, and one called Waterhoo, probably a Fleming or Brabançon was one of his lieutenants. His men were described as 'free-lances'. Such bands were useful when their commanders paid them, and they sought wealth as they went.

No documentation exists of what Venables and his men did during the Orleans campaign, but it is easy to surmise that they did not benefit as much as they expected. It looks like he and his band eventually went as freelance as could possibly be and resorted to brigandage, plunder and protection racketeering in Lancastrian Normandy. He commandeered the monastery at Savigny in the Cotentin region, previously an important Benedictine house and later a Cistercian. In 1334 John Duke of Bedford heard disturbing stories of the band's activities.

The Regent considered the Duchy of Normandy as a high priority in the conquest of France. It was under direct control by the English and was significant as his king's 'historic domain'. He did all he could to win over its people to the Lancastrian monarchy; he created a standard currency, founded a university at Caen and sought to involve the military class of the duchy in government and defence. He had heard that Venables' men had descended on the village of Vicques and slaughtered a dozen peasants, no doubt part of their mission to extort money from the villagers. He had also heard from some quarters that a general rising against the English was imminent, and decided to make an example of these brigands. He mounted a full military campaign against Savigny and destroyed this threat. Venables and Waterhoo were brought to Rouen and hanged like common criminals.

This act was hypocrisy. Both English and French commanders encouraged these loose cannons, turning blind eyes to looting. Venables would have been more acceptable if he had fought nearer the front line, but he carved out his territory where there was little resistance from the French, and in a sensitive region for support of the English conquest. Venables was in fact one more reason for not settling to rule under the Lancastrian kings and Bedford was fearful of this mass revolt that never came.

For the rest of his life La Hire served both his king and himself. There was a time in 1438 and 1439 that he campaigned in Lorraine in the service of Count René of Anjou. René was conducting a dispute over Lorraine with Antoine de Vermandois and appealed to Charles. The king sent La Hire and others to enforce his Support, but once that duty was discharged, they ravaged Alsace. In 1440, he worked with Dunois to capture Pontoise from the English and the following year he assisted the Duke of Orleans to capture La Réole, which proved his last ever action in the field. Poton de Xantrailles was still active too, although he had become a committed conventional soldier in Charles's service.

Etienne de Vignolles died at Montauban on 11 January 1443 in the presence of Charles VII, of an unknown illness. He had not increased overly in wealth and position and had scarcely changed his tactics in all this time.

About then, France and England agreed to a twenty-year truce. Charles allowed the marriage of his niece Margaret of Anjou to King Henry VI; a union that would be fateful for England once Margaret had acquired enough political know-how. There was also a secret agreement that the English would hand over the county of Maine, which was also disastrous in the long term when it left Normandy poorly defended to the south. The truce was broken in 1449, as it would have been sooner or later, and on this occasion by the English. Normandy was lost within a year, as was Guyenne in 1453. There only remained the town and environs of Calais that the English held, until the siege of 1558.

La Hire was revered as a hero of the reconquest, once the English had gone. He was particularly honoured by the presentation of his likeness. or what was believed to be so, as the Knave of Hearts in the playing card pack. This model first appeared in the late 15th century and the image, with long hair and moustache, has been a familiar format ever since. This does not in itself say that La Hire looked like this, but many believed it. In this edition he is named as La Hire, and the other knaves are presented as Lancelot, Hector and Ogier, all known as valiant warriors.

La Hire was not exactly a sympathetic character. He was very much a military commander of his time and had no option but to behave as he did. Even Fastolf recognised how important it was to wage 'sharp and cruel war' in order to achieve victory. Such men did not give much thought to the peasants they harmed; they held other perspectives. La Hire was only one of many irregular military leaders that had their time in the century and more that these wars were waged. They fought the wars of their kings, and alternately or at the same time sought material gain through the harshest of means, and the kings found them useful. Unlike Richard Venables, La Hire was unmistakeably in his king's service, and what he did would advance the Valois cause. When Bedford sought the acceptance of his king from the people of Normandy, Venables was such a stumbling block that the duke decided to eliminate him.

When Joan of Arc urged the army on, it was in fact Alençon, Dunois, Gilles de Rais and La Hire, together with others, that did the real fighting. La Hire was the real victor at Patay, and was the executive arm of her crusade. He was an effective warrior who for a time did well from the appearance of the Pucelle, but miraculous happenings aside, he and his men won many a fight and perhaps he deserves more credit than he gained.

If La Hire had survived to the end of the wars it is hard to see how he could have lived then. He was anger personified and peace would not have suited him. He was hardly chivalrous: once he availed himself of the hospitality of a Burgundian lord and after drinking the wine he served him, clapped his host in irons and demanded a colossal ransom.

Still, chivalry was becoming outmoded by the early fifteenth century and the times called for a Machiavellian address rather than a chivalrous one. He was a harsh, cynical fighter who produced results and was useful to the Valois cause because of it.

17

Eleanor Cobham

Scarlet Woman or Dupe?

The place that history gives to Eleanor Cobham is unflattering. As wife to Humphrey, Duke of Gloucester, her obsession with the occult apparently brought an unwitting association in 1441 with a plot against Henry VI and destroyed her husband's political career. Eleanor herself is sometimes regarded as an innocent, simply venturing into a prohibited realm because she wanted to give Gloucester an heir, an attempt which ended with her performing a humiliating public penance and imprisonment for the rest of her life. She is also thought of as a scarlet woman, a social climber in a rigid age of social degree, who was preparing to make her husband king by killing his royal nephew with black magic.

Eleanor Cobham, or Eleanor of Sterborough, or Eleanor, Duchess of Gloucester, was born some time before 1412, but almost certainly after 1400. Her father was Reynold de Cobham, third Lord Cobham of Sterborough. She lost her mother Eleanor Culpeper at an early age and her father remarried. Probably in her early teens, Eleanor, as was the usual practice for girls born into noble families, was sent to a household of higher social rank. To perform light services to a lady of similar age and act as one of her companions and confidantes was a common opening for a young aristocratic girl in those days, often leading to an education in the ways of high society and to possible social advancement.

At some time between 1420 and 1423 Eleanor became a lady-in-waiting to Jacqueline of Holland, herself a pawn in the political events of the Low Countries at the time. While in this household she came to the attention of her future husband, Humphrey, Duke of Gloucester, who had entered into a dubious marriage with Jacqueline. Eleanor's father had served on one of Gloucester's expeditions to France and through this connection he might have found his daughter this position.

Jacqueline, daughter and heiress of the Count of Holland, Zealand and Hainault, had been married first to Dauphin John, for a time heir to the throne of France, but after his mysterious death she was married again in 1419 to the Duke of Brabant, but soon decided she would be a pawn no longer. Within a year she found her husband impossible to live with and fled to England, and once there she applied for a papal dispensation to have this marriage dissolved. While Jacqueline stayed in England, Eleanor, then more than eight but unlikely to have seen twenty, entered her household.

Duke Humphrey, youngest of the four sons of Henry IV, had fought on the campaigns of his brother Henry V in France; he had suffered wounds at Agincourt and only because the king rescued him did he survive the battle. From August 1422, when Henry V died of dysentery, Humphrey's nephew became King Henry VI, succeeding his father at the age of nine months. Before he died, Henry V had dictated codicils to his will stating that during the minority Gloucester would be regent in England while his elder brother John Duke of Bedford commanded the continued war of conquest in France. Duke Humphrey was highly educated, handsome and well-regarded by many. The names of his illegitimate children Arthur and Antigone reflect his interests in literature. On receiving Jacqueline in England as Warden of the Cinque Ports, Humphrey found her company pleasant, as she did his.

Almost immediately after Gloucester accepted the regency, a faction headed by Bishop Beaufort wrested power from him by a radical redefinition of his powers. Henry Beaufort, Bishop of Winchester, later created a cardinal, was a legitimised bastard son of John of Gaunt and therefore Gloucester's uncle, and he had long served the Lancastrian monarchy. It was now ordained that Gloucester was only regent when Bedford was not in England, and even then had to submit his decisions to a council of regency for ratification. Bishop Beaufort was only one of this body, but his influence was strong. There was controversy over whether the dead king's will could be modified in this way, or even whether these codicils could override parliament. Some even questioned whether this is what Henry V did dictate. Some had serious doubts that Duke Humphrey was temperamentally suited to the office of regent. He had briefly been regent during his brother's last campaign, and he was no incompetent, but hindsight shows him as given to reckless adventures that took little account of the damage that such acts could cause. The Duke was popular in England but would certainly have ruffled too many feathers, and his behaviour concerning Jacqueline would confirm this. The council finally agreed to Beaufort's plan, leaving Humphrey muzzled and frustrated. For the rest of their lives, Gloucester and Beaufort fought incessantly; the duke never forgave him for this business.

While he was struggling with his uncle, Humphrey embarked on the grandiose scheme of becoming the new count of the three provinces once he gained Jacqueline's hand in marriage. Humphrey had little personal wealth; the estates awarded by his father and eldest brother had been modest, and this marriage seemed an ideal opportunity for him to gain what was almost a small kingdom, albeit in two geographical pieces. It was also the most irresponsible and potentially disruptive act an English prince could possibly commit at that time.

Philip the Good, Duke of Burgundy, had by siding with the English king enabled Henry V to make important gains in France. Following his father John the Fearless' murder by the opposing Armagnac faction in 1419, Philip had decided to recognise Henry's claim to the French throne, at least in name. The Burgundians did not always give their much-needed military aid to the English themselves and often made truces independently while the English fought on, but while they continued their civil war with the Armagnac faction the English cause could only benefit. Philip's brokering of the Treaty of Troyes in 1420 had established Henry V as heir to Charles VI, and his endorsement gave Henry access to Paris and nominal rule over much of northern France, where Burgundy's personal following was strong. The Armagnacs had fought on regardless, championing Charles's surviving son the Dauphin Charles as rightful successor. Bedford continued to campaign and made spectacular territorial advances throughout the 1420s.

But Philip was by no means fully committed to the English alliance, and in fact by 1422 was considering some accord with the Dauphin instead, for Philip's allegiance was determined by what he thought suited him best. John Duke of Bedford was labouring to keep Philip on side and even married his sister Anne for this reason. The Burgundian alliance had been the key to the English successes in France in recent years and although it did not ensure very much military cooperation between the Burgundian faction and the English, it at least kept the Armagnacs partially diverted by civil war.

When his brother Humphrey married Jacqueline in 1423 and soon after established himself at Mons, Bedford saw this as the worst possible turn of events. Philip had arranged the original marriage with Brabant, and he regarded the Low Countries as his own sphere of influence. Philip, as Count of Flanders, was engaged in the process of bringing the entire region under his control by a series of tactical marriages and other political manoeuvring. Humphrey, now styling himself with the comital titles that his marriage had brought, was close to destroying Bedford's labours and jeopardised the entire English conquest. In the event, Humphrey was removed before he had done much damage when in 1424 a combined Burgundian and Brabançon invasion force drove Gloucester out of Hainaut. Humphrey's ambitions was thwarted and the alliance was maintained. Philip would not desert the English side until 1435.

Jacqueline had in fact been economical with the truth over the dissolution of her previous marriage to John of Brabant and had not gained the expected papal sanction. Humphrey had only found out how vague his claim to the counties was when forced to defend them. He had been duped into a bigamous marriage, which in 1428 Pope Martin V finally ruled invalid. John of Brabant had been poisoned and Philip, who had captured Jacqueline, kept possession of her lands, granting her half the revenues while she lived. Thwarted in his plans to rule over this large area of the Low Countries, Humphrey promptly abandoned both the counties and the heiress. He then married again, but not for advancement.

By the time Humphrey returned to England he had Eleanor Cobham as a mistress. It was hardly unknown in those days for a noble to have an affair with a lady of his wife's household, but his marriage to Eleanor brought Humphrey nothing but herself. She was the daughter of a baron of modest means and not even an heiress, with no lands he could have gained. He had married beneath him, ignoring the convention that princes and nobles chose one of comparable rank that brought material or political gains with her. He must have cared for her at this time; she was very beautiful, accounts say.

Eleanor had some difficulty being accepted at court, as she was not of the same social standing as the wives of the greater nobles. Her past was definitely a subject for discussion among courtiers, and perhaps she was considered at best as one more of Humphrey's gaffes. In 1432 she was invested as a Lady Companion to the Order of the Garter, but could not have been welcomed by the Garter knights and their wives.

In fact, to see her on the town in a duchess's finery, often with a young noble on her arm, raised eyebrows. She was an upstart, one who had risen above her station by playing on the Duke's feelings, they said. Should have remained his whore...

Eleanor's rise does not now seem so dramatic, from daughter of a minor baron to royal duchess, but this was an age where degrees of gentility and nobility were becoming more clearly defined than ever before. Below the king and princes of the Blood the nobility ranked as duke, marquis, earl, viscount and baron, the gentry divided into knights, esquires and gentlemen, and their wives graded in the same way. There was a strict order of precedence where breaches were major insults. Parliament had laid down which materials one could wear as clothing according to rank. The common people were also divided, and always deferred to their superiors; a servant who dared to precede a noble through the door to a room could expect a beating. It was still possible at every stage to rise in rank, but those born to higher station resented newcomers. The tale of Cinderella is a nineteenth-century rehash of a much older story and does not take account of what Prince Charming's court made of the matter.

Eleanor's husband continued to struggle with the Cardinal for ascendancy. Known (undeservedly) as 'the Good Duke', Humphrey was personally very popular. He founded a magnificent library at Oxford, since absorbed into the Bodleian. His successful expedition to drive back the Burgundians when they besieged Calais in 1436 brought him acclaim, although it was the last time he took to the field, and the attackers had in fact been repulsed before he arrived. When Bedford died in 1435 with no issue from either of his two marriages, Humphrey had a new role: he was now heir presumptive.

Henry VI was now approaching manhood; his minority officially ended in 1437. He was still unmarried and therefore childless, and in an age where many died young this was cause for concern. With the Dukes of Clarence and Bedford now both dead without legitimate children and as the last surviving son of Henry IV Humphrey would be king if his nephew died without producing an heir. Humphrey had a clear claim to succeed, and the House of Lancaster had no other living males. The House of York, also descended from Edward III through a younger son, had a problematical claim and they were not the only contenders. As the civil wars later in the century would illustrate, the royal succession was dogged by controversy.

It is often assumed that Eleanor bore Humphrey's two bastard children while still his mistress, but this is unlikely given the short timespan, and what appears to have been Eleanor's inability to conceive after their marriage. Arthur and Antigone were probably the issue of a previous mistress. If Humphrey were to be king one day, Eleanor needed to produce at least one son if the Lancastrian succession was to continue, as these two were ineligible to succeed him. Did Eleanor's failure to produce issue after her marriage lead to her downfall?

Fascination with the occult was common among court circles in the early fifteenth century; in the French court of Charles VII it was rife at that time. In 1440, the year before the events unfolded, Gilles de Rais, Marshal of France and erstwhile companion in arms of Joan of Arc, was burned as a sorcerer, alchemist and satanist who had allegedly sacrificed children to the Devil. There was an air of fascination with this business, essentially illegal and condemned by the Church, but the daring would still experiment.

Accusations of occult attacks on kings were known before. In 1419, Joan of Navarre, formerly Henry IV's queen, was arrested on a charge of trying to kill her stepson Henry V by this method. Although she was never tried for this, she spent three years in comfortable confinement and thereafter returned to court as if nothing had happened. Both Humphrey and Eleanor were known to have been on good terms with Joan in her later years, and Eleanor was a mourner at her funeral in 1439.

There was a strong element of magic in people's lives and the ethics were somewhat muddy. Charms for toothache or to ward off evil were widely used without much question. Pilgrimages to saints' shrines for miracle cures and wearing of religious medallions were but a step away from placing pine-cones in windows or reciting obscure poems that invoked pagan deities. Psalms were recommended for various cures and desires. Excavations of seventeenth-century houses in London have shown that live birds were placed in cavities in their foundations. Prophecies, often obscure, would be remembered, or even invented, at convenient times.

The great all consulted astrologers. It was accepted without question that the stars governed people's lives. Princes, even popes, had stargazers resident in their courts for this purpose, even to the eighteenth century and, more rarely, even later. Copernicus, Tycho Brahe and other pioneer astronomers of later centuries made their living by interpreting royal horoscopes. Both Ronald Reagan and Diana Princess of Wales were known to have regular consultations with astrologers, the former making decisions on affairs of state after such sessions.

Fairy tales often feature court magicians who performed wonders on royal request. Such flamboyant and powerful characters did not exist, although some monarchs were known to have employed occult practitioners. Dr John Dee, Elizabeth I's court astrologer, is the best-known example. He was deeply involved in alchemy and scrying, and was even credited with the discovery of a magical language. Elizabeth eventually lost patience when Dee did not produce synthetic gold and offered him a teaching position in Manchester, then a town in the back of beyond.

It was a common belief, encouraged by the Church, that Satan went abroad granting such knowledge and power, and it was a customary accusation against sorcerers and witches that they did the Devil's work. Christopher Marlowe would write his *Dr Faustus* based on this supposition. Latter-day Wiccans, echoing the thesis of Margaret Murray, claim that witchcraft is a survival of pagan religion. There is also talk of a Hermetic tradition, old in the fifteenth century and believed to have originated in ancient Egypt, where the magicians' understandings and power came from knowledge of the correspondences between colours, planets, angels, symbols, and so forth. Psychologists and anthropologists have produced alternative explanations.

Whether the sorcerer had consciously abjured Christ and thrown his lot in with Satan, or whether he considered himself a scientist of ancient knowledge despite the censure of the established Church, is not the issue. Such practices had a reputation for extreme evil, often known as the 'dark arts,' or 'necromancy'. Such beliefs continue to the present day in one form or another and the Harry Potter stories contain references to a form of occultism known in the fifteenth century. Medieval practitioners trod an uneasy path on the edge of the law, always discreet and secretive in order to survive.

The Oxford scholar Master Roger Bolingbroke gained the position of chaplain in the Duchess of Gloucester's household and acted as her astrologer. Such occultists had an interest in finding a powerful protector, who may wish to avail themselves of their magical services. Bolingbroke was educated to be a simple household priest, and perhaps he valued her protection while he conducted his researches.

Bolingbroke, as it was revealed in 1441, associated with two others of his kind; Thomas Southwell, canon of St Stephen's Westminster, and one John Hume, or Hun, a canon of St Asaph's. Whether they were members of a secret society is not known and they could have simply been friends who shared an interest. The fourth person cited was Margery Jourdain, known as the 'Witch of Eye' (or Ebury) who lived close to Westminster, someone of a very different class.

Although it was said at their trial that the scholars conspired with the witch, no real evidence links her directly with the other three. Eleanor was said to have consulted Margery on a long-term basis. If Bolingbroke and the others did meet her, it was probably to hear her prophesy, as sorcery and witchcraft used different magical systems. Margery was also tried as a relapsed heretic; she might have been a Lollard in younger days. She apparently made a living as a wise woman, selling charms and potions to the great and the humble, an offence for which she was prosecuted as early as 1432. She was well-known for her prophecies. One could wonder who else of the court at Westminster consulted Margery, as love-charms, cures for ills and the telling of fortunes were much in demand, even in the highest circles.

During the 1430s the tide turned twice in the French wars. After the capture and execution of Joan of Arc in 1431, the English began to win back the lands they had been driven from in the previous two years. Cardinal Beaufort and the English delegation were confident enough to walk out of the Congress of Arras in 1435 when the French refused to recognise Henry VI as king of France. This act would prove disastrous when the Burgundians remained at Arras to make their peace with Charles VII and changed sides in the fighting. From that point, the English would gradually lose their territories in France.

Four years later, while the Cardinal and his party pressed for an orderly end to what was now an unwinnable war, it was Gloucester who championed the policy of continuing the struggle, with the support of many who had fought in the wars. Of course there was now little chance of Henry VI ruling all of France without many more years of long, onerous and expensive campaigning, but for the English to cut their losses was an unpalatable prospect to many. Gloucester roused parliament against such deliberations and also accused the Cardinal of trying to give away the king's French title, claiming that Beaufort had taken advantage of the king's 'tendre age', defrauding him to his own advantage. He also returned to previous objections he had made concerning the legality of Beaufort's holding the See of Winchester while a cardinal.

The Duke was now the champion of those whose anger had turned on Beaufort. He issued a manifesto demanding that the Cardinal and his supporters answer such charges. His enemies replied with a counter-manifesto, but the tide of opinion was rising against them. In 1440 and early 1441 it seemed that Humphrey was close to breaking his rival's hold on government.

Humphrey was on a roll with rising support. He had recently been appointed Chief Justice of South Wales as an attempt to appease him and there was also talk of him gaining a new command in France. Although disliked at court, Humphrey was too powerful to ignore. Early in 1441 he produced a second manifesto, now calling as much as his rivals had for peace, but for peace on favourable terms. The other side issued their new counter-manifesto, but they were very much on the defensive.

In June 1441 Gloucester was brought down in a spectacular manner, as the exposure of Eleanor and what looked like her involvement in a treasonable plot enlisting the powers of Hell to kill the king produced the best results Beaufort could hope for.

It appears that John Hume informed on his associates for some unknown reason. The other three were arrested and charged with employing their 'crafte of nygromancie' against the life of the king. Bolingbroke, suddenly very co-operative towards the authorities, claimed that his patron the Duchess had instigated the action, and from that point he insisted consistently that she had instructed him to bring about the young king's death.

Eleanor, who was dining at the King's Head in Cheapside when she heard of the arrests, ran for sanctuary to Westminster Abbey. This did not save her and in fact delivered her to her captors, and she was imprisoned at Leeds Castle in Kent before her trial in October. She denied throughout the proceedings any such plot against the king, and claimed that all she did was in order to conceive a child and ensure the royal succession. Unfortunately, books of magic had been found in her house, and Bolingbroke was testifying against her. Wax images were also found, and the charges included making an effigy of King Henry and allowing it to melt by the fire, slowly causing him to waste away. Images cast in silver and other metals were found. Sympathetic magic is one of its most widespread forms, making images and attacking those they represented through them. Again, Eleanor stated that they were aids to conception, but it is hard to see how they could have been, given the customary use of figures. The discovery of the mommets was a serious matter in an age where the Devil was believed to be always lurking close by.

Bolingbroke was brought to a platform before St Paul's Cross, dressed in his ritual robes. A brightly painted chair of his was put on display, described as having four swords at the corners with copper figures hanging from the swords. This was consistent with ritual magic as described in many books, although it does not appear to correspond with any specific activity or meaning; few chairs are mentioned in magic texts. There, before the Archbishop of Canterbury, Cardinal Beaufort and other bishops, Bolingbroke announced his abjuration of magic and other demonic acts.

It is not difficult to accept that as Bolingbroke had been caught engaged in sorcery and accused of attempting treason with its use, he could be prevailed upon to turn evidence. Perhaps he was led to believe that he could escape execution, and his public penance suggests that he expected leniency and might have bargained for it by accusing Eleanor of whatever Gloucester's enemies could dream up. There is certainly no evidence that this was the case, but if Cardinal Beaufort or his associates did not visit him in his cell and offer him this option, the outcome could scarcely have been better for them if they had.

Even the twenty-year-old and intensely pious Henry VI, often known for his clemency and regard of his kin, was more than horrified, not only at the thought of witchcraft but that Eleanor had sought to kill him, and called for retribution. There was then a tendency at the mention of the dark arts to abandon objectivity, and any who defended those so accused ran the risk of being accused of satanism themselves.

Given that she did not deny involvement completely, there is reason to believe that Eleanor herself was not entirely innocent in her intentions. Her husband would be king if Henry had met an early death. To beget a child was important in this context, especially while in her thirties, a late age to bear children. There is no real evidence that she did collude in or instigate an occult attack on the king, but as her chaplain was her astrologer too, she might have been seeking to know the future where the succession was concerned. There were a number of prophecies going about concerning the year 1441. Perhaps she had an interest in knowing what was to come: a *parvenu* duchess who saw becoming queen as the pinnacle. We have no way of knowing what her intentions were, but it is reasonable to think that she was simply asking for information through divination. Unfortunately for Eleanor, it was declared at her trial that it was treason even to speculate on or calculate how long the king would live, and this condemned her.

It was also claimed at the trial that Eleanor had used magic to make Gloucester marry her in the first place, through the use of potions which Margery had made for her. We do not know when she first developed her interest. It was an ill-conceived marriage, but Humphrey's own impetuous nature could more easily account for it than spells. Eleanor as a wife was ever a liability to him, and now in 1441 she would become his complete undoing.

Despite whatever he felt for Eleanor, Gloucester immediately dropped her as the scandal broke and began divorce proceedings. His support collapsed around him, for few would wish to associate with either treason or satanism, and the king refused to have any dealings with him. The duke knew he could be easily accused of complicity himself and Beaufort with his following rejoiced at the end of Gloucester's political career, dramatically cut down when so close to defeating the Cardinal and his associates.

The trials took place in the autumn. Southwell had died in the Tower. Margery Jourdain was tried and on 17 October burned at Smithfield. Bolingbroke's act of contrition and co-operation with the authorities against Eleanor did not save him from an equally terrible death. On 27 November he was dragged to Tyburn, hung, drawn and quartered, his head placed on London Bridge and his body parts exhibited in four cities simultaneously.

Eleanor had already been sentenced on 9 November. She was ordered to do public penance before beginning her life imprisonment; a less serious penalty than could have been, for she might easily have suffered execution. Only her high rank brought her clemency, or perhaps Beaufort and his affinity contented themselves with Gloucester's fall. For three days Eleanor, clad in her shift, barefoot and her hair unbound, walked the streets of London with a one-pound wax taper in her hand, which she presented to St Paul's and on the other days to other churches. The mayor, the sheriffs and other dignitaries followed her in procession. Her state provoked sympathy among the crowd. The chroniclers say that her 'meke and demure countenaunce' caused many to feel compassion. Afterwards she was committed to the custody of Sir Thomas Stanley, comptroller of the royal household, and sent under guard to Chester. Allotted fifty marks a year for her upkeep, she probably wanted for little in terms of comforts and entertainment, if she lacked her freedom.

Having ousted his rival of two decades, Cardinal Beaufort was easily the most powerful of the courtiers, but not for very long. After 1442 he lost much of his influence and as his advancing age made it difficult for him to attend council so often, a new generation came to the fore in King Henry's court. Soon, it was the Earl of Suffolk and Beaufort's nephew the Earl of Somerset, both later raised to dukedoms, who exerted the most influence on the king. Beaufort survived his enemy Gloucester by only a few months but was politically dead long before.

Humphrey Duke of Gloucester did not marry again. He did return from retirement in 1447 for one last act. Opposition to the peace made the previous year convinced the 'Good Duke' that he might advance his suit once more, and once again he championed the war veterans. But his comeback was short-lived: he was arrested that year on Suffolk's orders on vague charges of treason and died while in custody a few days later. Foul play was rumoured but never proven. Henry VI therefore survived him and had then married, but civil war began in the following decade and the Lancastrian monarchy eventually ended with him.

The affair was not over for the king. While he was at Blackheath in 1443 Juliana Ridligo, a woman of Gloucester's manor of Greenwich, screamed invective at Henry for his treatment of Eleanor and was sentenced to death for doing so. A number of times Eleanor was moved, including to Kenilworth, to Beaumaris Castle in Anglesey and then to Peel Castle on the Isle of Man, each time under royal household guard. There was a serious prospect of attempts to rescue her. When a raid from either France or Scotland was expected, she was returned in 1449 to Beaumaris.

Eleanor died on 7 July 1452 at Beaumaris. She might simply have been a pawn in the power struggle between her husband and the Cardinal. If she was in fact a Lady Macbeth who was seeking the king's death, as some have painted her, there is every reason to believe that she did little more than hope for chance to crown Humphrey without her involvement. The books of magic she possessed dealt mostly with medical issues, although the wax and metal figures are still to be explained away. Such books as she may have read were similar in nature to those now sold in the New Age section of a modern bookshop. Astrology and perhaps a little supernatural assistance were often employed in the fifteenth century, even if this was a grey area in terms of law and morality. The affair could easily have been a ruse by Beaufort and his following to discredit Gloucester, but still the lack of concrete evidence makes it unlikely that it was planned and suggests that they simply seized the opportunity.

Perhaps Eleanor's greatest mistake was to have married Gloucester. Rather than the discreet lifestyle of a royal mistress she chose the life of a duchess, which was an attractive opportunity. But to be the wife of a man like Humphrey Duke of Gloucester had its dangers; she might have otherwise pursued her interests in the occult with little consequence.

18

Prince Henry the Navigator

The Crusader with Telescopic Vision

There is often some question of perspective concerning the fifteenth century. It is either seen as a time of endings, when much that characterised medieval society declined, and alternatively as an age of ambition, of opportunities and new beginnings, the inception of the vibrant Early Modern period. It was in this century that Europeans set out into the world beyond Europe, and all would change.

Although Europeans were not entirely ignorant of what lay beyond the extent of Western Christendom, their knowledge even of Eastern Europe was at best vague. Of course, most in 1400 knew of Palestine and Egypt, at least at second hand. Many with some education had heard of Baghdad, India, China and possibly even Japan, but their knowledge of such places and even their approximate whereabouts was sketchy and buried in myth.

In the thirteenth century the Venetian merchant Marco Polo amazed Europe with tales of his twenty-year sojourn at the court of Kublai Khan in Peking, and his account of all the wonders of the east was taken as fact for many centuries. Only in the late 1990s was it plausibly suggested that Marco had probably never journeyed to China at all, and that some obvious anomalies in his account cried out for reassessment. That he apparently never noticed the Great Wall is one glaring example, and many other features remarkable to westerners such as the distinct form of Chinese writing also escaped his attention. He is noticeably absent from all records the Chinese had of that time.

A century after Marco the reputed travels of the English knight Sir John Mandeville set new parameters in tall tales. This account told of such wonders as the land of the Amazons and the Fountain of Youth in India, and spoke reverently of the wide and powerful Christian kingdom of Prester John, the priest-king. Fantastic tales of dog-men, Cyclopes and heathen peoples with outlandish customs had long appeared in European literature, and Mandeville's account was typical.

Mandeville was not himself responsible for the legend of this line of pious Christian kings who ruled deep in Asia, each called Prester John, who would be more than willing to join the Europeans in the crushing of Islam, but he devoted some of his work to this large, fantastic kingdom and all its wonders. There were in fact Christian kingdoms in Asia, either Nestorian or of other eastern persuasions, but none as large or as powerful as the mythical realm that Mandeville described. Ethiopia, the Christian empire in Africa far south of Egypt, could easily have been the basis for the myth, but if so it shows how poor a sense of geography the Europeans had. A letter allegedly sent by Prester John had reached the Byzantine Emperor in about 1165 proposing an alliance against Islam. This was obviously a forgery, but the idea persisted.

Even if there was any serious resolve for Europeans to proceed into Asia, the lands of Islam provided a discouraging barrier; that and the continual instability among various nomadic peoples at the edge of the Mamluk Sultanate, and even in Anatolia. There was still the lure of the east; the silks, precious metals and spices so highly valued in Europe that passed mostly through Egypt and acquired the stiff duties the Sultan's officials exacted en route. The Venetians held a near-monopoly on the spice trade from Alexandria to Europe, and their own cut of the profits made such desirable wares even more expensive.

How it fell to Portugal to initiate the exploration of the unknown was partially due to its position on the Atlantic, where the unknown lay a few hundred miles to the south, and even nearer to the west. It also resulted from the drive of one of its ruling family, Prince Henry, called 'the Navigator'. His reputation has since suffered through reassessment, but he still deserves the credit for what he began.

Prince Henry (or Henrique) was born on 4 March 1394. He was fourth son of King João I (or John) of Portugal and his mother was Philippa, a daughter of John of Gaunt. As a prince of the blood he was at first intended for a military role, which he fulfilled at least in his younger days. As any prince, he was trained in the ways of knighthood and warfare. In 1415 he and two of his brothers took part in an expedition which sailed to North Africa and captured Ceuta.

The ports of the Maghreb harboured Arab pirates who threatened ships passing through the straits of Gibraltar. At twenty-one he was knighted for this feat.

In 1418 Henry travelled again to relieve Ceuta from a Moslem siege. He returned to Africa in 1437 and led a disastrous attack on Tangier, which resulted in his brother Fernando's capture and subsequent death in captivity. In 1458, his life near its end, he came once more at the head of an army that captured Alcacer. These four campaigns in the Maghreb were the sum total of Prince Henry's own journeys by sea, one whose efforts did so much for Portugal as a maritime power.

The Kingdom of Portugal first appeared in the twelfth century as territory carved out from Moorish Spain, and the capture of Lisbon by English and Flemish knights during the Second Crusade counted much to its benefit, delivering to the new kingdom a permanent centre. For centuries Portugal survived mostly from agriculture and fishing, and although too far west to compete with the Italians for the Mediterranean trade, had a modest merchant marine.

For centuries ships had sailed down the African coast, but only so far south. Portuguese seafarers knew of Cape Bojador, the undoubted limit of the known world in western Africa, a feature now in the modern disputed territory of Western Sahara. Mariners venturing into its waters knew this bulge in the coastline well enough, and on sighting the cape they would automatically turn back towards Portugal.

Modern minds might wonder at this attitude. We are grateful to our pathfinders, and the idea of boldly going where none have gone before appeals to our imaginations. The world is mostly explored now, and the lure of voyaging into space and finding new worlds and possibly new life has inspired many a film and television series. The human race would eagerly travel to other worlds were it now technologically and economically possible. But in the early fifteenth century the sense of the unknown was discouraging, rather than an invitation to extend our knowledge. There were mariners' tales of what lay beyond Bojador that featured dark, terrible lands, boiling seas, cannibals and sea monsters. It was also said that the cliffs beyond were of lodestone, which would tear the bolts out of any ships that ventured there. Some less alarmist assessments still declared that the further coastline was certainly unnavigable, more easily understood when the cape itself was the most daunting place a seaman could think of. The currents about it were treacherous, the rocks and reefs dangerous, the whirlpools and storms putting sailors in mind of the end of the world. Any seasoned seafarer would think twice before venturing too close for fear of his vessel being dashed to pieces.

There was a further serious consideration, practical in its nature and probably more unnerving than any thoughts of sea monsters; the prevailing winds of that region blew from north to south. While it was comparatively easy to travel down the African coast, the journey back involved sailing in a zigzag motion, beating into the wind. It would depend heavily on weather conditions how long it took to return to safe territory, and the further a voyage went, the longer it would take to come back under such conditions, if a ship could return at all.

Lack of knowledge discouraged any attempt to find a way beyond Bojador, in an age when it was inadvisable to sail out of sight of land. Few questioned the validity of such dark tales when nobody ever claimed to have sailed beyond the cape, and it is surprising how serious a psychological barrier Cape Bojador really was. For seafarers who followed the well-known coastlines of the Mediterranean, and in an era where maps still showed in remote regions 'Here be Dragons' (none had seen dragons anywhere else, so it was assumed they must be there), it felt safer not to venture into waters where *nobody* had been before. Prince Henry's real achievement was to change such an attitude.

At first, and perhaps as a prime objective throughout, Prince Henry approached seafaring as a crusader rather than an explorer. His military ideals belonged to a tradition born in the centuries-old aspiration of the Christian peoples to regain the Iberian Peninsula from the Moslems. While besieging the ports of North Africa did little to roll back further the frontiers of Islam, at least it might provide footholds for further action and struck blows against the corsairs. Henry and his brothers persuaded King João to allow the 1415 expedition.

Not long after Henry's initial crusading he was made Grand Master of the Order of Christ. He in fact became a monk, but a monk with a warlike mission. Besides the monastic orders of knights, the Templars and Hospitallers, there were several other such crusading bodies, including a number of lay and clerical orders in the Iberian lands. It is believed that when the Templars were suppressed by King Philip IV of France and the Inquisition in 1314 the Order of Christ arose as a continuation of the Templars under another name.

The Templars had a base in Portugal at the Convento da Christo at Tomar. Following the suppression it appears that King Dinis of Portugal did not believe the charges of heresy, sodomy and satanism that were placed against the order and the Order of Christ, or the *Ordem dos Cavaleiros de Nosso Senhor Jesus Cristo*, was founded in 1319 with papal sanction. In 1357, the order moved their headquarters to Tomar, and many believe that the Templars in Portugal simply continued in this form. The Templars have more recently acquired reputation in popular literature as the keepers of arcane knowledge, and many books has appeared in recent decades linking the Order with all manner of outlandish theories. It was in Portugal that the red cross on a white field that the Templars had borne was still seen, often on the sails of Prince Henry's ships.

In 1417, on the death of Lopo Dias de Sousa, the last elected Grand Master of the Order of Christ, King João gained the assent of the Pope to endorse Prince Henry as his successor. From that point Henry was in part carrying on the mission of the order, and he used its financial resources to finance his seafaring ventures. He was also appointed lifetime governor of the Algarve, which also aided his life's work.

It was on the second Ceuta campaign that his interest began. In 1418 João Gonçalves Zarco, one of Henry's captains charged with patrolling the seas for Moslem shipping, returned from one voyage reporting his visit to the Madeira Islands, far to the south as they were. Henry took an interest from that point.

Did Henry's sights move from the North African coast to the limits of exploration? Not as such and to an extent he remained a crusader, for his ultimate goal was always the destruction of Islam and his drive to discovery was but a part of his mission. Or perhaps he would tell himself that, as his passion over seafaring and exploration took possession of his efforts. He might have planned to discover the extent of Islam and his voyages had an intelligence-gathering role, at least to begin with.

Some also credit Henry with wanting to search for Prester John, again to form an alliance against Islam. Although estimated distances and geographical position were subject in those days to wild miscalculation, it would hardly seem viable to take on such a mission; it was after all the wrong side of Europe. It might have been the plan to seek out allies against the Moslems, according to what peoples could be found, but Henry apparently said nothing about any such intention.

Nor was he known to be seeking the route to India. There was simply no knowledge of how far Africa went, and whether it was possible to sail to India from the Atlantic Ocean. Indeed, the maps that existed showed – as the Classical geographers believed – that the African land mass went on to the southern limit of the world. Henry was not known to think in such terms; it would have been thinking big, or rather wildly conjecturing at that time.

Some did at times wonder if there was a route from the Atlantic to the Indian Ocean. In 1291 the Venetians Ugolino Vivaldi and his brother Guido set out south from the Straits of Gibraltar hoping to find this route. They certainly travelled a distance down the African coast as evidence was later found that they had gone that way, but they were never seen again. Stories of where the Vivaldis went persisted for centuries, and it was believed that they ended up at the court of Prester John. Henry did look at the limits of geographical knowledge and seek to further them. The barrier that Cape Bojador presented to seafarers was his concern, and for many years he was almost obsessed with the breaking it down.

It is in fact untrue that certain Atlantic islands were discovered for the first time as a result of Henry's efforts. The Romans knew of both Madeira (which they called the Purple Islands) and the Azores. The Azores appear on a Catalan map of the fourteenth century, as do the Canaries (or the Fortunate Islands) in a map drawn in Majorca in the same era. At times the Madeiras were visited in the previous centuries for wood and a red dye called 'dragon's blood'. The Portuguese sent a number of colonists in 1418 headed by Zarco, Tristão Vaz Teixeira and an Italian, Bartolomeu Perestrelo, who between them governed the two main islands of Madeira and Porto Santo. They set about preparing the islands for grain and sugar production, which involved burning down forests and digging irrigation systems. Henry himself might have been involved in this project at the beginning, and certainly was from 1433, for in this year his father King João died and on his brother Duarte's accession Henry was created lord of Madeira for life. Henry confirmed the three colonist leaders and created provinces governed by hereditary captaincies. Perestrelo's daughter would later marry Christopher Columbus. The Cape Verde islands were a completely new find, in 1456, at almost the end of Henry's period of activity. They were not formally annexed to Portugal until 1495.

As soon as exploitation began, so did the transportation of slaves from Africa. Slavery and the trading of Arab, Berber and African captives was an acceptable practice by this time, for Europeans as much as Moslems. As the Atlantic colonies flourished, many free colonists from Portugal settled and slavery declined, as many slaves were freed. But the Portuguese later brought this practice to the New World and other Europeans emulated them. It places a stain on the legend of Prince Henry the Navigator, although he was in fact guilty not of initiating the slave trade, but of bringing it westwards.

While Henry lived there were many advances in naval technology. Although he was not at all responsible for any of these, his insistence on their implementation in his ships made all the difference. Ships were now being built that could stand longer voyages and carry far larger cargoes. Using the best features of northern and southern European naval technology, the vessels produced in Henry's time could last far longer against rough seas. They could carry more provisions for the crews and thus stay at sea longer. The rudder, now attached to the stern, replaced the steering oar. Fitting the new ships with both the large square sails and the lateen, or diagonal sails in the centre of the ship made it possible to take better advantage of the winds. As a product of the new shipbuilding knowledge the Portuguese caravel came about as a standard to meet the challenges of the Atlantic.

The compass had been in use for two centuries already, but new instruments were appearing. The quadrant enabled seafarers to navigate by the stars, and the astrolabe made some calculation possible where declination could be determined. The most significant development was in fact the use of the chart. The 'pontalon' as it was known provided a detailed picture of all features to be seen in an area, very much to scale. This appeared in stricter detail than maps had before and would show the compass points needed to orientate the charts. More reliable procedures of determining latitude and longitude still lay far in the future, but it would become easier to plan voyages more accurately. While it was still risky to sail out of sight of land for any length of time, mariners could take a calculated risk more often.

Assessment on what exactly Henry did with this new technology has been revised. It was long believed that he ran a school of seafaring at Sagres in the Algarve, but this is now thought unlikely. While Sagres was known as *Vila do Infante*; the Prince's town, it was mostly at Lagos that his operations took place.

In practice this 'school' was probably a more informal affair. Henry's patronage brought many interested parties to the Algarve.

Scholars, cartographers and travellers mixed with master mariners who also enjoyed the Prince's bounty. Henry made sure that his captains learned about the new methods of navigation, about Atlantic currents and wind systems. He even brought the map and instrument maker Jayme of Majorca to his court. Above all, he was patron to a number of lesser aristocrats who commanded his annual expeditions.

Henry sought every piece of relevant information. He studied the ancient maps and any recent charts, ordering them updated as new knowledge appeared. He questioned his men as they returned from voyages, seeking every detail. He even found ways of asking *Azenegues,* or captured Africans, what they knew of their lands, so that his mariners knew enough of the Senegal region to recognise the place when they finally reached it.

Yet for nearly two decades Henry was frustrated by the symbolic limitation of Cape Bojador. Again and again he urged his captains to round it, and each time they returned reporting storms and adverse conditions, or made excuses. Bojador was physically difficult to sail round as much as it remained a psychological barrier.

Finally in 1434, on a second attempt, Captain Gil Eanes accomplished this feat. He had grown up as a squire in Henry's household and had long lived with Henry's dream. Once he had sailed out to sea and returned landward on the far side of the cape, his report featured still more treacherous waters near the coast and a long expanse of desert, for the coastline immediately beyond was desolate and uninviting, lacking both vegetation and habitation; not much to see here. But the barrier was down, and seafaring was never the same afterwards.

In 1436 Afonso Baldava, another of Henry's captains, followed Eanes's route 300 miles south of Bojador and reached the Rio do Ouro. Five years later, Antam Gonçalves went further and brought back 200 captive Africans, and the same year Nuno Tristam sailed as far as Cape Branco. In 1441 Tristam reached Arguim Bay.

Now it was established that Portuguese ships would sail further south on each voyage, and they were taking longer and discovering more. From 1455 to 1466 Cadamosto and Diogo Gomes from 1458 to 1460 explored the Senegal and the Gambia rivers and sailed as far as Sierra Leone. While these, and the Cape Verde Islands in 1456, were all that was discovered in Henry's lifetime, it amounted to a large geographical area, and the unknown now beckoned to the Portuguese explorers more than it discouraged.

While he was promoting these voyages Henry was obliged to act in the internal matters of his country. In 1438, his brother King Duarte died, leaving a six-year-old son to reign as Afonso V. Duarte had arranged that his Queen, Eleanor of Aragon, serve as regent but this decision was unpopular, and the *Cortes* called for Pedro, Duke of Coimbra and brother to both Duarte and Henry, to take over the regency. It was Henry who mediated between the parties, and Pedro was finally chosen. Pedro proved an able governor, although his measures to curb some of the over-mighty nobles brought unrest.

Henry did not support Pedro when he revolted against Afonso after he came of age in 1448, and Pedro subsequently died at the Battle of Alfarrobeira fighting against his nephew the king. In all, where Henry intervened it was as a moderating influence. Afonso supported Henry's naval voyages, as he was clearly interested in both trade and expeditions against the Moslems. In 1458 Henry, now worn down by the passing of the years, sailed once more, in his nephew's service to capture Alcácer Ceguer, a Moslem fortress between Tangier and Ceuta.

Prince Henry the Navigator died on 13 November 1460 at Sagres, unaware that his life's work would change Europe and the world forever. Eventually, the Portuguese found their way down the African coast as a logical progression of the voyages he had sent forth. Afonso did little to promote further exploration after his last uncle died, but there was now a large body of mariners whose livelihood depended on Atlantic trade and some of whom continued to sail beyond the new limits. Before the century ended, the entire west coast of Africa was mapped.

In 1488 Bartolomeu Dias captained a voyage that rounded the Cape of Good Hope and reported a sea beyond, which was rightly believed the Indian Ocean. Although none followed up this discovery for some time, the courtier Vasco da Gama embarked in 1497 with Dias's charts and reached India the following year. Brazil was discovered in 1501 when the next expedition ventured further west on the return journey, and for centuries the Portuguese maritime empire brought prosperity and prestige.

This tendency to follow the route Prince Henry had opened proved an obstacle to Columbus when he tried to sell his own idea to King João II. Of course the Genoese seaman's theory was somewhat outlandish (and wrong in the event) as he believed China lay on the far side of the Atlantic, only three thousand miles to the west. The Portuguese were now haphazardly discovering the route to India the way Henry had begun, and by this route they were the first Europeans to reach India by sea. They were in no mood to be diverted once they were certain they had discovered the way.

Henry's achievement was the initiation of so many voyages which eventually lifted the lid on exploration. He provided the finance for all this, from his own resources and those of the Order of Christ, and died deep in debt. He also promoted the use of whatever nautical and geographical knowledge was available, and his mariners benefited from such efforts. His urging to sail further jump-started the Portuguese in their drive to reach India, then China, the Indies and Brazil. In fact, all those who explored the world beyond Europe owed a debt to Prince Henry. Although Henry was not, as far as we know, in search of a route to India, he was probing what was beyond the limits of knowledge and his burning question was how far the Islamic lands stretched. If he did not seek out Prester John, he might have thought some allies against the Moslems could be found.

It cannot be denied that his discoveries served much to the benefit of Portugal. He set up trading points wherever his ships sailed and, protected by the brethren of the Order of Christ, they brought much trade to Portugal. His efforts to develop the Azores and Madeira made sense economically and they showed profit from about 1450. The acquisition of wealth was not incompatible with his Christian ideals. The attacks on Ceuta and Tangier were as much planned to end piracy in the Straits of Gibraltar as to crusade against the infidels.

Henry was not guilty of initiating the slave trade; this was already under way in his time. In fact, he believed that it would fit well with his Christian mission, and he declared that the Africans captured would be employed in domestic service. He believed that Africans should be well treated and eventually brought to Christianity and freedom. This, as we all know, did not come about. Still, it would have been an original thought to challenge the concept of slavery in this time. As exploitation of the Atlantic islands progressed, slave labour became less appropriate for the farming methods used, and many slaves were eventually freed.

Henry's activities were essentially a crusade, a form of attack on Islam, and the desire for exploration developed from it. The Red Cross of the Templars was displayed on the sails of all the ships he sent, which adds even more fodder for the conspiracy theorists' deliberations. Henry held his role as a crusading monk above all, not that it was incompatible with exploration or trade. In 1460, King Afonso granted the Knights of Christ a five per cent levy on all merchandise from the new African lands.

Henry's personal motto was *Talant de bien faire*, 'the desire to do well' and this he followed. He set himself apart from the nobles of his land by what seemed his eccentric interpretation of crusading and turned that medieval endeavour into the early modern drive for exploration. It was only when Gonçalves brought back the slaves in 1441 that the Portuguese took any serious interest in voyaging, and Portugal led the Europeans to discover the whole world. It was Henry's energy and willingness to put large amounts of gold into these ventures that generated significant advances in his own lifetime.

19

John de Vere, Earl of Oxford

Persistent Lancastrian

As a second son, John de Vere was not expected to succeed as 13th Earl of Oxford when he was born on 8 September 1442. His father, also named John, was the 12th Earl and his elder brother Aubrey the designated heir. Their mother was Elizabeth Howard, daughter of the Duke of Norfolk, and there were six other children from two marriages. But the turn of events dictated otherwise, and mapped out the course of his life.

He came from a long and illustrious lineage. Aubrey de Vere, a Norman baron of the Cotentin, followed William the Conqueror to England and was rewarded for his services with lands in East Anglia. In the twelfth century his descendant was granted the earldom of Oxford and as one of the longest established noble families in England the de Veres served the kings in almost every generation. The events of the later fifteenth century put them, as most other nobles, in many an unenviable position.

From the early 1450s the ineptness of King Henry VI allowed for political dissent to escalate dramatically. The conflict between a 'court' party and the supporters of Richard, Duke of York, a claimant to the succession, and the resultant upheaval, is misleadingly termed the 'Wars of the Roses', growing from the myth that the two sides used red and white roses as their badges. The opening engagement at St Albans in 1455, a single day's fighting, temporarily resolved the dissent, placing York and his faction in control for a time, but this broke down and the two sides, the 'Yorkist' and 'Lancastrian' armies, fought openly between 1459 and 1461. The struggle for political ascendancy became a series of dynastic civil wars between the Lancaster and York branches of the ruling family, first over who should govern England, and then over who should be king.

Richard of York gained the support of a few powerful nobles, particularly his brother-in-law Richard Neville, Earl of Salisbury, and Salisbury's son and Namesake who became Earl of Warwick. Queen Margaret of Anjou, using her husband as figurehead, drew the Duke of Somerset and other greater nobles to wage war on York and his following and the Yorkist leader was killed at the Battle of Wakefield in December 1460. But York's party triumphed, and his son was proclaimed King Edward IV in March 1461, who confirmed his accession by defeating the Lancastrians decisively at Towton a few weeks later.

The 12th Earl of Oxford had pledged his support for the Lancastrian cause, although his real contribution was negligible. He is famed as having ridden to St Albans in 1455 to fight for King Henry but arriving a day too late. In 1460, he was excused from attending Parliament and similar duties at his own request when he pleaded infirmity.

The Yorkist victory at Towton in March 1461 forced the old earl to adapt to the new status quo and, like many others once Lancastrian resistance had practically collapsed, he made his peace with the new king. Edward IV, young, debonair and politically able, was all too willing to forgive his former enemies and although some of his attempts at reconciliation seem misconceived in retrospect, this policy worked on the whole. Too many had supported the previous regime, and it would have been disruptive to the peace and feudal framework of each county to wreak vengeance on all of them. Simply to receive their submission was the best policy of the time, and few Lancastrians were condemned. The early years of the Yorkist monarchy proceeded in a festive and positive manner.

But this spirit of self-congratulation the new regime displayed was tempered by serious concern that the Lancastrians could regroup and challenge them again. There was still opposition in Wales, and for three years the north of England saw intermittent fighting, rebellions and invasions from Scotland, which threatened to give Margaret and her party a foothold at least. Some of those Edward had pardoned and even given military commands turned their coats as soon as Lancastrian forces appeared. He took great pains to befriend the Duke of Somerset, only to hear of him re-joining Margaret in the north after a year in his court. There were allegations of plots among the nobles at Westminster, some of which were probably real.

In February 1462 the 12th Earl of Oxford and his heir Aubrey de Vere were arrested on charges of treason and placed in the Tower. The details are vague, but letters were said to have been intercepted between old Oxford and Margaret. There was talk of a planned landing of Lancastrian forces in Essex, where Oxford had estates and influence. John Tiptoft, Earl of Worcester and Constable of the same Tower, heard their case and speedily condemned them both to execution at Tower Hill on 26 February 1462. Sir Aubrey was said to have informed on his father, but this did not seem consistent with his character and allegiance. He might have been offered a pardon by 'turning king's evidence' when arrested himself, but if so, this was not honoured.

There is no way of knowing whether the allegations were true but given the elder John de Vere's usual behaviour it is unlikely that he would stir easily. That his son was plotting is more likely – he knew the favour of Queen Margaret in 1460 and before – but there is a shortage of evidence that confirms any such activities. Despite the official policy of reconciliation, the government was still unsure of those who had sided with the Lancastrian faction. There was also from 1461 widespread unease over the entire question of deposing a reigning king, and whether Henry VI, then a fugitive in Scotland, was still rightful ruler of England. The new government's attempts at conciliation were laced with paranoia.

Sir Aubrey was hung, drawn and quartered, a particularly bloody and extreme form of execution designed to discourage others from thoughts of treason. As his father was a peer of England, his own end was commuted to execution with a single blow of the sword. On that day, the younger John de Vere at nineteen found himself Earl of Oxford. Normally, treason would result in attainder, where to be declared a traitor by Act of Parliament would entail forfeiture of lands and titles and the stain of treason applying to one's heirs. No such process was followed in this case, and John simply received the lands and title his father had held. The king was still pursuing his policy of seeking the submission of his former enemies and was less keen on issuing attainders as he had been at the outset. It is not difficult to guess that the new 13th Earl had misgivings over the treatment of his father and brother.

When John married Margaret Neville, sister of the Earl of Warwick, still the most powerful supporter of the Yorkist monarchy, he seems to have integrated with the rulers well enough. John and Margaret remained married until her death in 1506, but if they had any children none survived them. Oxford held offices in the new regime. He was a justice of the peace in Essex, and also in Norfolk, Suffolk and Cambridgeshire, areas where he had influence. He was created a Knight of the Bath at Elizabeth Woodville's coronation and was then Queen's Chamberlain. However, this did not show very much favour from the new regime.

For some time after 1464, when the remaining Lancastrian rebels in the north were finally crushed, Edward IV sat more easily on the throne. But 1464 also saw the beginning of strains in the relationship between the king and Warwick, and events would once again become dramatic by the end of the decade. Oxford was not only the son and brother of executed Lancastrians, he was also Warwick's brother-in-law, but that in itself was neither here nor there. Perhaps when Edward revealed his secret marriage to Elizabeth Woodville, daughter of a reconciled Lancastrian baron, and an old enemy of Warwick, the dissent began. Or possibly when Edward decided he had made the earl too powerful and relied on him less after the Lancastrian resistance was mostly crushed, Warwick turned his thoughts to his own desires.

In November 1468 Oxford was arrested on charges of plotting against the king. He spent some months in the Tower before his pardon the following April. It appears that he 'confessed myche thinge' according to the Plumpton correspondence. Was he involved in Warwick's own conspiracies with the king's brother, George Duke of Clarence? It is not certain when Warwick first planned to revolt against Edward, and at what point he first conspired with Clarence to place him on the throne, but he first revolted later in 1469. It is not inconceivable from this reference that Oxford 'turned' as his brother is said to have done during his imprisonment, but Edward did not apparently act on any information he might have gained.

Warwick defeated the king's men at Edgecote on 26 July 1469 and captured Edward himself soon after. His control of the king could not last and Edward was soon out of his custody and seeking to limit his former ally's powers. A second clash at what was known as Losecoat Field in March 1470 caused Warwick and Clarence to flee for France. It is not at all clear what part John de Vere played in the proceedings, but he joined with a resurgent Lancastrian party who invaded England in the September of that year. Under Warwick's command this army outmanoeuvred Edward in East Anglia and forced him to leave the country to avoid capture.

Henry VI, who had since his capture five years before resided in the Tower, was restored to the throne, despite his apparent lack of coherent thought. The Readeption, as this restoration was dubbed, comprised in practice Warwick governing the country in Henry's name, while maintaining an uneasy alliance with the Lancastrian magnates. Oxford bore the sword of state at King Henry's recrowning. He was also auditor for Essex in this time. Besides Oxford, there were the long-term Lancastrian dukes of Somerset and Exeter, Warwick's brothers Marquis Montague and Archbishop George Neville of York, and Clarence, who now found himself on the wrong side with little gain. Queen Margaret and her son Edward had not yet returned to England.

The one noted act of revenge against a Yorkist noble during this Readeption was one Oxford himself must have called for. Oxford had been appointed Constable of the Tower in Worcester's place, and now condemned his predecessor to the same fate as the other de Veres had suffered. John Tiptoft had enforced the writ of the Yorkist monarchy with some horrific executions and was widely hated for it. A hostile and unruly mob forced a postponement of the execution by a day. Worcester requested he be beheaded by three strokes, in honour of the Trinity.

Not too much is in fact known of the six months of this Readeption, as the restored Yorkists later destroyed some of the vital records. In March 1471, it was known that Edward IV had landed in Yorkshire and was proceeding southwards, gaining support as he went. Clarence was an early defector to his brother, and the Percy Earl of Northumberland, restored by Edward the previous year to his estates and titles, finally appeared to fight for him. The renascent Lancastrian regime prepared to defend itself.

Oxford's men had repulsed Edward's first attempt to land shortly before, on 2 March, when the Yorkist king had sailed from Bruges and tried to land at Cromer. He had planned that the Dukes of Norfolk and Suffolk would aid him there, not knowing that both were in custody. A force under the command of Oxford's brother Thomas de Vere beat back Edward's scouts, and the Yorkists decided to sail on. Edward had more support in Yorkshire and his landing at Ravenser twelve days later proved more to his advantage. Soon, swelled with supporters from Yorkshire and Cumberland, the Yorkist army came south.

When he reached Nottingham, Edward offered a pardon to Warwick and his confederates. Oxford was not willing to enter into this dialogue, with the Duke of Exeter gathered troops at Newark, a 'great felowshipe'. The *Arrivall*, a pro-Yorkist chronicle, claims they had four thousand men from the East Anglian counties, but this is clearly an over-estimate. The commanders felt that what they had would not resist the enemy. As Edward advanced, Oxford and Exeter, with some of their army, stole away in the middle of the night. Soon after they sought to engage with the Yorkists at Leicester but were soon put to flight.

With Exeter, Oxford sought to link with Warwick, who was then defending Coventry. The Yorkists frustrated this for a time; they tried to goad the earl to come out and fight, eventually withdrawing to Warwick Castle when he would not. Clarence returned to the Yorkist fold at this point. Warwick and his confederates, Oxford included, eventually set out to confront Edward on the Great North Road, but the Yorkists eluded them and gained entry to London. The Yorkists then marched north again to meet their enemy at Barnet on Good Friday 1471. The Earl of Oxford was present, and unwittingly contributed to the Lancastrian defeat.

Oxford in fact scored the first success of the Lancastrian army when, commanding the left flank, his attack routed the Yorkist right, and Lord Hastings' men ran from the field and beyond the village. Oxford's forces, having killed many of the fugitive soldiers, halted their pursuit at Barnet and set about plundering. As a prudent commander, Oxford had his captains collect his dispersed troops and march them back to the battlefield, for the fight was not yet won.

The soldiers marching in an orderly fashion behind the Oxford banner of the Rayed Star cut a picturesque sight in the morning mists. Unfortunately, the Star looked too much like the motif of the Sun in Splendour, the badge of Edward IV, which also had rays, and some of Montague's musketeers fired on Oxford's men in error. Interpreting this as treachery, at a time when Montague's loyalties had been cause for suspicion, Oxford and his men decided to withdraw from the battle. The incident gave Edward an opportunity to turn around his position. Fighting between some Lancastrian troops and those of Montague, also over alleged treason, aided the Yorkists in their victory. Warwick, Montague and Exeter headed the list of those killed at Barnet. Oxford was at first believed killed.

When Oxford abandoned the field he rode straight for Scotland and afterwards went to France, taking his two brothers and Viscount Beaumont with him. In doing so he saved himself from the fate of the other Lancastrians. Margaret had landed the day of the Battle of Barnet and met with Somerset's army but was defeated and captured at the Battle of Tewkesbury, her son Edward killed in the fight and Somerset caught and executed. Henry VI died soon after, probably done to death in the Tower on Edward's orders.

Oxford was however still young and not ready for a life of obscure exile. He acquired ships and set out into the Channel as a privateer. The leaders of his cause were all now either dead or imprisoned, so he could do no more than damage the mercantile interests of the restored Yorkist regime. Edward IV had fewer enemies in England now, although Oxford's raid on Essex in May 1473 may have been disquieting for him. Oxford had little to gain but could do damage with his raids. Perhaps he hoped that his supporters in Essex would rally to him, but this invasion did not come to anything. This brings the narrative to the curious annexation of St Michael's Mount, near Penzance in Cornwall, in the same year.

What Oxford hoped to achieve by occupying this virtual island off the Cornish coast on 26 September 1473 is uncertain. It might have been a possible base for his activities, although it was so far west. We do not know where his flotilla was moored when not engaged in piracy, if it had a home. Still, the Mount would not have been used for a landing of troops, as no massed Lancastrian army awaited: the House of Lancaster was extinct and Henry Tudor still too young and too remote from the English throne to be taken seriously. There is no evidence of any intriguing between Oxford and the French and Cornwall was hardly a suitable place to land, given such poor communications. Either to establish a base, or simply as an attack in anger on this outlying piece of King Edward's territory, are the only possible motives.

The Mount had been returned to the possession of Syon Abbey by Edward IV in 1462, and was a place of pilgrimage. According to the legend Oxford's men came disguised as pilgrims and seized the Mount when they arrived. Oxford came with 597 men, including his younger brothers George and Thomas. The others were probably also dispossessed Lancastrians or mercenaries from France. Viscount Beaumont and Thomas Clifford, possibly a relative of the long-dead Lancastrian baron, are also mentioned among Oxford's following.

Sir Henry Bodrugan was soon commissioned to lead an army to retake the Mount. Pockets of Lancastrian resistance had been a problem in Edward's first reign. Sir Richard Tunstall had held Harlech Castle in the name of King Henry for seven years, and even now a Lancastrian foothold would be considered a real danger. Bodrugan did his duty, but took a pedestrian approach to the action. He allowed the other side a daily opportunity to parley and also stopped fighting at times to allow the defenders to bring in food supplies. Although chivalrous, this was hardly an effective way to deal with rebels, and Edward ordered Richard Fortescue, the Sheriff of Cornwall, to take over command.

It was still a difficult operation taking an island fortress, the Mount's Bay a natural moat with a causeway only passable at low tide. Warkworth's Chronicle called it 'a stronge place and a mygty, and can noght be geett yf it be wele vytaled with a few menne to kepe hit.' Bodrugan had perpetuated the siege by allowing the enemy to resupply themselves. Fortescue laid siege on Christmas Eve, taking a much more aggressive line but still allowing truces throughout, one to keep the Christmas festivities. The Mount was not the easiest stronghold to overcome and the king ordered ships and troops to be sent as reinforcements. During the truces Fortescue also made promises of pardons and gifts to the defenders on the king's behalf.

These offers probably caused Oxford's following to rethink their presence in a siege that could not lead to anything but eventual defeat. On 15 February 1474, Oxford, who apparently still had months of supplies, declared that he could only rely on the loyalty of eight or nine of his men, and surrendered. It is not said if he was ever personally offered a pardon, but there was none for him.

The same chronicler summed up the campaign as he closed the chronicle in a whimsical and somewhat sexist manner.

For ther is proverbe and a seying, '*that a castelle that spekythe, and a woman that wille here, thei wille be goten bothe*': for menne that bene in a castelle of war, that wille speke and entrete with ther enemyes, there conclusion therof the losing of the castelle, and a woman that wille here fully spokyne to her, if she assent noght at one tyme sche wille at another.

The writer concluded that Oxford was forced to surrender before his men rebelled, and the continual offers of incentives to them to give up had brought him down.

Oxford was not executed for his activities, which is surprising. Instead, he and his brothers were imprisoned in the fortress of Hammes in the Calais march, the only part of France that the English still held. Perhaps the king wanted to rehabilitate him at a later date, as he had kept Henry Percy incarcerated for eight years before restoring him to the earldom of Northumberland, which proved a successful policy in the long term. But Oxford remained his enemy and was attainted in 1475. It was perhaps an odd choice of a prison lying as it did within walking distance of enemy territory. Early in 1485, after twelve years, Oxford escaped in time to participate in the decisive events of that year.

Edward IV had died two years before, and after the short reign of his son Edward V, the Duke of Gloucester, Richard of York's youngest son, had usurped the throne as Richard III. Unpopular as this reign had become by 1485, the time was ripe for Henry Tudor, a distant relative of Henry VI, to advance his own vague claim.

Oxford not only escaped but had suborned his gaoler James Blunt, Captain of Hammes, and also Sir John Fortescue, gentleman porter of Calais. Hammes declared allegiance to the Tudor cause and Richard sent Thomas Brandon with a force to recapture it. Brandon finally took Hammes, but after Oxford had returned and negotiated successfully for the rebels to depart with him from the March.

Oxford disembarked with Henry when he landed at Milford Haven in August that year. When the two sides met at Bosworth later that month it was Oxford who commanded the archers, who did the Yorkists damage. Richard might have won at Bosworth if some of his army had behaved as expected. Lord Stanley changed over to Henry Tudor at a crucial point. Worse news came to Richard after he called in the reserves that the Earl of Northumberland commanded, and heard that they remained on the sidelines, ignoring his order. Richard fell in the battle, his men either dead, surrendered or fled. Bosworth is often taken to mark the end of medieval England; a good a year as any, and better than most.

After a lifetime serving what was often thought the lost cause of Lancaster, John de Vere now came into his own. Henry VII of a Lancastrian cadet branch valued the faithful and Oxford was now a loyal servant and protector of the Tudor monarchy. He led the van at the Battle of Stoke in 1487, when the Yorkists made one final attempt to regain the throne. He later fought in Picardy in 1492 and campaigned against the Cornish rebels in 1497. He was godfather to Prince Arthur in 1486. During this reign he was Lord High Admiral of England, Ireland and Aquitaine, High Steward of the Duchy of Lancaster south of the Trent, and even regained his position of Constable of the Tower. He was also appointed keeper of lions and leopards within the Tower. He became a Knight of the Garter.

Throughout the reign he served on many commissions. He presided over the court that condemned Edward Plantagenet, Earl of Warwick, son of Clarence, to execution in 1498. At the coronation of Henry VIII in 1509, Oxford officiated as High Chamberlain of England. This was probably his last important function as he approached his threescore and ten.

Unlike most of the commanders of the Wars of the Roses, John de Vere died in his bed at a good age. After his Countess had died, Oxford had remarried, to Elizabeth, daughter of Lord Scrope of Bolton and widow of Viscount Beaumont. This second marriage also without issue, so when John died at Headingham Castle on 10 March 1512 he was succeeded as earl by his nephew, also called John de Vere. Oxford was buried at Colne Priory.

Perhaps Oxford could be commended for his steadfast adherence to the cause of Lancaster. When so many threw their lot in with the new Yorkist monarchy, Oxford remained loyal throughout. Others who would quickly rally to Lancaster also professed allegiance to Edward. Oxford was as pragmatic as any other who lived under this new regime, but he could be credited with remaining loyal to Lancaster even when there was no House of Lancaster left, and no apparent possibility for its return.

It may be that Oxford despised the house of York rather than strove for the cause of Lancaster. The execution of his father and brother was almost certainly the cause. If he joined with Warwick as early as 1468 Oxford was not then acting for Lancaster, although certainly against Edward. He did support Warwick and Clarence in 1470, but these only went over to the Lancastrians when they escaped to France, and on the encouragement of Louis IX of France. While Oxford would have been glad to fight for the cause of Henry VI, it is unlikely that he took part in Warwick's revolt with that intention. Who would ever have thought before the summer of 1470 that the Yorkist kingmaker would then become the Lancastrian king-restorer?

The belief that Henry VI was the rightful king ran deep in the minds of many people. Could a king be deposed, unsuitable as Henry was? Even though the principle of legitimacy had been damaged by the House of Lancaster itself in 1399, Henry VI had the doctrine of the divinity that hedged a king on his side. Either way, not everyone had all they wished for under the Yorkist monarchy, and many disaffected elements were drawn to the idea of a Lancastrian restoration.

Oxford's occupation of the Mount in 1473 would have been the final retaliation on behalf of the House of Lancaster, if there were a House of Lancaster left. There was no Lancastrian invasion to follow it up. Harlech Castle had been held for all those years to facilitate a Lancastrian landing that would not come. Edward IV took the occupation of the Mount seriously, but there was little to fear from it, apart from raids on the mainland. After Oxford's surrender Edward IV had no more serious revolts to threaten his monarchy.

If any one event shaped the life of John de Vere, 13th Earl of Oxford, it was the execution of his father and brother. His hatred of Edward and the Yorkist monarchy shaped his actions throughout his life. His attacks after 1472 on the English coast had nothing to gain but revenge. Despite all, his efforts were eventually rewarded.

20

Vlad the Impaler

Not a Vampire, but a Horror Story in His Own Right

One morning in 1890 an Anglo-Irish gentleman took himself to a public library. Having brought his son to school in Whitby, he had a long wait for the next train home. He had no way of knowing what an impact his reading of that morning would have on the literary world, on the then-nascent moving picture industry, and on popular culture. The gentleman was Bram Stoker, and the book he chose on the obscure province of Transylvania would lead him to create Count Dracula.

The book that drew his interest featured the life of Valdislav Basarab, or Vlad III Prince of Wallachia, also known as *Vlad Tepes*, or Vlad the Impaler, and as *Vlad Drakula,* Vlad the Devilish. He read of the extreme harshness of his rule, and of his struggle to keep his petty state independent from the Turks, but it was the legend of the vampire, the *nosferatu,* the undead, that captured Stoker's imagination. Using Whitby as its setting the story as published seven years later was the final result of that day's reading. Stoker, a theatrical impresario, had been thinking of writing a horror story for some years before and apparently knew of vampire legends. We have all heard of Dracula, and have seen at least one film version and many a parody, but the real person behind the original story remains obscure. The Wallachian nobleman of the fifteenth century bore little resemblance to anything Stoker, Bela Lugosi, Christopher Lee or any other has portrayed in the past century. Historically speaking, Stoker missed the point.

The real Vlad the Impaler was certainly no vampire, but he could have easily been the subject of a horror story of his own. He has been hailed as a nationalist, a defender of Christendom against Muslim conquerors, but was certainly also the perpetrator of appalling atrocities. In a previous age he would have been revered as a crusader. His extremely cruel treatment of his enemies, in particular his fondness for exhibiting them still alive with spikes run through their bodies, is how he is mostly remembered in his homeland. There is no evidence that he ever drank blood, but he certainly spilled large amounts of it.

The modern state of Romania is a fairly recent creation, forged between the Crimean War and the Versailles Settlement. It consists of the three provinces of Moldavia, Wallachia and Transylvania, together with some smaller regions to its west and the Dobruja on the Black Sea coast. The Romanian language is Romance in origin, believed the legacy of Roman settlers in what was once Dacia and comprehensible to speakers of Italian. The Kingdom of Hungary had absorbed Transylvania by the fifteenth century, when all central Europe was menaced by the Ottoman Turks. By that time the Orthodox Romanians of the other two provinces lived under threat from both the Hungarian Catholics and Islam's newest champions.

From the fourteenth century the Ottoman Sultans had sent their conquering armies into the Balkans. Having surrounded the dying Byzantine Empire, they eventually brought it to an end with the capture of Constantinople in 1453 and then threatened the Bulgarian and Romanian lands. The princes of Wallachia maintained a constant balancing act paying tribute to the sultan and addressing Hungarian expectations in resisting the spread of Islam. Vlad the Impaler through his fictional representation as Dracula is associated with Transylvania, and he was certainly born in that province, but he was in fact Prince of Wallachia.

Since the days when Mircea ruled there as prince late in the fourteenth century, there had been division within the princely House of Basarab, and a collateral branch known as the Danesti seized the throne. The Ottoman threat to Wallachia had grown serious and immediate by the turn of the fifteenth century, and the princes were forced to pay tribute to maintain independence.

Vlad II, father of Vlad the Impaler, was born in 1390, the illegitimate son of Mircea. He grew up in the court of King Sigismund of Hungary, later elected Holy Roman Emperor. He was probably sent there as a hostage but eventually joined Sigismund's entourage, which was common practice in those days. In 1431 this elder Vlad was appointed military governor of Transylvania, then part of the Hungarian king's dominions. As an ethnic Romanian, Vlad would have been an astute appointment.

Sigismund also made this Vlad a Knight of the Order of the Dragon, which he had founded himself, and whose members would swear to uphold the cause of (Catholic) Christendom and resist the advance of Islam. The name 'Drakul', which can mean both 'Dragon' and 'Devil' in Romanian, was then attached to this Vlad by the Wallachian boyars or nobles. Vlad's second son would be known as Drakula, or 'son of the dragon' – or 'son of the devil'.

It was while this elder Vlad governed Transylvania from the castle of Sighisoara that this second son, also called Vlad, the subject of this chapter, was born in December 1431. His elder brother was named Mircea after his grandfather, and there was one younger, known as Radu the Handsome.

While the younger Vlad was still a child, his father staged a spectacular coup. From his base in Transylvania he gathered support in his homeland of Wallachia, building a following among the boyars of the principality. In 1437, with Hungarian assistance he invaded Wallachia, defeating and killing his Danesti rival Alexandru, and acceded as Vlad II.

But the new prince inherited all the problems of the old. To maintain independence from the Turks by paying tribute while at the same time living under Hungarian vassalage was always the same balancing act. The Hungarians objected to his neutrality when the Ottomans invaded Transylvania in 1442. The Hungarian commander Janos Hunyadi invaded Wallachia the next year, driving out Vlad II and replacing him with the Danesti contender Basarab II. But Vlad was restored in 1444 after a dramatic deal with the other side.

He formed an alliance with Sultan Mehmed II and soon regained Wallachia with Turkish military support. As part of the agreement Vlad left his two younger sons Vlad and Radu as hostages. Young Vlad lived for four years at the sultan's court before his moment of destiny arrived. Radu apparently opted to remain there.

The fundamental problem over suzerainty persisted. Vlad II was now the Sultan's placement, but was still sworn to the Catholic, pro-Hungarian cause as a Knight of the Dragon. In 1447, the Turks once again invaded Transylvania, and the Prince of Wallachia found himself with the same dilemma as his predecessors; bound to agreements on both sides. He sent his eldest son Mircea to fight in the province's defence, hoping this would not anger the Sultan.

But even this ambivalence was enough to annoy the Hungarians once again. When the Turks dealt them a crushing defeat at Varna, there were accusations on all sides and calls for reprisals. It is likely that Hunyadi had planned to allow the destruction of this unwilling vassal. There was a rising later in 1447 of boyars and merchants in the Wallachian city of Tirgoviste, probably with Hungarian complicity, during which Vlad II and his son Mircea were murdered. When Mircea's body was exhumed soon after, the facial contortion revealed hinted that he had been buried alive. Hunyadi then placed another Danesti Vladislav II on the throne in Wallachia, which he expected would fight alongside him against the Turks.

It was then, at the age of seventeen, that the one later known as Vlad the Impaler came into his own. When the Sultan learned that the Hungarians were regaining control of Wallachia in 1448 he placed the young hostage in command of a Turkish army and charged him with recovering the principality. Soon this Vlad was the new prince.

The reign of Prince Vlad III seemed short-lived, once Hunyadi quickly drove him out to Moldavia and reinstated Vladislav. There, Vlad remained at the court of Prince Bogdan until the prince was assassinated three years later. Vladislav II had changed sides, and Hunyadi now supported Vlad in retaking Wallachia. In 1456 Hunyadi attacked the Turks in Serbia, concurrently with Vlad's invasion of Wallachia. Hunyadi himself was killed on this campaign but Vlad killed Vladislav as he regained his principality.

Tales of Vlad the Impaler's activities as Prince of Wallachia survive, mostly of his atrocities. Public executions, mutilations, and ghastly ways of killing people characterised his rulership. He was most fond of impaling, hence his name. This extreme method involved passing a six-foot spike through the victim's body in such a way that none of the vital organs were damaged, but leaving them hanging to suffer an excruciating death over several days. Vlad apparently enjoyed eating his meals in front of those he impaled.

It must be remembered that public atrocities of this nature were far from rare. Not only in the lands of the Turks but also in western Europe public beheadings, burnings, blindings, castrations and flayings were all common occurrences, even popular spectacles. Public executions took place in Britain as late as 1868, and such severe penalties as the removal of a foot were still exacted in Belgium before crowds in the early nineteenth century. Even in 1977 the world was shown on television a Saudi princess put to death for adultery with a bullet in a public place, after seeing her lover beheaded. It is possible that Vlad III grew fond of atrocities while still a hostage at the Sultan's court. The Turks made much use of mass slaughter, beheadings and torture in order to enforce their rule. But atrocity was by no means the sole province of the Turks, and Vlad could have emulated much of Europe in his methods.

If the many anecdotes are at all true Vlad the Impaler seems to have delighted in the excessive use of spectacular executions, and that carnage was almost a daily occurrence. Vlad was not only quick to use such horrific punishments but was somewhat inventive in his actions and appeared to enjoy them.

One famous story features two Turkish envoys who refused to doff their hats to the prince. Vlad had the same hats nailed to the officials' heads. He invited 500 of the boyars to a banquet, and promptly enslaved them. Medieval rulers always had problems with the landowning classes and their vested interests, and their management was a complicated issue. Vlad apparently solved his problems by having the most troublesome executed, and the rest worked to death in building a mountain fortress.

Another story concerns a different banquet, for many aged, poor and sick. This time he offered them release from all their troubles, they would lack nothing they desired. They understandably accepted. He then left the hall, had the doors locked and the building set on fire; a cruel and predictable gesture.

The second story of the boyar enslavement does have some logic to it. He broke the power of the boyars, although in a harsh and horrific manner. Their strength and vested interests made it difficult for any prince to govern. He first asked the assembled boyars how many princes had reigned in Wallachia in their lifetimes. When they replied that had all seen many, even the youngest no less than seven, Vlad retorted 'It is because of your intrigues and feuds that the principality is weak,' and ordered their arrest. He rebuilt the cadre of boyars, in part from those he spared from his purge, but also raised many free peasants to nobility. He formed a personal bodyguard, the *shoji*, of boyars and mercenaries.

Other stories appear apocryphal, showing what seem to be pointless acts of cruelty, but perhaps he used atrocity as a tool of government. Of the burning of the poor and sick he is reported as saying 'I did this so that no one will be poor in my realm.' Such an act raises questions as to his sanity. It is said that he had a golden cup placed by a drinking fountain in a public square. Anyone could drink from it, it was declared, but whoever dared to take it away would suffer severe penalties. No-one did. Such an act was certainly illustrative of his success in maintaining law and order.

Vlad reputedly used the pettiest of excuses to inflict the worst penalties. It is said that he impaled merchants he believed cheated their customers. He executed women who had extra-marital affairs. One story has him ordering the impaling of a woman because her husband's shirt was too short. He would impale children. Tirgoviste was said to have had over 20,000 bodies rotting on spikes all around it at any given time. It was said that he had had killed over 100,000 people in his short reign, although reliable figures are not available.

To some Vlad is now considered a Romanian patriot, one who strove for the independence of his principality. He curbed the activities of foreign merchants in order to protect home commerce and set up strict trading laws, many with impalement as penalty. He was not at all enthusiastic over the activities of both the Orthodox and Catholic churches, as both were dominated by foreigners, which gave them too much power in Wallachia. He also sought to reduce the threat of the Turks. That he was the last ruler to resist Turkish domination gave him heroic status in later centuries when the Romanians, after centuries under the Turks, thought of him as their champion. Vlad may have been an autonomous ruler, but had agreed to pay 10,000 gold ducats annually, and the Sultan expected the *devshirme* or levy of men for his armies to be met. Some prudent princes paid such a high price as they thought it far more preferable than having their lands absorbed directly into the Ottoman Empire. Vlad was bold to defy the Sultan, and perhaps foolhardy too.

When Vlad refused to allow the annual conscription, the Turks began raiding and impressing men. As Turkish troops captured some castles on the Wallachian side of the Danube, Vlad retaliated. As relations with the Sultan deteriorated, Mehmed invited him to talks. But the prince learned while approaching his borders that Hamza Pasha, the Ottoman commander, was preparing an ambush. Vlad and his men entered the fortress of Giurgiu disguised as Turks and speedily overpowered the garrison. Afterwards he put the town to the torch and impaled the remaining Turks. Hamza Pasha had the longest spike reserved for him.

As this act could hardly go unnoticed in Constantinople, Vlad prepared for retribution. He wrote to other princes, even sending two bags of Turkish heads, ears and noses to Matthias Corvinus, King of Hungary. There was serious talk of a crusade against the Turks with the support of Pope Pius II, as Ottoman advances in the Balkans were disquieting for Europe. But the response from the princes of Europe was lukewarm. Most had one excuse or another, often with their closer enemies in mind. The Venetians asked for too much money, and only the Albanians under their leader George Scanderbeg fought their own defence. Vlad stood almost alone in the defence of Christendom. Surely he could scarcely expect another crusade from the West now that self-interest had killed the crusade as an effective institution long before.

The Turkish invasion, over 60,000 strong, came in the summer of 1462. As a major surprise, one of its commanders was Vlad's brother Radu, who had lived at the Sultan's court all this time, now leading a regiment of Wallachian exiles alongside the Turks. Vlad raised an army half this size, mostly of free peasants, and was able at first to frustrate the Turks' attempts to cross the Danube.

This only lasted a short time, and the Ottoman forces eventually gained a foothold. Their superior numbers and fire-power – the Turks had embraced the use of cannon and gunpowder and were using it well – soon convinced Vlad that he could hardly conduct conventional warfare. The Wallachians ran a guerrilla campaign, burning crops, taking livestock and harassing the Turkish army where they could. One Wallachian raid on the Sultan's own camp threatened Mehmed's own life. The raiders could not find him but killed two of his viziers and escaped with much loot. Vlad expected that another force led by some of the boyars would join and he could destroy the Turkish leadership, but this did not appear, and he withdrew into the forest. All Turks taken prisoner were tortured in the most inventive and horrific ways, and then impaled.

When Mehmed eventually approached Tirgoviste, it was said that he was sickened by a display of thousands of rotting bodies impaled on stakes, most of them Turkish. Even this man of blood was disgusted. Lack of supplies, disease and the attrition of the guerrilla war having also taken its toll. The Sultan lost heart in the campaign and redirected it. This was thought in the West as a major victory, even though at best it had only bought time. Vlad was enraged that his boyars' failure to rally had cost him his chance for a decisive and victorious counter-attack at the right moment.

As the main Turkish forces marched away, Radu the Handsome remained to fight on against an exhausted defending force.

He approached the Wallachian boyars and offered peace in return for tribute to the Sultan and his own recognition as prince. Those which Vlad had lately raised did not prove as loyal as expected, and many did not share Vlad's enthusiasm for independence, not after such a hard war. Perhaps they reasoned that the Ottoman Sultanate was so powerful that Vlad was mad to think he could resist it forever. Radu's offer was preferable to next year's invasion and the expected reprisals.

Vlad, deserted by many of his boyars and other supporters, fought on, driven into the Carpathians and eventually to Arges Castle in Transylvania. Soon faced by a major assault by a Turkish army on behalf of Radu, he came to the conclusion that little more could be done. His wife, declaring that she would rather be eaten by the fish than become a Turkish slave, threw herself from the battlements into the river below. Vlad escaped, the story says through a secret tunnel, and rode for Brasov, where Matthias Corvinus held his court.

His hope to gain an ally in Matthias was misplaced. The Hungarian king had already recognised Radu, and Vlad was no use to him at this time, even though he obviously saw his possible worth at a later date. Matthias had him arrested, escorted to Buda and thrown into prison. For a time, Vlad languished in his cell, where he was seen to catch mice and birds and impale them.

During the latter part of his twelve years in Hungary the former prince had much better treatment, as Matthias considered restoring him in Wallachia. For much of his time in Budapest Vlad lived in more comfortable circumstances, but under house arrest. Later still, as talk of a crusade against the Turks began once more, he was made a captain of the Hungarian army. It was said that Matthias would present Vlad to Turkish envoys to his court as a reminder. He was not forgotten.

Matthias also had Vlad initiated to the Order of the Dragon as his father had been, and married to a Hungarian princess. For the purposes of both, he became a Roman Catholic. Vlad had not shown much enthusiasm for either Orthodoxy or Catholicism when he was prince, but he needed the King's support if he would ever be prince again. This act provided the basis to the later legend: the Romanians believed that Orthodox Christians who converted to Catholicism would become vampires after they died. Whatever Stoker read in Whitby, it was this detail that gained more of his interest than the exploits of the factual Vlad Drakula.

In Wallachia, Radu was overthrown in 1473, and a Danesti, Basarab the Old, had taken his place, still as a Turkish vassal. Radu died of syphilis in January 1475. Later that year Prince Stephen of Moldavia approached Matthias with a planned crusade, with the intent of securing a Danube frontier against the Turks. Money from the pope eased the Hungarian king's assent, although he really did little when Stephen invaded Wallachia. He placed Vlad in command of the forces that would protect the Transylvanian frontier from possible Turkish or Wallachian raiding. The former prince immediately set about a military campaign across the Carpathians. He was reported by a papal envoy to have cut the Turks' bodies into pieces and impaled them a piece at a time; a variation on his long-standing obsession. It is not known if he fought at the Battle of Vashi where Stephen defeated the Wallachians, but he made a considerable impact on the war.

Matthias had kept Vlad as a card he could play, and now decided it was time. Late in 1476 he sent his general Stephen Bathory with an army to restore Vlad as prince of Wallachia. There were 25,000 troops, including many Transylvanians and Wallachian exiles. As Stephen of Moldavia invaded at the same time, Basarab's Wallachians could offer little resistance in the absence of Turkish support. Vlad himself led the attack on Tirgoviste in November. His large force soon convinced the defenders that resistance was futile, and he took Bucharest soon afterwards. Before the year was over, Vlad the Impaler was Prince of Wallachia once again. Before 1476 ended, he was murdered.

Exactly how Vlad died and by whose hand is not known. In December his headless body was found in the snow near Bucharest. There is a story of a Turkish assassin posing as a servant. It is also likely that many of the boyars who had returned to his side at this time had reason to kill him. There is no shortage of candidates. The body was taken to the nearby monastery at Snagov for burial, although archaeological excavations have not located his remains. His head made the journey to Constantinople to be shown to the Sultan and then placed on a pike, for the Turks had to be sure he was dead. Their possession of his head makes it likely that the Turks had arranged the assassination.

Wallachia's chances of independence from the Turks died with Vlad the Impaler. Other princes came and went after 1476, with less autonomy and only in the nineteenth century were Wallachia and Moldavia wrested from Ottoman overlordship. It was an act of pure folly to defy the Sultan in the fifteenth century without support from more powerful Christian nations. Vlad showed himself an able military commander, especially in his use of inadequate resources, and his 1462 campaign at least ended with his principality still independent. But there would have been another attack the following year if Radu had not overthrown Vlad and the Turks would have overrun Wallachia sooner or later.

The princes of Wallachia were often pawns of the Sultans and the kings of Hungary, and perhaps most saw little option but to cooperate with their powerful neighbours. Vlad was at first simply another of these puppets, but later sought to break the hold of foreign influences on his principality. To take on the Ottoman sultanate, even though he performed well on his campaign, was doomed to failure in the circumstances.

The Turks feared him even when he was in exile. It was to his undoing that his boyars, for all he gave so many of them, decided that loyalty to him brought such a high price that they accepted Radu's offer. Vlad was probably not so much a patriot, nor a champion of the Romanian people, nor even of Christianity, but simply an ambitious ruler.

It was his apparent love for atrocity, and for the metal stake, that characterises his reign and probably cost him support. As already said, public horrors were commonplace in the medieval period almost everywhere in the world. Vlad simply multiplied their use many times over.

His story brings to mind the Machiavellian maxim that a prince is better feared than loved. His law-and-order policy was certainly effective, and feared he certainly was. It also aided his military prowess. Such atrocities were often used in the East as a psychological weapon – the Mongols were particularly famed for this – and were effective. The Turkish army approaching Tirgoviste was said to have been horrified at the thousands of rotting impaled bodies around it. It did not, as some chroniclers believed, cause the Sultan to give up the campaign, to admit that he 'could not win this land from a man who does such things. A man who knows how to exploit the fear of his people.' It certainly demoralised the invaders as their campaign was otherwise suffering. The Turks would do the same to rebellious populations; it was the sheer volume of Vlad's atrocities that shocked them.

It was the fact that Vlad apparently enjoyed inflicting such pain and carnage that made him so infamous. He seems to have impaled on the pettiest pretext, with such enthusiasm that it pleased him immensely. Such acts throw his sanity into doubt. Without such a preoccupation Vlad Basarab might have been considered a patriot and defender of Christendom, even if his efforts proved futile in the long term.

21

Tomas de Torquemada

The Stuff of Nightmares

On the mention of the word 'Inquisition' a series of images, all unpleasant, invades our thoughts. Although some may know of a difference when 'Spanish' is prefixed to it, our perception of the entire affair involves torture, horrific death by burning, black-cowled inquisitors and an atmosphere of horror in dark places lit only by fire. Such has been the Inquisition in popular imagination, perpetuated by Edgar Allen Poe, Victor Hugo and Dostoyevsky. It has parallels with more recent outrages against humanity.

Although the Inquisition itself was a more diverse institution, the version practised in Spain from the fifteenth century to more modern times was in many ways consistent with this image. Whether this assessment requires revision, and whether it was the influence of its first Grand Inquisitor Tomas de Torquemada that set the perception, requires examination. Was he really the monster history depicts him, or simply a product of his society and age?

As an institution, the Inquisition already had a long history by the time Torquemada relaunched it in the late fifteenth century. The origins of this institution can be traced to the opening decade of the thirteenth century, and to the sanction of Pope Innocent III.

When he took office in 1198, there was a long list of abuses within the Church and in society that he wished to end, including the spread of heresy. Having seen his Fourth Crusade to restore Jerusalem hijacked into a cynical conquest of Constantinople, he sanctioned a new crusade against the Cathars in southern France, the first not directed against Islam. Strictly speaking, the Cathars were a new religion rather than a heresy, rooted in a Zoroastrian dualist perspective of good spirituality and the evil of the flesh. To justify the extermination of thousands and other atrocities committed under the guise of crusading, in 1209 the Church had decided that the doctrine must be eradicated, and this called for desperate measures.

Innocent III himself did not begin the Inquisition but the Third Lateran Council of 1216, which he convened the year before his death, laid the foundations. Among the assertion of doctrines and standards of behaviour made were harsh measures to be taken against heresy, including the assistance of the secular authorities in executing unrepentant and relapsed heretics. By the 1330s, during the pontificate of Gregory IX, there was a set procedure for a semi-permanent tribunal. Dominican and Franciscan friars were usually appointed as inquisitors.

The Church had its own courts for dealing with such issues as sodomy, incest, blasphemy, and of course heresy. There was already a body of canon law, in which was stipulated the accused's right to conduct a defence, to review witnesses, and to appeal, features designed to ensure that justice be done. The Inquisition as it emerged circumvented all such rights and procedures. The reasoning was that the Church was under attack, and its defence must be unhampered by such niceties. The accused were not told who their accuser was, or they might even be accused anonymously. They could be questioned on their faith without knowing of the charges, and if the tribunal decided they did not give unequivocal responses, they could be tortured until a straight answer was obtained. There was a range of penalties and the ultimate sentence was death by burning, but this was the last resort, reserved for those who remained unrepentant of their heresy, or those who returned to heresy after reconciliation with the Church.

This siege mentality is often perceived to have a modern echo. The Holy Church was in danger from these heretics, it reasoned, and any consideration of fair assessment and establishing the truth was cast aside. Just as when the Bush administration declared a War on Terror in 2001 – as if it were possible to declare war on a strategy or a state of mind – and produced such an affront to natural justice as Guantanamo Bay, the Church waged war on heresy. Forgetting common sense as quickly as they did Christian charity, they treated all their suspects as the enemy and thousands were arrested, questioned, imprisoned, tortured and, in comparatively few cases, met death by the flame.

Of course, there was much variation in treatment. Some inquisitors might proceed with caution and some may have understood it their primary mission to bring erring Christians back to the fold. Few were so fanatical as to seek to burn those brought before them. Many felt it was their duty to strike fear in the hearts of heretics, but at the same time there was always the hope that the heretics would see the light and resolve to remain good Christians ever after.

The inquisition in its medieval format had in fact run its course by the end of the fourteenth century. While the Cathar and Waldensian heresies were all but suppressed, few were now summoned for heretical views and the tribunals ceased to meet. The inquisition had assembled in 1314 when the Templars were accused of idolatry, heresy, sodomy and a vast range of other charges, from usury to deliberately losing the Holy Land to the Saracens, but seldom afterwards, The inquisition was only used a few times in England; when Archbishop Arundel finally gained the legal sanction to burn Lollards in 1402 he preferred to control the process himself and the standard ecclesiastical courts accordingly examined cases and exacted the penalties. There was no need for such an institution when those in charge of the conventional processes were as bent on seeking out the guilty.

The Spanish Inquisition revived the process, this aggressive stance that presupposed guilt and sought out the guilty without any hindrance from the episcopal establishment, but the principal target at this early stage was the insincere convert from Judaism. It would be an exaggeration to say that Fray Tomas de Torquemada single-handedly relaunched the Inquisition in Spain in the new dynamic form. He had widespread support for his actions, both clerical and lay, and from the top of the social hierarchy.

There are not many biographical details on Tomas de Torquemada. He was born in or about 1420 in Valladolid. His father was Don Miguel de Torquemada, a lesser Castilian noble; the family name means 'burnt tower'. Especially when Latinised to *Turra Cremata*, the reference to burning in his name had a sinister ring to it. One of the grandparents of the man who would become the scourge of Jews in Spain was a convert from Judaism.

The prime influence on the young Tomas was certainly his uncle, Cardinal Juan de Torquemada, the celebrated prelate and theologian, a Dominican. Tomas was clearly destined for a career in the Church under his influence, and was known for his powerful, almost aggressive, address to his studies. According to the usual practice, the original nepotism, he might have advanced on a fast-track route through his uncle's *familia* to become at least a bishop by his mature years. But Tomas was clearly bent on entering the Dominican Order without thought for higher office.

He would refuse doctoral honours and later episcopal office. As an only son, his taking Holy Orders ended his line. By joining the Black Friars he showed commitment to their mission for Christian orthodoxy, and between 1435 and 1440 Tomas entered the convent at Piedrahita.

Friars have already appeared in this work as sincere advocates of the simple Christian life as well as academics, but there was more than one order. While the original followers of Francis of Assisi conducted this anarchic, benevolent lifestyle as God's Holy Minstrels, the stance of the Dominican or Black Friars as appeared a little earlier was a world away. In the footsteps of their founder Dominic Guzman, the Order of Preachers as they styled themselves were men with a mission. Not for them as for the Order of Friars Minor extreme poverty and a simple Christian example; the Dominicans laboured to promote a rigid orthodoxy in the minds of the faithful.

Dominic, a theological scholar of Castile, had begun preaching in 1204, just as Innocent III turned his attention to the Cathar and Waldensian heresies that had taken hold in southern France, and long before Innocent first gave verbal endorsement of both the Dominicans and the Franciscans. Just as the crusade he proclaimed had assaulted the bodies of these heretics, the Dominicans became the shock troops in the battle for the minds of the laity. From an early stage many Friars of both the early orders were appointed as inquisitors, the Dominicans in particular, their black cowled habits one more sinister detail of the affair.

There was no doubt of Torquemada's commitment and skill in the ways of the Order. His biographers talk of his sincerity and his drive. He was cook in the convent at one stage, but within twenty years became Prior of the Convent of Santa Cruz de Segovia. It was said that later in life Torquemada was known for his superstitious behaviour. He would not eat unless the horn of a unicorn or the tongue of a scorpion was placed by his plate as a guard against poison. The horn probably came from a narwhal or an ibex.

Events in the Iberian Peninsula in the 1470s would afford Torquemada and the Inquisition fertile ground for their activities. The area we know as Spain then comprised three separate states. Castile was the largest and covered most of the northern and central regions. The Kingdom of Aragon, itself a union of three small kingdoms looking out onto the Mediterranean, had territories in southern Italy, Sardinia and the Balearics. The kingdom of Navarre had been absorbed by Aragon.

In the south was the Emirate of Granada, the only remaining Moslem state in Europe. A remnant of Islamic rule over all the peninsula, this land had changed little since the time of Ibn Khaldun, apart from further loss of territory. The *Reconquista* had shown little further impetus in nearly two centuries and even when the Castilians took Gibraltar in 1462 the remaining Islamic territories still felt fairly secure.

The marriage of Isabella, heiress of Castile in 1468 to Ferdinand, heir to the throne of Aragon, did not immediately unify Spain but began a centuries-long process of radical transformation. Their energy at the time they succeeded to their kingdoms in 1474 and 1479 had them reassert their respective monarchies, gain the support of the nobles and embark on a systematic war of conquest against Granada, which they finally completed in 1492. Ferdinand and Isabella are known for their patronage of Christopher Columbus, and how this eventually led to Spain's empire in the New World. Torquemada himself played an important role in in creating the personal union and the completion of the *Reconquista*. He would soon declare war on what he thought was the greatest danger, in the minds of the people

For centuries, Spanish Christianity had lived in a close association not only with Islam, but also with Judaism. The treatment of Jews in Europe throughout this period was appalling, as anti-Semitism was a persistent theme from Roman times to the present day. We are all too aware of its excesses in Nazi Germany, and perhaps loath to admit that until 1945 anti-Semitism was not unfashionable throughout the civilised world. By the twelfth century at least, many Jews lived in European cities, for most of the time going about their ordinary business without fear, but seldom at ease with the Christians. It was common for European Jews to live in a separate walled neighbourhood, a Jewry or *ghetto* with gates that closed at night. Such enclosures were primarily designed for the Jews' own protection and the rabbi usually locked the gates at sunset.

The tendency to demonise the Jew came and went in waves. The race who killed Christ was accused of every horrific crime that could be conceived; they kidnapped and ritually murdered children, spread diseases and plotted to destroy Christianity. In 1255, a boy later canonised as Little St Hugh of Lincoln disappeared, and the authorities tortured a Jew of the town called Copin until he confessed to crucifying him; Jews sacrificed a child that way every year, he told the court. He was executed and a pogrom against Jews followed. This was repeated in several other towns all over Europe in the following centuries. When the Moslems led by Saladin retook Jerusalem in 1187, the people of York reacted by massacring the Jews of the city. When the Black Death ravaged Europe, mobs lynched Jews as they blamed them for spreading the plague by poisoning wells. There was no evil act a Jew was incapable of, many believed, and the Dominicans preached this incessantly.

Innocent III presiding, the Fourth Lateran Council approved measures prohibiting Christians from marrying Jews, or associating closely with them at all, and ordered that Jews would wear the Star of David on their dress, together with several other restrictions that the Nuremberg Laws of 1935 echoed.

By tradition, Jews were often moneylenders, which is a key to understanding their role in medieval society. For a Christian to lend money and charge interest constituted the sin of usury, and this hardly encouraged the financing of enterprise. Not so for Jews, and this was for some a route to material success, especially as in some countries Jews were forbidden to practise most trades. Rates of interest could be fixed by law. Before banking was established the Jews played an essential role in society and even kings undertook to protect them, and a few grew rich and were often resented for their wealth and demands for repayment. Shakespeare's Shylock is a caricature of this popular image. When Edward I decided he no longer needed to rely on his Jewish creditors, in 1290 he expelled all Jews from England, seizing their property, and it was only under Cromwell that they were allowed to return four centuries later. Jews could be victims of extreme fanaticism with little warning.

It is believed that Spain in the passage of the *Reconquista* was a haven of religious tolerance. While this is misleading, it could be said that Jews and Moslems living in the Christian-held regions saw comparatively less persecution at this time. As the Christian kingdoms expanded southwards, Moslem peasants were still needed for their labour and enforced mass conversions were impracticable. Persecution in the Moslem lands caused many Jews to move north, bringing their expertise with them.

Many Jews made a living from their scholarship, too, such as Maimonides, or Rabbi Moshe ben Maimon, the celebrated Torah scholar and philosopher of the twelfth century. There were many other accomplished men of letters, doctors, teachers of mathematics, philosophy and of the Holy Books, and the period from 900 to 1200 is deemed a golden age of Jewish culture and learning in Spain.

However, Castile and Aragon were already going the way of other European states by the fourteenth century, and the same privations and waves of persecution followed. When the Black Death ravaged Europe in 1348 and 1349, and often during its recurrences its impact on the psyche of Christendom was almost as powerful as the toll in lives. Obsession with sin and with mortality became the norm. The Dance of Death where all estates, knight, lady, peasant and priest, line-danced together while the last dancer was a skeleton with a scythe, became a popular subject in ecclesiastic painting. There were outbreaks of plague in Castile in 1440 and 1467, and as elsewhere in Europe complacency vanished. To rationalize what was seen as divine wrath there was a tendency to seek out what sins or omissions were the cause, or to look for culprits. Thus the preaching of the Dominicans, who put all ills down to heresy and the machinations of the Jews, gained wide attention.

In Castile the first significant persecutions began in the 1380s. In June 1391, the Castilians rose in response to the preaching of a fanatical deacon and the ghetto in Sevilla was attacked. Synagogues were burnt down or converted into churches, many Jews massacred and others sold into slavery, the violence spreading to Madrid, Cordova, Burgos and Cuenca. It was obvious that the authorities would do little and the kings were no longer interested in protecting Jews. In July, similar pogroms broke out in Aragon where the death toll was massive. In the Balearic Islands, whose governor turned a blind eye, some 300 Jews died. In Valencia, with the murder of about 250, the Jewish community was eradicated from the city.

This phase of extreme persecution ran its course, and life returned to normal. But soon in Castilian lands there came a flood of restrictions, some petty but mostly intended to deny Jews a normal life. In 1412, Jews were restricted to living in designated quarters, excluded from posts in public office and forbidden to practise commerce. They were no longer to be addressed by the honorific title of 'Don' and prohibited from cutting their hair or beards, so that they might stand out in public. They also wore the Star of David. In Aragon there were even more onerous demands. Practising Jews had to attend three Christian services a year where they were hectored each time on the error of their ways.

Yet as the fifteenth century progressed it was possible for a practising Jew, as much as a practising Moslem, to live and work in both Castile and Aragon, even with so many privations. Common sense allowed them to continue as moneylenders and scholars. Commerce and society could not easily do without them, and thus persecution was less acute most of the time.

It was those Jews who converted to Christianity that now lived a precarious life. Many had been forcibly converted in the pogroms, and to return to Judaism would mean death for apostasy. As in previous times, many Jews voluntarily sought baptism and adopted Christian names and lifestyles to integrate, and by the mid-fifteenth century the *conversos* or 'New Christians' formed a large segment of the population. Many prominent people, such as Hernando del Puglar, chronicler at the Castilian royal court, were *conversos* and many a family, Torquemada's included, had one Jewish ancestor or more.

It is not hard to conclude that many converts came to the font pragmatically. While there were Jews who embraced Christianity enthusiastically and even zealously called for further persecution of their former co-religionists, many others decided to avoid persecution with what was to them a meaningless ritual and changes in outward lifestyle. Who would blame them in the circumstances?

Suspicion was growing, however, that many of the New Christians were far from sincere in their conversion; they may attend church and profess the Christian faith, but in secret they remained Jewish. Perhaps they would simply refrain from eating pork, but others felt strongly enough of the religion of their fathers as to keep kosher, observe the Sabbath on Saturdays and the festivals of Yom Kippur, Succoth and Rosh Hashanah, or study the Torah, all in secrecy. A few kept secret libraries of the Holy Books of their religion.

The Dominicans behaved like a secret police, constantly monitoring *conversos* for signs that they had not abandoned their previous faith: whether they did not eat pork, or refrained from various actions on certain days. One friar observed that a convert's chimney did not smoke on Saturdays, and this was taken as evidence that he kept the Jewish Sabbath by not lighting fires on that day.

Many, the Dominicans in particular, seriously believed that such New Christians were not only using their conversions to hide their continued Judaism, but were Judaizing, encouraging converts to return to the old religion and even subverting Christians. Judaism is not a religion that actively seeks converts and although they must have resented the unwarranted persecution, it is an impossibility that the Jews really were seeking to undermine Christianity in Spain. While many *conversos* probably did keep their old religion in private, this was hardly doing Christianity any harm.

Tomas de Torquemada could not have lived at a better time in terms of his personal mission. As fanatically Anti-Semitic as any Dominican, he was the best-placed of all when the Infanta Isabella chose him as her confessor. It was Torquemada who supported the plan of her marrying Ferdinand of Aragon and urged her to agree to it. After her marriage he showed some skill in keeping Ferdinand calm when he had problems with the Castilian nobles, and Ferdinand eventually made Torquemada his own confessor too.

In the guise of a wise cleric counselling a young girl who would one day be queen, he persuaded Isabella that radical action was needed. Not only should Islam be driven from the peninsula, but war should be declared on all those elements that sought to undermine the Church in the kingdoms: Saracens, heretics, idolaters and above all, Jews, The Jewish peril was the most acute: in particular the *conversos* who practised their former religion while professing Christianity, and the Judaizers who sought to convert Christians. Torquemada convinced her not only that Christianity was in the gravest danger and urged that the Inquisition be brought to the kingdoms, but that a lax approach to religious observance was an obstacle to the unification of Spain.

Aragon had already established the inquisition there a long time before. It followed a medieval framework overseen by the bishops and had not summoned anyone for decades. Castile had never had the inquisition, for like England it had never seen the need to import the procedure. But from 1474, when Isabella and her husband succeeded to the Castilian throne, the hunt for secret Jews and their persecution intensified.

Torquemada still declined appointment to a bishopric; he was not even seen at court more than a few times up to this point. He did agree to take a place on the royal council, but in reality he enjoyed an influence on the new king and queen similar to that which Rasputin would have on the Tsar and his family in pre-revolutionary Russia. Isabella followed his instruction in matters of her conscience and entrusted him with various sinecures that the crown could grant. Torquemada did not ask for much himself, only the means to declare war on the Jewish threat.

After preparing Isabella for this mission while she waited to succeed, Torquemada wasted little time and soon after her accession he and Gonzales de Mendoza, Archbishop of Toledo, approached her and Ferdinand with their revolutionary plan. With the sanction of the joint monarchs, they then submitted a petition to Pope Sixtus IV to establish an inquisition with modifications of their own. This new form had Ferdinand and Isabella in ultimate control of the proceedings, rather than the bishops. The two monarchs found this arrangement attractive as it circumvented the participation of the nobles and the Church, traditional constraints on the monarchy. They were happy to allow Torquemada to direct proceedings.

Sixtus, a Franciscan who, once elevated to the papal chair, behaved like a Renaissance prince, and who was responsible for building the Sistine Chapel and other fine buildings of Rome, had misgivings; but he was himself bent on plans to reassert the power of the papacy. After considerable intriguing, a Papal Bull was issued in 1479 authorising the appointment of two inquisitors at Seville at the monarch's discretion. Torquemada, who effectively directed the Inquisition from that point, immediately set to work with great energy, using the power of the state. There were Commissaries of what would be called the Holy Office sent to every part of Castile, their brief to investigate instances of heresy, apostasy, sorcery, sodomy and polygamy, where the Dominicans operated independently of the bishops' tribunals. Although the rhetoric of the Inquisition still spoke of heresy, Torquemada's energies were primarily directed against the false *conversos* while he was in charge.

His mandate obtained, Torquemada convened a general assembly of inquisitors at Seville on 29 November 1484, where he presented a code of articles. Most were similar to the medieval guidelines, but his own modifications were harsh. Every Spanish Christian, including boys over fourteen and girls over twelve, was declared subject to the Inquisition. Absolution in secret was forbidden even after voluntary confession, and a public declaration of error would be made. In particular, a thirty-day period of grace was allowed, and those who confessed their heresy in this period were only fined and otherwise kept their goods.

At first Torquemada and others set up the seat of the Holy Office in the convent of San Pablo in Seville, but the Friars established there resented its presence. The Inquisition then moved to the fortress of Triana, a gloomy and forbidding construction. Those released from the custody of the Holy Office were forced to swear never to reveal what went on inside the fortress. It added to the sense of menace the place posed, and those who left it alive were often too afraid of being returned there to break their oath.

Under Torquemada's leadership, permanent tribunals were established at Valladolid, Seville, Jaen, Avila, Cordova, and Villa-Real. He also established one at Salamanca in Aragon in 1484, despite the opposition of the bishops and with Ferdinand's support. There were many others of an *ad hoc* nature. The inquisitors and their following were allowed free board and lodgings wherever they travelled and were allowed to buy provisions at a reduced rate. He also set up a High Council of five who would assist him in his role as Grand Inquisitor.

Torquemada first invited all of Castile's Jews to present themselves before the tribunal and avow their faults, and assured all who did of grace and pardon. Many immediately fled the country – one source says as many as 17,000 – and many Castilian *conversos* settled in Portugal and France. Many actually accused themselves, for fear their enemies would accuse them anonymously.

Most of the evidence we have of the procedures conducted dates from later centuries and it is not certain how much was under Torquemada's watch as Grand Inquisitor. Most of the Inquisition's own archives were destroyed during the Napoleonic occupation of Spain.

Some talked of being led from their cells to the place of the Inquisition by a route that usually involved passing the instruments of torture. The sight of the principal Inquisitor in black robes and a hood that put his face in darkness also figured. Charges would be pronounced and witness statements read without naming their sources. There would follow a verbal duel during which the accused would seek to acquit themselves while the court was seeking to catch them out. Those before the Inquisition were often unable to guess who was accusing them, and it was difficult to offer a defence of false witness. This interrogation stage was designed to establish the theological basis of the charges, and the accused's response. It gave the defendants few opportunities to establish their innocence.

'The Question', or physical torture, was always the option most feared. Strictly speaking, it could be used when the defendant pleaded neither guilty nor innocent and only until they made a clear statement of either. In practice the defendant was put to The Question if the tribunal decided they were being misled, and it was not difficult to reach such a decision.

The rack, where the body was drawn by pulleys and the vertebrae damaged, was one of the standard methods. The *strappado* was a similar device, which involved hanging the subject by the arms, together with similar instruments that inflicted excruciating pain and could cripple and otherwise incapacitate those who suffered. The practice of pouring water down the victim's throat, ancestor of 'waterboarding' used in recent years, was common, often with the mouth filled with silk cloth, which bloodily chafed the inside of the mouth when withdrawn. According to the guidelines, the inquisitor and other officials would be present at each torture session. According to the rules, too, the accused could be tortured only once, and it was declared that torture was 'suspended' at the end of each session.

Yet the Spanish Inquisition, even during the height of its terror, was the subject of many myths, and it was not so inventive in its means of inflicting pain as literature depicts. When Edgar Allen Poe wrote *The Pit and the Pendulum* in 1842 he used historical licence in the tradition of the pulp horror stories of his day. While it is true that many left the houses of the Inquisition as cripples, with damaged bones and ligaments and minus some of their fingers, proportionately few of the prisoners were actually tortured. It was said that many, on being brought to the torture chamber, instantly confessed to all the charges, and others did so on the mere mention of The Question. Such a reaction is to be expected. Very few died under torture.

The trial itself was usually short, for guilt was usually assumed from the outset. Defence lawyers could be called, but these were eventually appointed by the court. It was far from easy to be acquitted, and it was probably the best option to confess even when innocent and hope for the mercy of the tribunal.

Maria Gonzalez was the first of the *conversos* burned by the Spanish Inquisition. She had already confessed during the period of grace in 1484, but it appears that her husband had forced her to keep Jewish practices. She was denounced and hauled up before the Inquisition charged with keeping the Jewish Sabbath, wearing her best clothes on a Saturday, saying Jewish prayers, lighting an oil lamp on Friday evening and eating meat and unleavened bread in Lent. Many others soon followed with a tedious roll of the same and similar activities.

Those who went to the stake formed a small percentage of the accused. Figures from the later period for some tribunals give 'Reconciliation' as the outcome of the majority of cases. Ideally, this would mean that the suspects had confessed to their erroneous beliefs and expressed the contrite desire to return to the fold of the righteous. This might incur other charges or penalties, including confiscation of property or imprisonment. The Reconciled were still denied all honourable employment and forbidden the use of gold, silver, jewellery or fine wool.

Less fortunate were those who received the sentence of *sanbenito*. For the rest of their lives they wore yellow crosses on their chest and their shoulders. At least the penitent survived, but this was the ultimate badge of shame. In later records other penalties appear: scourging and slavery in the galleys for a number of years, banishment and loss of goods.

The stake was always present as the ultimate penalty. Torquemada wished, as in the strict interpretation of the guidelines, that 'Release' should be reserved for extreme cases. Only those who refused to recant their wicked ways and those who had been 'reconciled' and then lapsed were to burn. But as for all penalties, there was considerable variation between the tribunals, and the rules were interpreted differently. There is a consensus among historians that about 2,000 people were burned between the beginning of the Spanish Inquisition and 1530. Probably less than half were so executed while Torquemada was Grand Inquisitor.

Death by burning was one of the most terrible ends known in the Middle Ages and it was usually the practice for the executioner to strangle the condemned before the flames reached them. Such a merciful release was confined in Spain to those who went to the stake as contrite Catholics. Unrepentant heretics, Jews and Moslems died screaming.

In Torquemada's time the ceremony known as the *auto-da-fé* appeared. This Act of Faith, usually known by its Portuguese name, would be held whenever the Inquisition decided. Usually on a feast-day in front of the assembled public, a procession would take place, of priests, often of monks and holy relics, followed by all those condemned by the Inquisition in yellow robes and with nooses around their necks. Once the procession reached the central square of the city – the Plaza Mayor in Madrid was the best-known venue for such a spectacle – the sentences were announced. Once the minor penalties were either carried out or the penitents released, the burnings would take place. It is likely that the inquisitors felt honour bound to order *some* burnings, to show an example to those whose Christian faith was wavering.

There was also a practice of burning in effigy only: a symbolic act. This could serve if the condemned was not present, or dead, for posthumous condemnations were common. In some places more were burned in effigy than in person in the early days. The Inquisition also ordered the burning of books. An act again echoed in Nazi Germany, a long list of writings, those in Arabic and Hebrew, particularly the Talmud and writings of Jewish and Moslem authors, went to the fire.

Over the centuries to come the Spanish Inquisition proceeded very much as Torquemada had ordained, some details varied over time and between localities, but the institution remained brutal in its ways and knew little humanity. In Valencia in 1607 a man of eighty-six and a thirteen-year-old girl each suffered a hundred lashes. Heretics were still the designated target, along with sorcerers, idolaters, sodomites and other enemies of Christianity, but the *conversos* who were still Jews at heart, or even those who were sincere Christians, had the most to fear.

Ironically, it was those Jews who continued to practise their religion that escaped the clutches of the Inquisition for a time. Despite a multitude of restrictions and periodic persecutions, at least the moneylenders could expect some protection from the monarchs. Torquemada had not forgotten them: in these earlier years he urged Ferdinand and Isabella to ensure that all Jews would be either expelled or forced to convert, but to his dismay he was confronted with a pragmatic unwillingness to act on his exhortations. The monarchy often borrowed from Jewish moneylenders and they financed the ongoing war of attrition against Granada. When Ferdinand and Isabella agreed to fund the voyage of Christopher Columbus in 1492, they obtained the finance from Jewish lenders.

Torquemada and the Dominicans saw the Moslems also as a threat to Christian Spain. Throughout the *Reconquista* many who had fallen under Christian rule found this made little difference to their own lifestyle. Men such as the philosopher and historian Ibn Khaldun found a blurring between the two cultures in the fourteenth century. There were also converts from Islam to Christianity whose sincerity may have been questionable, although few came to the Inquisition's attention in this early phase. Again, although their Catholic Majesties, as the Pope had designated them, wanted a fully Christian Spain, it would be impracticable to forcibly convert all their Moslem subjects given their large numbers, and inopportune while waging war on Granada. Their more pragmatic ministers no doubt counselled the king and queen thus, and they reluctantly denied Torquemada's demands.

The anti-Semitic lobby, in which Torquemada was prominent, exploited two events in this time. Pedro de Arbués, an inquisitor whom Torquemada had appointed to his home town of Saragossa, was murdered while praying in the cathedral in 1485, even though he was wearing a helmet and mail armour at the time. It was decided it was the work of certain *conversos* and heretics, and several were executed for it, although it is far from certain that any were guilty. Pedro received a controversial canonisation in 1867.

The Aragonese resented what they considered a Castilian imposition. Of course, many, Jewish or otherwise, abhorred the entire idea of the Inquisition, and there would be no shortage of suspects for the murder. Torquemada himself never travelled anywhere without a bodyguard of several hundred soldiers, hated as he was above all other Inquisitors.

The affair of the Holy Child of La Guardia in 1491 was also explosive, when once again the Jews were accused of the ritual murder of a child. No body was found – and in fact no child was reported missing at the time – but several Jews and *conversos* were condemned to death after admitting to the sacrifice under torture. The child was created an unofficial saint and is still venerated in La Guardia, even though it never existed. After this, the call to expel all Jews was strong. It would almost coincide with the final destruction of the Granada state. At Torquemada's urging all Jews were expelled from Andalusia, on the border of this remaining Moslem territory, for fear that they may seek to sabotage the final conquest.

Although Torquemada's management of the 'home front' in this holy war was concerned mostly with secret Jews, it was not difficult to correlate the relentless campaigning against Granada with the divine mission. Torquemada always went to meetings of the Estates-General and urged support for the completion of the *Reconquista*. He also lobbied the papacy for all the spiritual favours accorded to crusaders in previous centuries.

When the last Amir of Granada finally surrendered in January 1492, Torquemada rode with Ferdinand into the city. He then ordered the founding of a Dominican convent in Granada, no doubt preparing to extend the activities of the Inquisition, but in this he was disappointed.

Under the terms of the surrender Ferdinand had agreed not to bring the Inquisition into the new lands, which would have caused serious dissent while the territory was assimilated. But Ferdinand did agree that he no longer needed Jewish finance; the wars were over, and three ships sailed that year, with Columbus in the prow of the first. Torquemada was at least content with sanction for his plan to drive the Jews out of Spain entirely. No doubt counselled by their ministers, Ferdinand and Isabella were reluctant to agree to this expulsion. Jews were rich in expertise and on the whole did the country much good as traders, financiers and teachers. The Jews offered a payment of 300,000 ducats in return for their continued residence, which the sovereigns were inclined to accept. Torquemada exploded when he heard this and burst in on the joint monarchs bearing a large crucifix. 'Judas Iscariot sold Christ for thirty pence; and your highnesses wish to sell Him again for 300,000 ducats. Here He is; take Him and sell Him.' He left, leaving the crucifix on the table. His hectoring finally produced the result he wished for; it is hard to argue with a fanatic by advocating common sense.

On 31 March 1492 the sovereigns issued their decree that every Jew must either submit to baptism or leave the country on pain of execution. They were given four months grace in order to make their decision, or at least to sell their property and settle their affairs. This comparatively humane concession did not escape intervention from the Grand Inquisitor, and Torquemada ordered that Christians were forbidden to communicate with the Jews in this period of grace, which made it almost impossible for Jews to sell their goods and left much forfeit to the Inquisition. At least 800,000 Jews are estimated to have left Spain that year.

The human cost was severe and did Spain much harm in the long term. Most of those who opted to remain as *conversos* were at best reluctant converts, and fearful of the Inquisition ever after. Many of those expelled did return to Spain within a few years and accepted baptism. The expulsion had cost Spain thousands of merchants with their trade connections, scholars, teachers, doctors and other experts. Many Jews skilled in cartography and navigation moved to Portugal, which as the era of world exploration was just beginning, did Spain no good. The disappearance of the Jewish moneylender made itself felt within a short time, and his place was later filled by Dutch and Italian bankers.

Complaints flooded to Rome over the activities of the Inquisition in Spain and Torquemada sent Fray Alfonso Badaja to defend his actions. Even Ferdinand and Isabella expressed concern that property confiscations of the condemned were not rendered to them. Torquemada had channelled much of it into the expense account for the Inquisition. When the monarchs complained a second time, the pope ordered that the monies go to the royal treasury.

As early as 1482 Pope Sixtus had made his concerns felt over the Spanish Inquisition's undue zeal and obvious obsession with seeking out faults. He remarked that the Inquisitors at Seville,

...without observing juridical prescriptions, have detained many persons in violation of justice, punishing them by severe tortures and imputing to them, without foundation, the crime of heresy, and despoiling of their wealth those sentenced to death, in such form that a great number of them have come to the Apostolic See, fleeing from such excessive rigour and protesting their orthodoxy.

Yet Sixtus still did not attempt to curb the excesses, nor did his successor of 1484, Innocent VIII. The new pope both confirmed Torquemada and sanctioned the opening of a new front in the Church's war against its imagined enemies. The year of Innocent's accession saw a serious cold spell, now known as the Little Ice Age, the effects of which were put down to the agency of Satan. The Papal Bull that year talked of sorcery and witchcraft.

The Inquisition then opened for business in Germany, where the same methods were used to smoke out witches and magicians. The inquisitors Kramer and Sprenger soon produced the *Malleus Maleficarum,* The Hammer of the Witches, which acted as a training manual for the discovery of Satan's agents. The Witch Craze as began under this pontificate would continue for two centuries and more, resulting in as horrific a persecution of innocents as had happened in Spain.

Innocent died in 1492 and Cardinal Roderigo Borgia succeeded as Alexander VI. The Borgia pontificate is arguably the lowest point in the history of the papacy, at least morally. The papal curia saw orgies and unbridled licentiousness, and intrigue, treachery, nepotism, corruption and every un-Christian trait was unashamedly displayed. Alexander came from Valencia, but was unsympathetic towards Torquemada, as the Spanish Inquisition functioned independently of Rome.

This Spanish papacy had little effect on Torquemada in his mission, although he had serious opposition from the prelates close by, who at times complained to Rome about his fanaticism. There was a severe clash with Juan Davilia, Bishop of Segovia, when it was alleged that his long-dead grandfather, a *converso,* was a Judaizer and Torquemada ordered the bones dug up and burned. Davilia appealed to the pope, who overturned the charge and gave him a position in the household of the then Cardinal Cesare Borgia.

Torquemada then accused another convert, Pedro de Aranda, Bishop of Calaborra, of personal Judaizing, who also appealed successfully to Rome; but Pedro was still deprived of his see and later died in prison on Torquemada's sentence. Alexander then sought to remove Torquemada. He suggested in 1496 that four 'helpers' be appointed to take over his duties, given his advancing age. Torquemada protested, and it was during the confiscation controversy that Ferdinand raised his objection to the new men, who were forced to climb down. Having been Grand Inquisitor for fifteen years, Torquemada had enemies all the way to Rome, but none could easily remove him.

Time was taking its toll on Torquemada, for he was now in his seventies and suffered an acute form of gout. Soon after the clash with Alexander he relinquished his office by choice and retired to the convent at Avila. But his influence did not diminish even then. Even in this retirement he was revising further the guidelines of the Inquisition, and almost to the day he died he worked on further modifications. He stipulated that two inquisitors would hear the cases, one a jurist, the other a theologian, and wrote down other proposals, constantly tightening up the rules and procedures.

His influence with the royal family continued to the end. Ferdinand and Isabella's eldest daughter, also called Isabella, had married the king of Portugal and the marriage settlement stated that Portugal expel all Jews, as in Spain. In October 1497, the joint sovereigns were supported by Torquemada when Juan, their only son, died. Torquemada visited the dying prince, who had suffered a severe chill from sleeping on a bed of ice in a heatwave. Torquemada attended his last general assembly to promote his changes and soon after returning to Avila he died, on 16 September 1498.

His death certainly did not diminish the prowess of the Inquisition or cause a rethink of its stance. In 1507 Cardinal Francisco Ximines (or Jimines) de Cisneros, a Franciscan whose zeal in aggressively furthering Christianity was no less than Torquemada's, had taken on his mantle as Grand Inquisitor. In his time and after, the Inquisition changed little in its outlook and methods, and a sickening litany of arrests, tortures, penalties, and burnings continued for centuries. Ferdinand set up the Inquisition in his overseas domains: Sardinia, the Canary Islands and even the New World. His attempts to do so in Sicily and Naples were frustrated by rebellions.

The Jews remained the principal target in Spain, although from 1507 Ferdinand, sole monarch from Isabella's death in 1504, repudiated agreements made in Granada and demanded that all Moslems also either converted or left the country. Now the hunt for witches and sorcerers as elsewhere in Europe took up the Holy Office's attentions. By the early sixteenth century the Lutherans and other Protestant groupings joined the list of the demonized and the agents of the

Inquisition sought them out within the lands of their jurisdiction. The Holy Office took extreme care that no books came to Spain that could promote heretical thought. Millions lived in a state of terror, those with Jewish or Moorish blood in particular. For all its efforts over the centuries, the Inquisition did not succeed in suppressing Judaism in Spain. Although many were arrested, there were still secret Jews in Spain when the entire business ended.

The children of the Enlightenment saw the Inquisition as the epitome of the evils of ignorance, a gross medieval institution that promoted every abuse for which reason was believed the remedy. Joseph Bonaparte ordered it abolished on becoming king of Spain, but even then the Inquisition was reinstated with the Bourbon restoration of 1814. The last heretic was executed in 1826.

The Inquisition became an issue between the liberal and conservative politics of the time and in 1836 was finally abolished by royal decree. Even then it was not easy to address the issue in modern Spain. Scholarly investigation of the affair was much restricted until after the death of Franco in 1975. There is no doubt of its effect on popular culture ever since. It was said that during the 1973 right-wing coup in Chile, those arrested were confronted by interrogators in hoods, an image clearly reminiscent of the inquisitors.

Torquemada was first interred at the Dominican monastery at Avila, but was later translated to the cathedral. In 1836, his tomb was violated and his bones scattered. Dead for centuries, he was still despised for his actions.

What can be said in his favour? He and his creation are both viewed as bywords in fanaticism, ignorance and extreme cruelty, his indictment rather than his achievement. For his life's work Torquemada can be placed in the company of some the worst authors of atrocities the world has known. But he grew up under extreme Dominican influence, where he gained a conviction that the Holy Church was under threat from Jews and other subversive elements. This he believed wholeheartedly and spent his life in the struggle against this believed threat.

The Catholic Encyclopaedia does allude to his harsh and cruel methods but defends the need to preserve Christianity in Spain as justification. It even ends its entry with the quote of the Spanish chronicler Sebastian de Olmedo, describing Torquemada as the 'hammer of heretics, the light of Spain, the saviour of his country, the honour of his order'. It gives the impression that on the whole the

Catholic Church grants him their seal of approval, despite reservations over his methods. He was never canonised.

Of course, even though the peninsula was a frontier, there was no plot to return Spain to Islam, and certainly none to convert everyone to Judaism. It must be remembered that Europe was in a state emotional turmoil after the Black Death, and cool reason was one more casualty. Torquemada was voicing the beliefs rising at the time, outrageous at they were, and attacking the enemy with a total 'There is No Alternative' approach.

We have seen that Torquemada's reputation was exaggerated in places as he became a figure of anti-Catholic propaganda. The numbers who suffered while he was Grand Inquisitor were clearly much inflated. This is hardly justification, and figures are meaningless when such crimes against ordinary people are examined. Suffice to say that many felt the wrath of the Inquisition as a result of who they were by birth.

When Torquemada died and the Inquisition continued without him there were no significant changes to the method and ferocity with which the Holy Office went about its mission. Torquemada was not alone in all he believed; he had the support of the Spanish monarchy, the Church and perhaps most of the Christians of Spain. He was a man of his time, his paranoia fuelled by the soul-searching that pervaded all Europe and many about him harboured the same unease. It is likely that some thought the milk of human kindness, or at least a more unbiased approach to the accusations, should temper the manner of the Inquisition, but few said so, mostly for fear of being accused themselves. The Spanish Inquisition continued for four centuries with the same ferocity against the imagined menace as if Torquemada was in charge throughout.

Torquemada was a supporter of the Aragon-Castile marriage and the consequent reunification of Spain. He is not credited as the architect of the scheme, but his influence on Isabella was at least in part the cause for her agreement. The Reconquista was an ongoing theme in Christian Spain. Along with many, Torquemada included, the king and queen saw Catholicism as the unifying factor in their country.

Although Torquemada deserves some of the credit for this new impetus, his own achievement cries out for condemnation. His obsessive siege mentality resulted in crimes against humanity that can never be justified.

22

Margaret, Countess of Salisbury

Last of the Plantagenets and English Catholic Martyr

Historical epochs are artificial, mostly created for the convenience of historians. One could say that many features associated with the Middle Ages continued far beyond 1500, even into the nineteenth century in some cases. While it is true that there was less concern over kingship and power and more over religious dissent by the sixteenth century, there was really no one date on which everything changed. But so many people must have seen the world change so much in their lifetimes. One was Margaret Countess of Salisbury, whose life began during the Wars of the Roses and ended in the Reformation. She played a role in both.

Margaret was born into the royal family of the Yorkist monarchy and was by the reign of Henry VIII the last surviving Plantagenet. Her father was George, Duke of Clarence, younger brother of King Edward IV. For almost two decades before Margaret's birth the nobles of England had been engaged in intermittent civil war, centring on the rival claims of the descendants of Edward III for the kingship. In 1461, the House of York had triumphed when the young Edward IV succeeded as king and soon defeated the Lancastrians decisively. After his accession he created his eldest surviving brother George as Duke of Clarence, while the other, the future Richard III, became Duke of Gloucester.

Clarence, seven years Edward's junior, was ambitious and somewhat gullible. He was forever frustrated by his brother the king's refusal to allow him to marry any of several desirable heiresses. At the same time Edward gradually ceased to be as well-disposed towards Richard Neville, Earl of Warwick, who had been the most powerful supporter of the House of York. As relations between king and earl deteriorated, Warwick exploited Clarence's frustrations.

In 1469, Clarence married Isabel Neville, Warwick's eldest daughter, in defiance of his brother; an act that heralded the first of three armed uprisings against Edward, the second revolt intended to make Clarence king. The events of the next two years first had Warwick and Clarence flee into exile, then saw them return as decisive supporters of the successful Lancastrian campaign in September 1470 which restored the deposed King Henry VI to the throne. By the spring of 1471, this brief restoration was reversed when Edward regained the kingdom, defeating the Lancastrians first at Barnet where Warwick fell, and then at Tewkesbury where the other Lancastrian leaders were killed or captured.

Clarence, who had returned to his brother's side at a crucial point in the campaign, was at least nominally forgiven. His marriage had brought him considerable estates and for the next seven years he lived in comparative ease and raised his family. Apart from one child born on shipboard while Warwick, Clarence and Isabel were fleeing to exile, who did not survive, there was Edward, who would become the Earl of Warwick, born in November 1475. Margaret herself was born in August 1473 at Farley Castle in Somerset, a niece of the Yorkist king. Her deceased grandfathers were Richard Duke of York and Warwick the Kingmaker.

While she was still a small child events changed much for the worse. Her mother died in December 1477, having given birth to a fourth child who only survived her by three weeks. In 1478 her father fell from grace in a spectacular manner. Clarence was condemned for taking part in yet another plot against his brother and this time put to death. The story of his drowning in a butt of malmsey is probably myth, but he was certainly found guilty of treason and executed on the quiet, his estates forfeit and his line tainted. Both Edward and Margaret, Clarence's surviving children, appear to have lived reasonably well in the circumstances and grew up at court. They were excluded from the succession by their father's treason.

When Edward IV died in 1483, and the Duke of Gloucester became Lord Protector, the validity of the succession of his son the twelve-year-old Edward V was soon challenged by claims that the marriage of his parents was void in canon law. Any claim on behalf of Margaret or her brother was also ignored, and nobody emerged to champion them; even if any such suit were not sullied by their father's attainder, their status as minors was an added disadvantage. Gloucester therefore became King Richard III.

Young Edward, still known as Earl of Warwick even if his titles and lands were technically forfeit, was not entirely forgotten. In early 1485, King Richard, a widower whose only son had died the previous year, agreed that Edward should be considered his heir, should his plans to remarry and produce more children not come to fruition, and he ordered the attainders reversed. Edward rode to battle with his uncle the king against Henry Tudor in August 1485, and when Richard fell at Bosworth the victorious Henry VII had the boy arrested and confined to the Tower, where he remained for the rest of his life.

During his long imprisonment Edward was still a possible candidate for the throne as some Yorkists believed, and during the revolt of 1487 a schoolboy named Lambert Simnel impersonated Edward. Still the real Edward remained imprisoned; the king could not decide what to do with him. When he and another pretender Perkin Warbeck tried to escape in 1498, Henry finally decided to have both executed, for now he understood how dangerous it was for either to remain alive.

There is little said of Margaret in this period. She may have been the last of Clarence's children alive and at liberty but showed no inclination to join with the remaining Yorkists. As in the reigns of Edward IV, Edward V and Richard III, she did not appear to suffer under the new regime. As a woman she was not as much of a threat to the new monarch, and there is no sign of her causing any trouble, nor of anyone taking her part in the controversy over the succession. Throughout the 1480s and early 1490s she remained at court; perhaps the king thought it best to keep her in sight, but he did little else.

Margaret next appears on record when she marries Sir Reginald Pole at some time between 1491 and 1494, when she was around twenty. Pole was a Knight of the Garter and a distant kinsman of King Henry on the Beaufort side, and he served as Chamberlain to the household of Prince Arthur, the king's eldest son. Pole and Margaret attended Arthur's marriage to the Spanish princess Katherine of Aragon in 1501. But Arthur died the following year, and Katherine, daughter of Ferdinand and Isabella, was remarried to his brother Prince Henry. Margaret was close to Katherine from an early stage and the princess apparently thought highly of her.

Sir Reginald Pole died before December 1505. Margaret had borne him five children and her widowhood left her in straitened financial circumstances. When Henry VIII acceded in 1509 Margaret gained prominent appointments in royal service, at first as a Lady of the Bedchamber to the new Queen Katherine of Aragon. Given the positions she held, she was certainly valued as an organiser of the household. As a widow she was now a career woman, and did not remarry but devoted herself to her responsibilities. Margaret's friendship with Katherine turned her circumstances round dramatically and she was first granted an annuity of £100. When Princess Mary was born, Margaret was given custody of her household and from 1520 was appointed her governess. She was godmother to the princess.

The new king held her in more regard than his father had. Henry VIII on her petition granted her the title in October 1515 of Countess of Salisbury. He also restored to her many of the lands forfeited on her grandfather the Kingmaker's death and even reversed the attainder on her family. Besides her closeness to Katherine, Margaret was a useful royal servant who attended to the upbringing of his daughter.

All of her children were well provided for. Her eldest son Henry Pole, Lord Montague, was also in royal service. He was knighted on the Tournai campaign in 1513 and appeared several times on the king's business. Another son, Arthur Pole, was first a gentleman then an esquire of the bedchamber to the king and in 1523 himself knighted. He apparently died young, sometime after May 1527. Reginald, the scholar of the family, also benefited from royal patronage. Her daughter Ursula Pole was mostly spared the harm that later befell the family. She married Henry Lord Stafford fairly early and lived until 1570. Little was seen at this time of Geoffrey Pole, the youngest son.

In the early sixteenth century there were a number of nobles whose grandfathers had been peers at the courts of the Yorkist kings, as in the 1460s some had 'bought into' the new regime by marriage with the new king's close family or had been otherwise prominent. Some such as the Cavendish family were descendants of the House of York, just as Margaret was. This grouping was known as the White Rose party, but this is potentially misleading, for as a group they did not act together in any political capacity. Many in fact were careful not to rouse Henry VIII's suspicion, but the king was always wary of these people as a possible focus for conspiracies against him.

Of this number, Edmund de la Pole was the most prominent at first. He and his brother Richard were sons of Elizabeth, who had been Duchess of Suffolk and sister to Edward IV and Richard III. Her husband was not related to Margaret's family but she and the brothers were first cousins. Edmund had been a prisoner of Henry VII. Richard fought against Henry VIII in the French army and was known in France as Richard IV of England. Henry had Edmund executed in 1513 and Richard died much later, in 1525.

Despite their general unwillingness to assert themselves, an incident brought many of the 'White Rose' nobles under suspicion, Margaret and her family included. Edward Stafford, second Duke of Buckingham and son of the Duke who led the revolt against Richard III, had lived on good terms with the Tudor monarchy. Late in 1520, Cardinal Wolsey received an anonymous letter accusing Buckingham of wishing Henry dead and for a Yorkist restoration. The king took this very seriously and the Duke was arrested. Although no charges against him could be proven, this accusation was enough and despite pleas from the queen for clemency, Buckingham was eventually executed in 1523.

Margaret came under suspicion in 1521 as a known associate of Buckingham. She was not arrested but was dismissed from the Princess's household. Wolsey tried to replace her, approaching the dowager Countess of Oxford who pleaded infirmity, and a lasting replacement was not found. Margaret was allowed to return to her duties in 1525. This business raises questions. Was Margaret involved in a Yorkist plot against the king? There is no evidence that she did more than appear in the company of a known plotter. Once again, her parentage put her under suspicion, for it was dangerous being the last of the Plantagenets under a Tudor monarchy fearful of its own continuance.

Although Margaret had survived the White Rose scare, her fortunes would later turn for the worse again, but this time as a result of a change in the standing of the Queen. There was in addition much dissent and controversy in England in the coming years, this time in the sphere of religion. Although her parentage appeared to no longer to affect her, it would once again. All three factors would bring about her downfall.

In the late 1520s, Henry's fears of leaving his realm without a son, Katherine having failed to produce surviving children other than Mary, led him to seek a divorce. The events that followed the said divorce, his marriage to Anne Boleyn and the severance of the English church from Rome, are well known. The effect on Margaret and her family is complex.

If anything, her prime concern was her goddaughter and charge. She did all she could to shield Princess Mary from the upheaval leading to the divorce. The Princess's household, which included her tutor Dr Richard Featherstone and a number of Spanish servants formerly of Katherine's entourage, was looked on with suspicion as both the divorce and the English Reformation loomed. Margaret was probably as Catholic as many, but beyond recognition of Henry as head of the Church of England there were fewer differences that Catholics had at this early stage. We do not know for certain if Margaret was either a Catholic die-hard or a Yorkist plotter and it is more likely that she was no more than a defender of her Princess's interests, despite some circumstantial evidence. In 1533 Henry ordered that Mary's household be dismissed. Both she and Margaret protested, but there was nothing to be done now that the king had disinherited his daughter and saw this household a possible centre for dissent. It is not certain what Margaret did for the next few years. Her refusal to give up Mary's jewels and plate certainly angered the king, but she was allowed to return to court in 1538 for a short time.

It was the activities of one of Margaret's sons that placed her and her family under renewed and more serious suspicion. Reginald Pole had emerged as one of the most able theological thinkers of this time. Having studied under the king's patronage he was urged to accept a bishopric in 1530, for Henry thought highly of him, but his opposition to the king's divorce soured relations, as did his refusal to endorse the breach with Rome. Despite his displeasing the king, Pole was allowed to travel to Italy to study but did not return.

In 1536, after the English Church broke with Rome, Pole was created a cardinal by the papacy and voiced his opposition to the English Reformation. His treatise *De Unitate Ecclesiae* was vociferous in his attack on Henry, where he even urged that France and Spain should invade England to restore Catholicism. In the years that followed he carried on as an active papal legate and theologian, playing a significant part the proceedings of the Council of Trent. He was by 1549 considered a possible candidate for the papacy itself, although for some reason he was still slow to take Holy Orders. Even as a cardinal he was still a deacon and was only ordained priest on his triumphant return to England.

When Mary did become Queen of England in 1553, it was Cardinal Pole who came to mastermind the restoration of the Catholic Church in the realm. As the last Catholic ever consecrated Archbishop of

Canterbury, he sought an easy transition, his attempts to moderate the persecution of Protestants mostly coming to naught. He died on 17 November 1558, the same day as Mary, just before Protestantism returned to stay in England.

His activities once created a cardinal while in Rome were were a great irritation to Henry, as was the Pilgrimage of Grace of 1536. This rebellion in northern England was inspired by fears over Henry's attack on the Church. Believing that the revolt represented the true feelings of of the people of England about its new religious direction, Pole produced his contentious treatise, and this sealed the fate of his mother and brothers.

Geoffrey Pole, the youngest of Margaret's children, was arrested and finally confessed to plotting, implicating some of his family. There is no way of knowing whether the Poles were really engaged in any conspiracy and it is likely that after months of imprisonment and possibly torture Geoffrey was forced into signing the confession. Lord Montague and even his small son Henry were arrested and sent to the Tower early in 1538.

Soon it was Margaret's turn. The Earl of Southampton, High Admiral of England, and Bishop Goodrich of Ely invaded her home at Warblington, Hampshire, and had the Countess of Salisbury hauled before them and questioned. Without obtaining a confession, Southampton had Margaret sent first to his own home, and then to the Tower.

There was no trial for Margaret. An Act of Attainder was passed against her, and she was declared guilty by act of Parliament on 12 May 1539. Thomas Cromwell produced one piece of what was considered evidence, a strangely decorated white silk tunic found in Margaret's house. On the front was embroidered the lions of England without the lilies of France that quartered the Royal Arms. Around this was a wreath of pansies (the badge of Pole) and marigolds (for Mary Tudor). On the back of the shirt was a badge of the Five Wounds. Such a garment was construed to have political significance for it apparently hinted at Margaret's claim to the throne and the links to Princess Mary suggested her discredited cause. The Five Wounds were used as a particular icon of the rebels in the Pilgrimage of Grace.

None of these symbols incriminated Margaret for certain. She had made no secret of her devotion to Mary or of her Plantagenet parentage, and like Mary she had remained Catholic. But the Five Wounds had recently acquired an explosive significance. The French ambassador believed that her parentage had doomed her, but it appears that her Catholicism was enough to bring about her arrest. In 1540, Richard Featherstone, Catherine's chaplain and Mary's tutor, and Thomas Abell, also chaplain to Queen Catherine, were hung, drawn and quartered. Now Catholicism was becoming equated with treason.

When Margaret's son Lord Montague was arrested, so was Hugh Cavendish, Marquis of Exeter, another descendant of the Plantagenet kings. Both were beheaded. Montague's son Henry was still in the Tower in 1542 when he was excluded from the general pardon and he was either executed on the quiet or died while still imprisoned. Sir Geoffrey Pole was pardoned in 1539 and was then allowed to live out his life quietly, payment for having effectively betrayed his own mother and brother.

On 28 May 1541, Margaret Countess of Salisbury was beheaded. She had been kept in the Tower for two years with no warrant for execution served. A new rebellion in Yorkshire prompted action, ill-advised as it turned out.

The French ambassador Maraillac claims it took place in a corner of the Tower grounds with few in attendance; a 'strenge and lamentable execution'. Another source says she was executed in the presence of the Mayor of London and a large crowd. It was still done within the Tower confines, probably on the green, for a public execution of an old and venerable lady might have shown the regime in an undesirable light. The closed nature of the Tower made such a controversial act easier to carry out.

The regular executioner was in the north at the time, so it was said that a 'wretched and blundering youth was chosen, who literally hacked her head and shoulders to pieces in the most pitiable manner.' The story told says that when Margaret was ordered to bow her head she replied 'So should all traitors do, but I am none.' She was subsequently asked by the executioner to turn her head to the side for an end with a single blow, but she again refused, telling him to do 'as he could'. Declining to cooperate with the executioner, she protested her innocence to the end while prolonging her own suffering. Stories of her defiant end circulated, giving the appearance of martyrdom.

Of course there is no real evidence that Margaret engaged in any attempt to dethrone Henry VIII. She was a devout Catholic of course, and the mother of the king's most vociferous opponent. Whether she seriously wished to see Henry overthrown cannot be known, or whether she was involved in any discussion of it, but she was not recorded at any time as acting in such a cause. She was said to have shown anger at her son Reginald's seditious writings, as her servants testified.

She was what remained of the House of York, but whether she believed she or her sons should rule instead of the Tudor kings she was certainly devoted to the Princess Mary. It was reasonable at that point to consider that Mary might still become Queen after Henry's death despite her disinheritance. Mary's father did indeed later restore her and Elizabeth to the succession once the ill-health of Prince Edward called for contingencies. Mary did eventually succeed as queen.

Margaret was sixty-eight when she died. She had grown old in the service of Princess Mary and had thrown caution to the wind when she protested against her charge's treatment. In such times even such a minimal act of protest could have serious consequences. Otherwise, she was not known to have said or done anything of a treasonable nature. She was probably as Catholic as her princess and would not have agreed with the divorce of Mary's mother or the break with Rome. Whether her views went so far as to wish for revolt and Henry overthrown is uncertain, but she certainly had the good sense not to speak openly of it if she did.

But these were unsure times and it was easy to evoke royal wrath simply for being someone rather than doing something. She was Warwick the Kingmaker's granddaughter, and a Plantagenet of the House of York and that was enough to put her in her in danger, as was being a known Catholic. Worse still, she was Reginald Pole's mother and his verbal attacks on the regime were heard in England. Margaret was in a precarious position simply by virtue of who she was, and she was careful. But she risked censure by defending her goddaughter at the worst time in the religious conflict, and all these factors produced for her a lethal trap.

Select Bibliography

Primary Sources
Arrivall of King Edward IV (Camden Society 1838)
Christine de Pisan *The Treasure of the City of Ladies* (Penguin Classics 1985)
Dante Alighieri *The Divine Comedy: Hell* (Penguin Classics 1949)
Foxe's Book of Martyrs 1563 (Whitaker House, U.S., 1981)
Geoffrey Chaucer *The Canterbury Tales* (The Riverside Chaucer OUP 1987)
Jean Froissart Chronicles (Penguin Classics 1978)
The Brut, or *The Chronicle of England* Vol 2 (Early English Texts Society London 1908)
The Illustrated Chronicles of Matthew Paris ed. Richard Vaughan (A. Sutton, 1984)
Warkworth's Chronicle (Camden Society 1839)

Secondary Sources
Geoffrey Barraclough *The Medieval Papacy* (Thames & Hudson 1968)
F R H du Boulay *An Age of Ambition* (Thomas Nelson 1970)
Patricia Carson *James van Artevelde: the Man from Ghent* (Story-Scientia 1980)
S. B. Chrimes *Henry VII* (Methuen 1972)
G L Harriss *Cardinal Beaufort A Study of Lancastrian Ascendancy and Decline* (Clarendon 1988)
James Hutton *James and Philip van Arteveld. Two episodes in the History of the Fourteenth Century* (John Murray 1882)

Select Bibliography

Andrew Jotischy *Crusading and the Crusader States* (Longman 2004)

Maurice Keen *Chivalry* (Yale University Press 1984)

Thomas E Kelly 'Eustache the Monk' in *Medieval Outlaws* ed. Thomas H Ohlgren (Sutton Publishing 1998)

C H Lawrence The Friars (Longman 1994)

A A Ledieu *Esquisses Militaires de la Guerre de Cent Ans* (Lille 1887)

Gordon Leff *Medieval Thought from St Augustine to Ockham* (Pelican Books 1958)

Philippe de Mézières *La Vie de Saint-Pierre Thomas* (Rome 1954)

'Miscellanea Relating to the Martyrdom of Archbishop Scrope', ed. James Raine, in *Historians of the Church of York*, Rolls Series 71 (London 1886)

Jonathan Phillips *The Fourth Crusade and the sack of Constantinople* (Vintage Digital, 2011)

Anders Piltz *The World of Medieval Learning* (Basil Blackwell 1981)

Jean Richard *The Crusades c.1071-c.1291* (Cambridge 1996)

Desmond Seward *The Last White Rose* (Constable and Robinson 2010)

M J Trow *Vlad the Impaler* (Sutton Publishing 2005)

John Ure *Prince Henry the Navigator* (Constable and Company 1977)

George Vickers *Humphrey Duke of Gloucester* (Archibald, Constable & Co 1907)

Marina Warner *Joan of Arc* (Weidenfeld & Nicolson 1982)

Bertram Wolffe, *Henry VI* (Methuen 1981)

Jeffrey Lee *God's Wolf: The Life of the Most Notorious of All Crusaders. Reynald de Châtillon* (Atlantic Books 2016)

James Ross *The Foremost Man of the Kingdom: John de Vere, Thirteenth Earl of Oxford 1442-1513* (Boydell Press 2015)

Index

Also available from Amberley Publishing

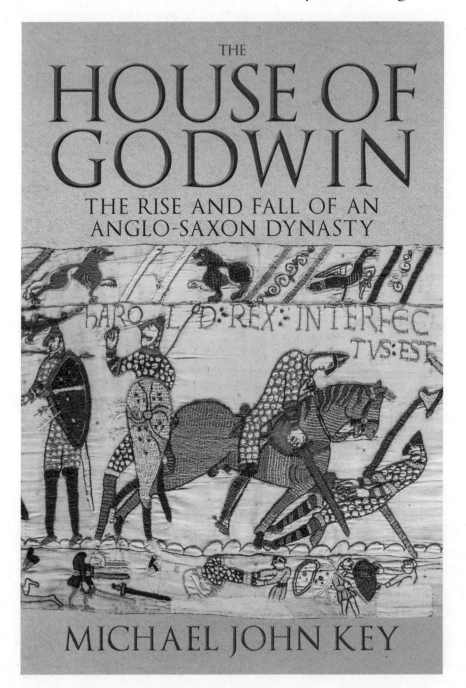

THE

HOUSE OF GODWIN

THE RISE AND FALL OF AN ANGLO-SAXON DYNASTY

MICHAEL JOHN KEY

Available from all good bookshops or to order direct
Please call **01453-847-800**
www.amberley-books.com